AF575541

TRADIVOX

VOLUME XVII

TRADIVOX

CATHOLIC CATECHISM INDEX

VOLUME XVII

Peter Geiermann
John M. Farley
Henry Cafferata

Edited by
Aaron Seng

SOPHIA INSTITUTE PRESS
MANCHESTER, NEW HAMPSHIRE

South Bend, Indiana
www.Tradivox.com

This book is an original derivative work comprised of newly typeset and reformatted editions of the following Catholic catechisms, once issued with ecclesiastical approval and now found in the public domain:

Geiermann, Peter. *The Convert's Catechism of Catholic Doctrine.* St. Louis, MO: B. Herder Book Co., 1910.

Farley, John M. *Catechism for First Communicants.* Rev. ed. New York: Frederick Pustet Co., Inc., 1911.

Cafferata, Henry. *The Catechism Simply Explained.* St. Louis, MO: B. Herder Book Co., 1932.

Scripture references follow the Douay-Rheims Bible, per the imprint of John Murphy Company (Baltimore, 1899).

Cover and interior design by Perceptions Design Studio.
Unless otherwise noted, all illustrations are in the public domain.

Sophia Institute Press
Box 5284, Manchester, NH 03108
1-800-888-9344

www.SophiaInstitute.com

ISBN 978-1-64413-382-8
LCCN 2023940093

Dedicated with love and deepest respect
to all the English Martyrs and Confessors.
Orate pro nobis.

CONTENTS

ACKNOWLEDGMENTS

THE publication of this series is due primarily to the generosity of countless volunteers and donors from several countries. Special thanks are owed to Mr. and Mrs. Phil Seng, Mr. and Mrs. Michael Over, Mr. and Mrs. Jim McElwee, Mr. and Mrs. John Brouillette, Mr. and Mrs. Thomas Scheibelhut, Mr. and Mrs. Kyle Barriger, as well the visionary priests and faithful of St. Stanislaus Bishop and Martyr parish in South Bend, Indiana, and St. Patrick's Oratory in Green Bay, Wisconsin. May God richly reward their commitment to handing on the Catholic faith.

FOREWORD

The Catholic faith remains always the same throughout the centuries and millennia until the coming of our Lord at the end of the time, likewise "Jesus Christ is the same yesterday, today and forever" (Heb 13:8). The Catholic faith is "the faith, which was once delivered unto the saints" (Jude 1:3). The Magisterium of the Church teaches us solemnly the same truth in the following words of the First Vatican Council: "The doctrine of the faith which God has revealed, is put forward not as some philosophical discovery capable of being perfected by human intelligence, but as a divine deposit committed to the spouse of Christ to be faithfully protected and infallibly promulgated. Hence, too, that meaning of the sacred dogmas is ever to be maintained, which has once been declared by holy mother Church, and there must never be any abandonment of this sense under the pretext or in the name of a more profound understanding. May understanding, knowledge and wisdom increase as ages and centuries roll along, and greatly and vigorously flourish, in each and all, in the individual and the whole Church: but this only in its own proper kind, that is to say, in the same doctrine, the same sense, and the same understanding (cf. Vincentius Lerinensis, *Commonitorium*, 28)."[1]

An authentically Catholic catechism has the function of learning and teaching the unchanging Catholic faith throughout all generations. The Roman Pontiffs indeed, taught: "There is nothing more effective than catechetical instruction to spread the glory of God and to secure the salvation of souls."[2] Saint Pius X said, that "the great loss of souls is due to ignorance

[1] Vatican I, Dogmatic Constitution *Dei Filius de fide catholica*, Ch. 4

[2] Pope Benedict XIV, Apostolic Constitution *Etsi minime*, n. 13

of divine things."[3] Therefore, the traditional catechisms have enduring value in our own day and age, which is marked by an enormous doctrinal confusion, which reigns in the life of the Church in the past six decades, and which reaches its peak in our days.

I welcome and bless the great project of the "Tradivox" in cataloguing and preserving the hundreds of long-lost Catholic catechisms issued with episcopal approval over the last millennium. This project will convincingly show the essentially unchanging nature of the apostolic doctrine across time and space, and so I invite the faithful of the entire world to support this historic effort, as we seek to restore the perennial catechism of the Church. The project of a catechism restoration on behalf of "Tradivox" will surely be of great benefit not only to many confused and disoriented Catholic faithful, but also to all people who are sincerely seeking the ultimate and authentic truth about God and man, which one can find only in the Catholic and apostolic faith, and which is the only religion and faith willed by God and to which God calls all men.

+Athanasius Schneider, O.R.C.,
Titular Bishop of Celerina
Auxiliary Bishop of the Archdiocese of Saint Mary in Astana

[3] Cf. Pope St. Pius X, Encyclical *Acerbo nimis*, n. 27

SERIES EDITOR'S

PREFACE

SOME are surprised to find that when a given Catholic is asked to "look something up in the catechism," he may well respond: "Which one?" The history of the Catholic Church across the last millennium is in fact filled with the publication of numerous catechisms, issued in every major language on earth; and for centuries, these concise "guidebooks" to Catholic doctrine have served countless men and women seeking a clear and concise presentation of that faith forever entrusted by Jesus Christ to his one, holy, Catholic, and apostolic Church.

Taken together, the many catechisms issued with episcopal approval can offer a kind of "window" on to the universal ordinary magisterium — a glimpse of those truths which have been held and taught in the Church *everywhere, always, and by all.* For, as St. Paul reminds us, the tenets of this Faith do not change from age to age: "Jesus Christ yesterday and today and the same for ever. Be not led away with various and strange doctrines" (Heb 13:8-9).

The catechisms included in our *Tradivox Catholic Catechism Index* are selected for their orthodoxy and historical significance, in the interest of demonstrating to contemporary readers the remarkable continuity of Catholic doctrine across time and space. Long regarded as reliable summaries of Church teaching on matters of faith and morals, we are proud to reproduce these works of centuries past, composed and endorsed by countless priests, bishops, and popes devoted to "giving voice to tradition."

In This Volume

The decades leading up to and following the First Council of the Vatican (1869–70) saw tremendous growth in the number of official catechisms being composed and published across the world. Perhaps nowhere was this more evident than in the United States of America, where Catholic immigrants from many lands drove demand for religious textbooks (and schools to use them) in their various native tongues, as well as in the traditional Latin and vernacular English of the North American "melting pot." Bishops accordingly promulgated a growing number of older catechisms in fresh editions, composed or approved new catechisms on their own authority, and joined brother bishops in council to promulgate new regional catechisms (e.g., those of Baltimore, Maynooth, or Quebec[1]).

This interest, combined with growing literacy rates and massive advances in the rapidity of book publication and distribution (stereotyping, the steam press, and transportation changes having the most significant impact in these years), saw an astronomical rise in publishing: some estimates indicate an 800% increase in the number of titles in print from the early to mid-1800s. By the turn of the twentieth century, it had become common for Catholic priests to compose catechisms of their own, often with very specific demographics in mind. Catechisms of Catholic doctrine began to appear with custom tailoring to audiences of particular age groups, levels of sacramental initiation, states in life, and stages of conversion. Among these, perhaps the most popular were the "convert's catechism" and the "first Communion catechism," of which this volume takes a representative sampling.

The first is Fr. Peter Geiermann's *The Convert's Catechism of Catholic Doctrine*, first published by Herder in 1910. Born to Catholic parents in southeast Michigan, Geiermann joined the Redemptorist Order in 1892, eager for a life of study and apostolic work, much of which consisted in instructing adults and converts in the faith. His *Convert's Catechism* proved so helpful throughout the Saint Louis Province that it was soon being used

[1] For these famous regional catechisms, see Volumes XVI, IV, and XV, respectively.

in several dioceses of the American Midwest, running in over one dozen editions and remaining in print until 1957—nearly thirty years after the author's death. The original text merited the attention of the eminent Rafael Cardinal Merry Del Val, who conveyed to the author the apostolic blessing of Pope Pius X for his efforts. The body text of 1910 has been retained here in its entirety, along with a number of additional subheadings to render the arrangement more clear.

THE SECOND IS the little *Catechism for First Communicants*, one of many catechisms printed in New York (not a few of which, confusingly, have gone under the moniker "New York Catechism" over the past two centuries) under the imprimatur of Archbishop John Murphy Farley. Published by Frederick Pustet in 1911, the exact authorship of the original text remains unclear, although it may likely be attributed to one of Archbishop (later Cardinal) Farley's attending priests. Elevated to the cardinalate by the "Pope of the Eucharist," St. Pius X, Farley shared the supreme pontiff's zeal for preparing children to receive Holy Communion at an early age. The *Catechism for First Communicants* approved by His Eminence reflects this solicitude, as it is prefaced by excerpts from *Quam singulari* (1910), including the decree: "For first confession and first Communion, a complete and perfect knowledge of Christian doctrine is not necessary. The child will, however, be obliged to gradually learn the whole catechism according to its ability." The charming text accordingly adopts the educative method common to small children: that of question and answer, in which the answers reformulates the question:

> **21. What do we receive in Holy Communion?**
> In Holy Communion, we receive the true body and the true blood of our Lord Jesus Christ.

The body text of Archbishop Farley's 1911 original is presented here without change, allowing the reader to glimpse a prior century, in which little children could recite by heart certain doctrines that have become obscure to many adults in our own.

The third catechism included in this volume is Canon Henry Cafferata's *The Catechism Simply Explained*, one of the most successful "short catechisms" published in prewar England. First appearing in 1897, Cafferata's concise and incisive little text was reissued with many subtitles (and from several publishers) in subsequent decades: "for Converts," and "for Little Children" among the most popular. In just seven years, it had already sold over 10,000 copies and was in its fourth edition—a success that continued for many years in England and America, as variations of the original continued in print until 1959, just before the opening of the Second Vatican Council (1962–1965). The "revised and enlarged" Herder edition of 1932 is recovered here without change, and reflects the temper of the time in England, in which Catholics were engaging in more straightforward dialogue with the Church of England, presenting "reasons for their hope"[2] with clarity and conviction. Many passages remain instructive for those in our own time who claim to be "spiritual, but not religious":

> It is difficult sometimes to get protestants to realize that they are bound to worship God, and that by religious worship. They have been accustomed, more or less, to do as they like about religion, and they cannot quite get rid of the idea that they are not bound to attend to it; but all this is very much opposed to what God requires. He did not leave it a matter of option or choice to us. His words are very strong and forcible: "He that believeth and is baptized shall be saved, but he that believeth not shall be condemned."[3] We are, therefore, bound, under pain of eternal loss, to believe all that God has taught us; and this means also doing all that he has told us to do, whether by his own divine lips or by the voice of his Church.

Editorial Note

Our *Catholic Catechism Index* series generally retains only the doctrinal content of those catechisms it seeks to reproduce, as well as that front matter most essential to establishing the credibility of each work as an

[2] Cf. 1 Pt 3:15
[3] Mk 16:16

authentic expression of the Church's common doctrine, e.g., any episcopal endorsement, *nihil obstat*, or *imprimatur*. However, it should be noted that especially prior to the eighteenth century, a number of catechisms were so immediately and universally received as reliably orthodox texts (often simply by the reputation of the author or publisher), that they received no such "official" approval; or if they did, it was often years later and in subsequent editions. We therefore include both the original printing date in our Table of Contents, and further edition information in the Preface above.

Our primary goal has been to bring these historical texts back into publication in readable English copy. Due to the wide range of time periods, cultures, and unique author styles represented in this series, we have made a number of editorial adjustments to allow for a less fatiguing read, more rapid cross-reference throughout the series, and greater research potential for the future. While not affecting the original content, these adjustments have included adopting a cleaner typesetting and simpler standard for capitalization and annotation, as well as remedying certain anachronisms in spelling or grammar.

Woodcut depicting an early method used in the production of Catholic catechisms, circa 1568.

At the same time, in deepest respect for the venerable age and subject matter of these works, we have been at pains to adhere as closely as possible to the original text: retaining archaisms such as "doth" and "hallowed," and avoiding any alterations that might affect the doctrinal content or authorial voice. We have painstakingly restored original artwork wherever possible, and where the rare explanatory note has been deemed necessary, it is not made in the text itself, but only in a marginal note. In some cases, our editorial refusal to "modernize" the content of these classical works may require a higher degree of attention from today's reader, who we trust will be richly rewarded by the effort.

We pray that our work continues to yield highly readable, faithful reproductions of these time-honored monuments to Catholic religious instruction: catechisms once penned, promulgated, and praised by bishops across the globe. May these texts that once served to guide and shape the faith and lives of millions now do so again; and may the scholars and saints once involved in their first publication now intercede for all who take them up anew. *Tolle lege!*

Sincerely in Christ,
Aaron Seng

TRADIVOX

VOLUME XVII

THE CONVERT'S CATECHISM OF CATHOLIC DOCTRINE

BY

REV. PETER GEIERMANN, C.SS.R.

ST. LOUIS, MO. AND FREIBURG (BADEN)
PUBLISHED BY B. HERDER
1910

THE CONVERT'S CATECHISM OF CATHOLIC DOCTRINE

BY

REV. PETER GEIERMANN, C.SS.R.

ST. LOUIS, MO. AND FREIBURG (BADEN)
PUBLISHED BY B. HERDER
1910

IMPRIMATUR
St. Louis, Sept. 1st, 1909.
THOS. P. BROWN, C.SS.R.
Sup. Prov.

NIHIL OBSTAT
Sti. Ludovici, die 30, Nov. 1909.
F. G. HOLWECK,
Censor Librorum.

IMPRIMATUR
Sti. Ludovici, die 1, Dec. 1909.
O. J. S. HOOG, V.G.

PRAYER TO THE HOLY GHOST

Come, Holy Ghost, fill the hearts of thy faithful, and enkindle in them the fire of thy love.

V. Send forth thy Spirit and they shall be created.

R. And thou shalt renew the face of the earth.

Let us pray.

O God, who hast taught the hearts of the faithful by the light of the Holy Ghost, grant that by the same Spirit we may be always truly wise, and ever rejoice in his consolation, through Christ our Lord.

R. Amen.

INTRODUCTION

The Convert's Catechism aims at presenting religious truths in the order of their relative importance to the sincere non-Catholic. It emphasizes controverted points in a special manner, while stating the Catholic doctrine clearly.

There are two views of life: the divine and the human. The one is true, eternal, and immutable; the other false, temporal, and changeable. The former is in perfect accord with right reason, enlightened by faith; the latter, the result of reason alone, is invariably distorted by ignorance, prejudice, or passion. Catholics take the former view of life; men of the world, the latter. Between these two classes, there are many honest souls groping in darkness or semidarkness, seeking the light. It would be demanding too much to require these to embrace the Catholic view in all details before receiving the light of faith. They can, however, be expected to follow the guidance of right reason and the promptings of grace, and thus advance gradually on the right way, to the realization of the truth, and the possession of divine life.

For these reasons *The Convert's Catechism* does not follow the beaten path in imparting religious instruction, but is composed on an entirely new plan, to facilitate the labor both of the inquirer and of the instructor. Part I insists on the necessity of serving God, as God ordains in revelation, especially as taught by his divine Son. It shows the necessity of a divine Church, infallibly guided by God, to teach man how to live as a child of God and heir to the kingdom of heaven. When he has once mastered this principle of divine authority, the inquirer is prepared to accept whatever the divine Church teaches on faith, morals, and the means of grace, all of which is clearly stated in Part II of this catechism. The scope of this little work prevented the author from entering into the reason and authority of religion. For additional reading, he therefore refers the convert to his *Manual of Theology for the Laity*, of which six editions have been issued in three years.

The Convert's Catechism of Catholic Doctrine

SECTION I

The Catholic Doctrine in General

Natural Truths

Fundamental Truths

1. **What religious truths can man discover by his own efforts?**
By his own efforts man can discover especially the existence of these four religious truths: 1) there is a God, Creator and preserver of the universe; 2) man has a free will; 3) God rewards the good and punishes the wicked; 4) the human soul is immortal.

2. **What is God?**
God is a Spirit, who exists of himself, and on whom all things depend.

3. **What is man?**
Man is a creature composed of a material body and a spiritual soul.

Obligation of Religion

4. **What relationship exists between God and man?**
Between God and man there exists a fourfold relationship: 1) God is the Creator, man is his creature; 2) God is the benefactor, man is his beneficiary; 3) God is the supreme ruler, man is his subject; 4) God is the end of all creation; in God alone man can find lasting happiness.

5. **What obligation flows from this relationship?**
From this relationship flows man's obligation of religion.

6. **What is religion?**
Religion is man's obligation to know, to love, and to serve God.

7. **Is man free to serve God as he pleases?**
Man is not free to serve God as he pleases; he must serve God, as God, his supreme master, ordains.

Religion Leads to Happiness

8. **For what does every human heart crave?**
Every human heart craves for happiness.

9. **Can man acquire perfect happiness on earth?**
Man cannot acquire perfect happiness on earth.

10. **Why cannot man acquire perfect happiness on earth?**
Man cannot acquire perfect happiness on earth: 1) because his soul will live after his fleeting life on earth is ended; 2) because God put in every human heart a longing for an endless possession of an infinite good, which he alone can satisfy in eternity.

11. **How then can man acquire perfect happiness?**
Man can acquire perfect happiness by seeking the friendship of God in this life, so that he may enjoy the same fully in the next life.

12. **How does God reward the good?**
God rewards the good with his blessings on earth, and shares with them the joys of heaven.

13. **How does God punish the wicked?**
God punishes the wicked with his enmity during this life, and consigns them to the torments of hell after death.

14. **What is heaven?**
Heaven is the state of everlasting life, in which the good see God face-to-face, are made like unto him in glory, and enjoy eternal happiness.

15. **What is hell?**
Hell is the state of never-ending torments.

Revelation, Tradition, the Bible, the Canon of the Bible

Revelation

16. **Has God ever spoken to man?**
"God, who, sundry times and in diverse manners, spoke in times past to the fathers by the prophets, last of all, in these days hath spoken to us by his Son."[1]

[1] Heb 1:1-2

17. **What do we call the truths which God has spoken to man?**
We call the truths which God has spoken to man "divine revelation."

Tradition

18. **How was divine revelation preserved and transmitted to man?**
In the beginning of the world's history, divine revelation was preserved and transmitted only by tradition or the reverential belief and teaching of succeeding ages. In the course of time, God inspired holy men to record many of his revealed truths. Finally, Jesus Christ made his Church the custodian and interpreter of revelation.

The Bible

19. **What has become of the truths recorded under the inspiration of God?**
The truths recorded under the inspiration of God have been collected into the Bible and translated into every known language.

20. **When was the first complete collection of the inspired writings made?**
The first complete collection of the inspired writings was made only toward the close of the fourth century of the Christian era.

The Canon of the Bible

21. **What is the list of the various inspired writings called?**
The list of the various inspired writings is called "the Canon of the Bible."

22. **When was the present Canon of the Bible officially declared authentic?**
The present Canon of the Bible was officially declared authentic by the Universal Council of Trent, August 8, 1546.

Faith, Good Works, the Rule of Faith, Motives of Faith

Faith

23. **How does man accept divine revelation?**
Man accepts divine revelation by faith.

24. **What is faith?**
Faith is a divine gift which enables man to believe firmly all that God has revealed.

25. **How does man dispose himself for the gift of faith?**
Man disposes himself for the gift of faith by humility, sincerity, obedience, and sacrifice in the service of God.

26. **How will man obtain and preserve the gift of faith?**
Man will obtain and preserve the gift of faith by submitting his mind and heart to the influence of God by prayer.

27. **What prayers should every Christian commit to memory?**
Every Christian should commit at least the following prayers to memory: 1) the Lord's Prayer, 2) the Angelical Salutation, 3) an act of contrition, 4) the Christian acts of faith, 5) hope, and 6) charity.

The Lord's Prayer.—Our Father who art in heaven, hallowed be thy name. Thy kingdom come. Thy will be done, on earth as it is in heaven. Give us this day our daily bread. And forgive us our trespasses as we forgive those who trespass against us. And lead us not into temptation: but deliver us from evil. Amen.

The Angelical Salutation.—Hail, Mary, full of grace, the Lord is with thee; blessed art thou among women, and blessed is the fruit of thy womb,

Jesus. Holy Mary, Mother of God, pray for us sinners, now and at the hour of our death. Amen.

Act of contrition.—O my God, I am heartily sorry for all my sins, because by them I have lost heaven and deserved hell, but, more than all, because I have offended thee, my God, who art infinitely good and worthy of all my love. I am firmly resolved, with the help of thy grace, never to sin again and to avoid all the occasions of sin.

Act of faith.—O my God, I firmly believe all the sacred truths which the holy Catholic Church believes and teaches, because thou hast revealed them, who canst neither deceive nor be deceived.

Act of hope.—O my God, relying on thy infinite goodness and promises, I hope to obtain the pardon of my sins, the assistance of thy grace, and life everlasting, through the merits of Jesus Christ, my Lord and Redeemer.

Act of charity.—O my God, I love thee with my whole heart above all things, because thou art infinitely good and worthy of all my love; and for the love of thee I love my neighbor as myself.

28. **Where are the chief truths which man must believe summed up?**
The chief truths which man must believe are summed up in the sign of the cross and in the Apostles' Creed.

The sign of the cross.—In the name of the Father, and of the Son, and of the Holy Ghost. Amen.

The Apostles' Creed.—I believe in God, the Father Almighty, Creator of heaven and earth; and in Jesus Christ, his only Son, our Lord; who was conceived by the Holy Ghost, born of the Virgin Mary, suffered under Pontius Pilate, was crucified; died, and was buried. He descended into hell; the third day he arose again from the dead; he ascended into heaven, sitteth at the right hand of God, the Father Almighty; from thence he shall come to judge the living and the dead. I believe in the Holy Ghost, the holy Catholic Church, the communion of saints, the forgiveness of sins, the resurrection of the body, and life everlasting. Amen.

29. **Why will man go to heaven if he perseveres in prayer?**
Man will go to heaven if he perseveres in prayer, because God is infinitely good, has created all men for heaven, and has promised to hear their prayer.

Good Works

30. **Will faith alone save man?**
Faith alone will not save man, for "faith, if it have not works, is dead."[2]

31. **How does man perform good works?**
Man performs good works by keeping the commandments. "If you love me, keep my commandments."[3]

32. **What is hope?**
Hope is a divine gift by which man firmly trusts that God will give him eternal life and the means to obtain it.

33. **What is charity?**
Charity is a divine gift by which man loves God above all things for his own sake, and his neighbor as himself, for the love of God.

The Rule of Faith

34. **What is the rule of faith?**
The rule of faith is a divine guide whereby man can infallibly possess revealed truth.

35. **Why is a rule of faith necessary?**
A rule of faith is necessary: 1) to discover revealed truth; 2) to preserve purity of doctrine; 3) to settle religious controversies with divine authority.

[2] Jas 2:17
[3] Jn 14:15

36. **What is this guide or rule of faith with divine authority?**
This guide or rule of faith with divine authority is a teaching body sent by God, and guided by him, in leading the faithful to life eternal.

The Motives of Faith

37. **How has God safeguarded the genuineness of his revelation?**
God has safeguarded the genuineness of his revelation by miracles and prophecies.

38. **What is a miracle?**
A miracle is an evident, supernatural, and extraordinary effect produced by God for the benefit of religion.

39. **What is a prophecy?**
A prophecy is an exact prediction of an event that can be foreseen only by God.

40. **Why should man accept divine revelation?**
Man should accept divine revelation because God neither can nor will deceive.

41. **On what does man today base his faith in revelation?**
Man today bases his faith in revelation on the divinity of Jesus Christ, of his teaching, and of his Church.

Jesus Christ: His Personality, His Mission

His Personality

42. **Who is Jesus Christ?**

Jesus Christ is the Son of God, the second Person of the Blessed Trinity, true God and true man.

43. **What is the Blessed Trinity?**

The Blessed Trinity is the union of three divine Persons in one God.[4]

44. **Why is Jesus Christ true God?**

Jesus Christ is true God: 1) because in him were fulfilled the prophecies made concerning the Messias; 2) because he proved his divinity by his miracles, especially by his resurrection from the dead; 3) because his Church has triumphed over the powers of hell as he predicted.[5]

45. **Why is Jesus Christ true man?**

Jesus Christ is true man because he has a human Mother, and a human body and soul like ours.[6]

46. **Had Jesus Christ a human father?**

Jesus Christ had no human father: he was conceived by the power of the Holy Ghost.[7]

47. **Who is the Mother of Jesus Christ?**

The Blessed Virgin Mary is the Mother of Jesus Christ.

[4] See Mt 28:19.
[5] See Mt 3:17; Lk 3:22.
[6] See Lk 1:26-39; 2:1-52; 23:1-47.
[7] See Is 7:14; Lk 1:35.

48. **Give an outline of the life of Jesus Christ.**

The advent of Jesus Christ was announced by the angel Gabriel. His birth in the stable of Bethlehem was proclaimed by angels to shepherds. He spent about seven years of his childhood in exile in Egypt. Up to his thirtieth year, he then lived in seclusion at Nazareth. His public ministry lasted three and one-half years. He lived in poverty and privation, and died on the cross on Mount Calvary on Good Friday.

49. **How many natures are there in Jesus Christ?**

In Jesus Christ there are two natures: the nature of God and the nature of man.[8]

50. **Is Jesus Christ more than one person?**

Jesus Christ is but one divine Person.[9]

51. **Why is there but one person in Jesus Christ?**

There is but one person in Jesus Christ, because his human nature never existed independently of his divinity, but was united to it at the moment his soul was created.[10]

52. **What do we call the union of the divine and the human nature in Jesus Christ?**

The union of the divine and the human nature in Jesus Christ we call "the incarnation of the Son of God."—"The Word was made flesh."[11]

53. **How many wills are there in Jesus Christ?**

In Jesus Christ, there are two wills: a human and a divine will.[12]

[8] See Jn 6:70; 7:12.
[9] See Mt 22:41-44.
[10] See Ps 71:11; Apoc 1:5; 1 Jn 4:3.
[11] Jn 1:14
[12] See Mt 8:29; 9:27.

His Mission

54. **Why did Jesus Christ come into the world?**
Jesus Christ came into the world: 1) to make atonement to his heavenly Father for the sins of the world; 2) to effect the redemption of the human race from the slavery of Satan; 3) to begin the sanctification of mankind by the application of his merits.[13]

55. **Why are the merits of Christ infinite?**
The merits of Christ are infinite because he is a divine Person.[14]

56. **How did Jesus Christ make atonement for the sins of the world?**
Jesus Christ made atonement for the sins of the world by his suffering and death.

57. **What were the chief sufferings of Jesus Christ?**
The chief sufferings of Jesus Christ were his bloody sweat, his cruel scourging, his ignominious crowning with thorns, and his painful death on the cross.

58. **What are the effects of Christ's triumph over Satan?**
The effects of Christ's triumph over Satan are: 1) Christ became Lord and master of the world; 2) he made it possible for man to be justified.

59. **What is justification?**
Justification is that application of Christ's merits to man, which: 1) frees him from the slavery of Satan; 2) gives him spiritual life; 3) makes him a child of God and an heir to the kingdom of heaven.[15]

60. **What is sanctification?**
Sanctification is man's growth in grace, virtue, holiness, and merit.

[13] See 1 Jn 3:8; Lk 2:11; 13:34; Mt 23:37; Eph 2:18.

[14] See Col 1:20.

[15] See Rom 4:25; 5:18.

61. **How is man sanctified?**

Man is sanctified by avoiding evil, and, by using the means of grace which Christ has left him, to do God's will in all things.

62. **What did Jesus Christ to facilitate man's sanctification?**

To facilitate man's sanctification, Jesus Christ did chiefly six things: 1) he completed divine revelation, thus clearly indicating the way to heaven; 2) he promulgated a new law, defining how man should make the journey of life; 3) he instituted special means of grace, called sacraments, to enable all to keep the law; 4) he organized his followers into a society, which he called his Church; 5) he gave that Church the unerring guidance of the Holy Ghost in helping all of good will to sanctify themselves; 6) he promised to watch over that Church to the end of time.

The Church: A Divine Society, Her Attributes, Her Marks, the True Church Today

A Divine Society

63. **What is the Church?**

The Church is a divine society composed of all who profess to pay God the debt of religion as prescribed by divine authority.

64. **Of whom is the Church composed?**

The Church is composed of all who profess the faith of Christ, partake of the same sacraments, and are governed by their lawful pastors under one visible head.

65. **Has the Church a divine and a human element?**
The Church has a divine and a human element.

66. **Why is the Church divine?**
The Church is divine: 1) because she is the mystical body of Christ; 2) because she has Christ for her founder and spiritual head; 3) because she has the Holy Ghost for her soul or principle of undying life; 4) because she is instituted to lead mankind to God.[16]

67. **Why is the Church visible and human?**
The Church is visible and human because she is composed of visible human beings.

Her Attributes

68. **Which are the inherent attributes of a divine Church?**
The inherent attributes of a divine Church are four: authority, infallibility, indefectibility, and necessity.

69. **What do these attributes mean?**
These attributes mean that the true Church must 1) be authorized to act in the name of God; 2) be preserved by him from error; 3) last to the end of time; 4) be the gate to heaven for all of good will.

70. **When did Jesus Christ give his divine authority to his Church?**
Jesus Christ gave his divine authority to his Church when he said: "As the Father hath sent me, so I send you."[17]

[16] See Col 1:18; 1 Cor 3:11; Eph 4:15.
[17] Jn 20:21

71. **Why must a divine Church be infallible in teaching faith and morals?**
A divine Church must be infallible in teaching faith and morals, because she is intended by God to lead all of good will to heaven with divine certainty.

72. **How is the Church of Christ made infallible?**
The Church which Jesus Christ established is made infallible by the power of the Holy Ghost.[18]

73. **Why is the Church of Christ indefectible?**
The Church of Christ is indefectible: 1) because he sent the Holy Ghost to abide with her to the end of time; 2) because he promised to remain with her to the consummation of the world.[19]

74. **Why is the Church of Christ necessary to mankind?**
The Church of Christ is necessary to mankind, because: 1) no one can go to the Father except through Christ; 2) this is the only Church instituted by Christ for the salvation of mankind.

75. **Are all, therefore, bound to belong to the Church which Christ established?**
All are bound to belong to the Church which Christ established, to share in his merits and thus attain life everlasting.[20]

76. **Can those who know the Church of Christ be saved outside of her fold?**
Those who know the Church of Christ cannot be saved outside of her fold.[21]

77. **How can those be saved who do not know the Church of Christ?**
Those who do not know the Church of Christ can be saved by belonging to her in spirit.

[18] See Jn 14:26; Mt 28:20.
[19] See Mt 28:20; Jn 14:16.
[20] See Acts 4:12.
[21] See Mt 18:17.

78. **How can a sincere non-Catholic belong to the Church in spirit?**
A sincere non-Catholic can belong to the Church in spirit by having an efficacious desire of doing all that God has ordained for his salvation; that is, by faith, prayer, perfect sorrow for his sins, and a sincere effort to do the will of God as he understands it.

Her Marks

79. **Are there any marks by which the Church of Christ can be recognized?**
There are four marks by which the Church of Christ may be recognized. It must be one, holy, catholic, and apostolic.

80. **How must the Church of Christ be one?**
The Church of Christ must be one in faith, one in worship, one in obedience, and one in the means of grace throughout the world.

81. **How is the Church of Christ holy?**
The Church of Christ is holy, because: 1) her founder, Jesus Christ, is holy; 2) she teaches a holy doctrine; 3) she invites all to live a holy life; 4) she has aided countless souls to attain great holiness.

82. **How is the Church of Christ catholic or universal?**
The Church of Christ is catholic or universal, because: 1) she teaches all the doctrine of Jesus Christ; 2) she teaches all nations; 3) she subsists in all ages; 4) she was established by Jesus Christ to bring salvation to all of good will.

83. **Why is the Church of Christ apostolic?**
The Church of Christ is apostolic, because: 1) she was founded by Jesus Christ on his apostles; 2) she is governed by their lawful successors; 3) she can never cease to teach their doctrine.

The True Church of Today

84. **What Church of the present day can prove her claim to be the divine Church founded by Jesus Christ?**
The only Church of the present day which can prove her claim to be the divine Church established by Jesus Christ is the Catholic Church.

85. **Which is the Catholic Church?**
The Catholic Church is the Church governed by the pope, the bishop of Rome.

86. **Why is the Catholic Church called "Roman"?**
The Catholic Church is called "Roman," because the pope, her head, resides in Rome.

87. **Why is the Catholic Church the true Church of Jesus Christ?**
The Catholic Church is the true Church of Jesus Christ because: 1) she alone has apostolic succession; 2) she alone possesses the attributes and marks of the true Church; 3) she alone exercises that authority, which is necessary for the Church of God.

88. **How did the other churches, sects, and denominations originate?**
All the other churches, sects, and denominations are of purely human origin.

The Pope, the Primacy of Peter, the Infallibility of the Pope

The Pope

89. **Who is the holy father or pope?**
The holy father or pope is the visible head of the Church, the successor of St. Peter and the vicar of Christ on earth.

90. **Why is a visible head necessary for the Church?**
A visible head is necessary for the Church to maintain her unity of faith, her unity of worship, and her unity of government.

91. **Why must the visible head of the Church today be the successor of St. Peter?**
The visible head of the Church today must be the successor of St. Peter, because Jesus Christ made St. Peter the visible head of his Church.

The Primacy of Peter

92. **When did Christ promise to make St. Peter the head of his Church?**
Christ promised to make St. Peter the head of his Church when he said: "Thou art Peter and upon this rock I will build my church, and the gates of hell shall not prevail against it. And I will give to thee the keys of the kingdom of heaven. Whatsoever thou shalt bind on earth shall be bound in heaven, and whatsoever thou shalt loose on earth shall be loosed in heaven."[22]

[22] Mt 16:18-19

93. **When did Christ make St. Peter the head of his Church?**
Christ made St. Peter the head of his Church when he appeared to his disciples after his resurrection, and solemnly said to Simon Peter: "Feed my lambs—feed my sheep."[23]

94. **Did Christ give St. Peter authority over the other apostles?**
Christ gave St. Peter authority over the other apostles.

95. **What scriptural proofs are there for the primacy of Peter?**
The principal scriptural proofs for the primacy of St. Peter are: 1) St. Matthew calls St. Peter the first apostle;[24] 2) St. Peter proposed the election of a successor to Judas;[25] 3) St. Peter was the first to preach;[26] 4) the first to perform miracles;[27] 5) the first to rebuke civil authorities;[28] 6) the first to receive Gentile converts;[29] 7) in the Council of Jerusalem, there was much disputing until Peter spoke, "when all the multitude held their peace";[30] 8) when the chief pastor was in prison, prayers were offered for his delivery.[31]

The Infallibility of the Pope

96. **Was St. Peter infallible in teaching faith and morals?**
St. Peter was infallible in teaching faith and morals.

[23] Jn 21:15-17
[24] Cf. Mt 10:2
[25] Cf. Acts 1
[26] Cf. Acts 2
[27] Cf. Acts 3
[28] Cf. Acts 4
[29] Cf. Acts 10
[30] Acts 15:12
[31] Cf. Acts 12

97. **Why is the pope an infallible teacher in faith and morals?**
The pope is an infallible teacher in faith and morals because the attributes of a divine Church are necessarily found in their fullness in her headship, which the pope inherits from St. Peter.

98. **When does the pope teach with the infallible guidance of the Holy Ghost?**
The pope teaches with the infallible guidance of the Holy Ghost only when he acts in his official capacity as vicar of Christ, that is, when he publicly teaches a doctrine of faith or morals to be held by all the faithful.

99. **Who are the successors of the other apostles?**
The successors of the other apostles are the bishops of the Catholic Church.

100. **Why does the Catholic Church use the Latin language in the Sacrifice of the Mass and in the administration of the sacraments?**
The Catholic Church uses the Latin, a dead language, whose words always retain the same meaning: 1) to preserve the original doctrine in all its purity; 2) to safeguard the proper form of the sacraments; 3) to obtain clearness and precision in her laws.

SECTION II

The Catholic Doctrine in Particular

On God

101. **What does the Catholic Church teach about God?**

About God the Catholic Church teaches as divinely revealed, that:

1. There is one God, infinitely perfect, who exists of himself from all eternity.
2. In God there are three Persons: Father, Son, and Holy Ghost, equal in all perfections.
3. The Son proceeds from the Father, and the Holy Ghost from the Father and the Son from all eternity.
4. God loves to show his goodness and mercy to mankind.

On Creation and the Fall of Man

102. **What does the Catholic Church teach on the creation of the world and the fall of our first parents?**

On the creation of the world and the fall of our first parents, the Catholic Church teaches as divinely revealed, that:

1. God created all things in time, for his glory and the welfare of his creatures.

2. God created angels and men in original justice, endowed them with intelligence and free will, and subjected them to a trial.
3. The supernatural joys of heaven were to be the reward of the fidelity of angels and men.
4. Some angels rebelled against God and were cast into hell.
5. God gave a man a guardian angel.
6. Man, tempted by Satan, ate of the forbidden fruit, and lost his right to heaven.
7. Human nature was weakened but not essentially changed by original sin.
8. All mankind is descended from Adam and Eve.
9. God creates every human soul.
10. The guilt of original sin is transmitted to the children of Adam by generation.
11. God promised mankind a Redeemer.

On Redemption

103. **What does the Catholic Church teach on the redemption of mankind?**
On the redemption of mankind, the Catholic Church teaches as divinely revealed, that:

1. God the Son assumed human nature from the Virgin Mary, uniting the human and the divine nature in one divine Person, Jesus Christ.
2. Jesus Christ has a human and a divine will.
3. Jesus Christ died for the redemption of all mankind.
4. The merits of Christ are infinite.
5. Jesus Christ rose from the dead and ascended into heaven by his own divine power.
6. The Virgin Mary gave the God-man, Jesus Christ, his body, and is therefore truly the Mother of God.

7. To make Mary worthy of her divine maternity, God preserved her from original sin.
8. In consequence, Mary's body did not taste corruption, but was reunited after her death to her soul, and both taken to heaven.

On Sanctification

104. **What does the Catholic Church teach on the sanctification of mankind?**
On the sanctification of mankind, the Catholic Church teaches as divinely revealed, that:

1. In Christ's merits is salvation for all of good will.
2. Christ established the one, holy, catholic, apostolic Church to teach, guide, and govern the faithful.
3. Christ made St. Peter the head of his Church.
4. The pope is the lawful successor of St. Peter.
5. Christ gave his Church the infallible guidance of the Holy Ghost.
6. The Catholic Church is the guardian of revealed truth as contained in divine tradition and sacred scripture.
7. The Holy Ghost keeps the pope, the vicar of Christ on earth, from error when he teaches a doctrine of faith and morals to be held by all the faithful.
8. Public revelation was completed with the apostles.
9. Faith alone will not save man, but good morals or good works, are necessary.
10. God gives sufficient grace for salvation to all mankind.
11. Prayer is the universal means of obtaining God's help.
12. Christ instituted seven sacraments as special fountains of grace.
13. Every sin can be forgiven.
14. Charity unites God's friends on earth with those in heaven and in purgatory.

15. Due veneration of angels and saints is pleasing to God.
16. It is a holy thought to pray for the souls in purgatory.
17. The pious use of sacramentals disposes us for and draws down God's special blessing upon us.

The Last Things

105. **What does the Catholic Church teach on the last things?**

On the last things, the Catholic Church teaches as divinely revealed, that:

1. Man's probation ends with death.
2. The particular judgment follows immediately after death.
3. The good go to heaven and the wicked go to hell after the particular judgment.
4. Those who are not entirely purified go to purgatory after the particular judgment.
5. This world will come to an end when God wills.
6. The dead will rise again on the last day.
7. On the last day, Jesus Christ will come again to judge the living and the dead.
8. After the general judgment, the elect will enter life eternal, but the reprobate will go into the everlasting torments of hell.
9. The thought of the last things inspires man with the fear of the Lord and the love of God.

Knowledge of the Word of God

106. **What is the word of God?**
The word of God is all that God has revealed for man's salvation.

107. **What does the knowledge of God's word do for man?**
The knowledge of God's word 1) enables man to know what to believe, what to do, and what means to use to please God; 2) it moves all of good will to seek to please God.

108. **Is the knowledge of God's word necessary to man's salvation?**
Some knowledge of God's word is necessary to man's salvation.

109. **How can man obtain a knowledge of God's word?**
Man can obtain a knowledge of God's word: 1) by listening to the Sunday sermons; 2) by reading the Bible and books of instruction; 3) by consulting his pastor or father confessor; 4) by cultivating the society of intelligent and practical Catholics.

110. **What knowledge of God's word is essential for man's salvation?**
For man's salvation, it is essential to know: 1) that there is one God, infinitely perfect; 2) that God will reward the good and punish the wicked forever; 3) that in God there are three divine Persons, Father, Son, and Holy Ghost; 4) that God the Son became man and died for our salvation.

111. **What additional knowledge is necessary for the proper reception of the sacraments?**
For the proper reception of the sacraments, it is besides necessary to know: 1) that Jesus Christ established the Catholic Church to lead men to heaven; 2) that he instituted seven sacraments as fountains of grace; 3) that God promised to hear our prayer; 4) to have a knowledge of the Our Father,

Hail Mary, Apostles' Creed, ten commandments, and the six precepts; 5) to have a knowledge of the nature of the sacrament to be received.

The Law of God

112. What is the law of God?

The law of God is the will of God, binding the liberty of man in conscience.

113. Where is the law of God summed up?

The law of God is summed up principally in the ten commandments of God and in the six precepts of the Church.

114. Which are the ten commandments?

The ten commandments are:

1. I am the Lord thy God; thou shalt not have strange gods before me.
2. Thou shalt not take the name of the Lord thy God in vain.
3. Remember thou keep holy the sabbath day.
4. Honor thy father and thy mother.
5. Thou shalt not kill.
6. Thou shalt not commit adultery.
7. Thou shalt not steal.
8. Thou shalt not bear false witness against thy neighbor.
9. Thou shalt not covet thy neighbor's wife.
10. Thou shalt not covet thy neighbor's goods.

115. Which are the six precepts?

The six precepts are:

1. To hear Mass on Sundays and holy days of obligation.
2. To fast and abstain on the days appointed.
3. To confess at least once a year.

4. To receive the Holy Eucharist during the Easter time.
5. To contribute to the support of our pastors.
6. Not to marry non-Catholics, nor those who are related to us within the fourth degree of kindred, nor privately without pastor and two witnesses, nor to solemnize marriage at forbidden time.

116. **How did Christ sum up the law of God?**
Christ summed up the law of God in three points: 1) "If anyone will come after me, let him deny himself and take up his cross and follow me."[32] 2) "Thou shalt love the Lord thy God with thy whole heart, with thy whole soul, and with thy whole mind."[33] 3) "Thou shalt love thy neighbor as thyself."[34]

117. **Has the Catholic Church the power to make laws that bind man in conscience?**
The Catholic Church has the power to make laws that bind man in conscience, for Jesus Christ gave her that power when he said: "As the Father hath sent me, so I also send you."[35] "If he will not hear the Church, let him be to thee as the heathen and publican."[36]

118. **In what matters can the Catholic Church bind her subjects in conscience?**
The Catholic Church can bind her subjects in conscience in all matters that pertain directly or indirectly to the salvation of their immortal souls.

[32] Mt 16:24
[33] Mt 22:37
[34] Mt 22:39
[35] Jn 20:21
[36] Mt 18:17

Sin

119. **What is sin?**

Sin is any willful breaking of God's law.

120. **Which are the seven capital sins, or sources of sins?**

The seven capital sins, or sources of sin are: pride, covetousness, lust, anger, gluttony, envy, and sloth.

SIN OF THE ANGELS, CONSEQUENCE OF THEIR TRIAL

Sin of the Angels

121. **Who committed the first sin?**

The rebellious angels committed the first sin.

122. **What are angels?**

Angels are pure spirits created to adore, love, and serve God in heaven.

123. **Why did God try the angels?**

God tried the angels that they might earn the reward of heaven.

124. **How did God try the angels?**

God tried the angels by giving them a commandment.

125. **What commandment did God give the angels?**

It is a probable opinion that God revealed to the angels the mystery of the incarnation and commanded them to adore the God-man.[37]

[37] Cf. Heb 1:6

126. **What sin did the angels commit?**
Some of the angels committed a sin of pride and disobedience in transgressing God's commandment.

Consequence of Their Trial

127. **What was the consequence of the trial of the angels?**
The consequence of the trial of the angels was that the good angels were taken to heaven and the rebellious angels were cast into hell.

128. **What do we now call the rebellious angels?**
We now call the rebellious angels, "demons," "devils," or "bad angels."

129. **Who was the leader of the rebellious angels?**
Lucifer was the leader of the rebellious angels.

130. **What do the bad angels do now?**
The bad angels oppose the designs of God by tempting man to sin.

131. **What do the good angels do for us?**
The good angels pray for us, oppose the designs of the devils, and are appointed by God as our guardian angel.[38]

ORIGINAL SIN, CONSEQUENCE OF THE FALL OF OUR FIRST PARENTS

Original Sin

132. **What is original sin?**
Original sin is the sin we inherit from Adam, the father of the human race.

[38] Cf. Mt 18:10

133. **In what does original sin, as we inherit it, practically consist?**
Original sin, as we inherit it, practically consists in the privation of the friendship of God.

134. **Why do we inherit the sin of Adam?**
We inherit the sin of Adam because by God's positive design, revealed to Adam, Adam, as head of the human race, was to act in the name of mankind in preserving or losing original justice and holiness.

135. **Who were our first parents?**
Our first parents were Adam and Eve.

136. **Were Adam and Eve innocent and holy when God created them?**
Adam and Eve were innocent and holy when God created them.

137. **What commandment did God give Adam and Eve?**
To try their obedience, God commanded Adam and Eve not to eat of a certain fruit which grew in the garden of paradise.

138. **How did Adam and Eve sin?**
Eve was tempted by Satan under the form of a serpent, and ate of the forbidden fruit. She then persuaded Adam to do the same.

Consequence of the Fall of Our First Parents

139. **What befell Adam and Eve on account of their sin?**
On account of their sin, Adam and Eve lost innocence and holiness and were doomed to sickness and death.

140. **Which were the chief blessings intended for Adam and Eve, had they remained faithful?**
The chief blessings intended for Adam and Eve, had they remained faithful, were a state of constant happiness in this life, without pain or death, and everlasting happiness in heaven.

141. **What do we now inherit from Adam?**

We now inherit the sin of Adam and its punishment, just as we would have inherited the happiness of our first parents if they had remained faithful.

142. **What other effects flow from original sin?**

In consequence of original sin, the nature of man is corrupted, his understanding darkened, his will weakened, and his whole nature inclined to evil.

143. **Who alone was preserved from incurring original sin?**

The Blessed Virgin Mary alone was preserved from incurring original sin.

144. **Why was the Blessed Virgin Mary preserved from incurring original sin?**

The Blessed Virgin Mary was preserved from incurring original sin because she was the woman destined to crush the serpent's head by becoming the Mother of God.

145. **What is this privilege of Mary called?**

This privilege of Mary is called her "immaculate conception."

MORTAL SIN, HELL

146. **What is actual sin?**

Actual sin is any willful thought, desire, word, deed, or omission forbidden by the law of God.

147. **How is actual sin divided?**

Actual sin is divided into mortal sin and venial sin.

Mortal Sin

148. **What is mortal sin?**

Mortal sin is a grievous offense against the law of God.

149. **How is mortal sin committed?**

Mortal sin is committed by transgressing the law of God, 1) in a serious or grievous matter; 2) while adverting to the gravity of the transgression; 3) and acting with a bad will.

150. **What are the consequences of mortal sin?**

The consequences of mortal sin are: 1) the loss of sanctifying grace; 2) the enmity of God; 3) the slavery of Satan; 4) the penalty of the torments of hell.

151. **Is mortal sin a great evil?**

Mortal sin is the greatest evil in the world, because it robs man of God and heaven, the greatest good.

152. **Which are the six sins against the Holy Ghost?**

The six sins against the Holy Ghost are: presumption, despair, resisting the known truth, envy of another's spiritual good, obstinacy in sin, and final impenitence.

Hell

153. **What do the reprobates suffer in hell?**

In hell, the reprobates suffer an agony of remorse and despair for having lost eternal happiness. They are the slaves of Satan, imprisoned, and tortured by an avenging fire.

VENIAL SIN, PURGATORY

Venial Sin

154. **What is venial sin?**

Venial sin is a slight offense against the law of God.

155. **How is venial sin committed?**
Venial sin is committed by transgressing the law of God, 1) in a light matter; or 2) without sufficient knowledge or full consent of the will.

156. **What are the consequences of venial sin?**
The consequences of venial sin are: 1) the lessening of the love of God; 2) disposing the soul to mortal sin; 3) the penalty of temporal punishment.

157. **What is temporal punishment?**
Temporal punishment is the punishment that will have an end either in this world or in the next.

158. **Of what does temporal punishment consist?**
Temporal punishment consists of remorse, sickness, and reverses in this life, and of the pains of purgatory in the next life.

Purgatory

159. **What is purgatory?**
Purgatory is the state in which those suffer for a time who die guilty of venial sins, or who die without having fully satisfied for the punishment due to their forgiven sins.

160. **How can we satisfy in this life for the temporal punishment due to sin?**
In this life, we can satisfy for the temporal punishment due to sin by prayer, fasting, almsdeeds, by the spiritual and corporal works of mercy, and by the patient suffering of the ills of life.

JUDGMENT: PARTICULAR, GENERAL

161. **When will man be judged?**
Man will be judged at the moment of death and at the end of the world.

162. **Who will be man's judge?**
Jesus Christ will be man's judge.

163. **Why will Jesus Christ judge man?**
Jesus Christ will judge man because he has acquired dominion over man by paying the price of his ransom.

164. **How will Jesus Christ judge man at the hour of death?**
Jesus Christ will judge man at the hour of death as God.

165. **How will Jesus Christ judge man at the end of the world?**
Jesus Christ will come with great power and majesty as the God-man at the end of the world and judge angels and men.

166. **Why will man be judged at the hour of death?**
Man will be judged at the hour of death to receive his reward or punishment.

167. **Why will man be judged at the end of the world?**
Man will be judged at the end of the world: 1) to vindicate the providence of God before the world; 2) to reward the elect publicly; 3) to overwhelm the reprobate with public confusion.

168. **What will take place before the general judgment?**
Before the general judgment, the resurrection of the dead will take place.

169. **How will the dead rise on the last day?**
The dead will rise on the last day through the power of God, their Creator.

170. **Why will man's body rise on the last day?**
Man's body will rise on the last day to share in the reward or punishment, as it shared in the good or wicked deeds of life.

Conscience

171. **What is conscience?**

Conscience is the judgment of man's reason regarding the morality of his actions.

172. **Why did God give man a conscience?**

God gave man a conscience to discern good from evil, and to judge himself so that God may not judge him unfavorably after this life.

173. **How is conscience divided?**

Conscience is divided into true, right, wrong, erroneous, and doubtful.

174. **What is a true conscience?**

A true conscience is one that agrees with the mind of God.

175. **What is a right conscience?**

A right conscience is one which is sincerely dictated according to the law of God.

176. **What is a wrong conscience?**

A wrong conscience is one that is knowingly dictated contrary to the law of God.

177. **What is an erroneous conscience?**

An erroneous conscience is one that is sincerely dictated contrary to the law of God.

178. **What is a doubtful conscience?**

A doubtful conscience is that state of mind in which man has not sufficient knowledge of a particular right or duty to form a just judgment of the morality of his action.

179. **Is it right to act with a doubtful conscience?**
It is not right to act with a doubtful conscience.

180. **How can man dispose of his doubt?**
Man can dispose of his doubt: 1) by further investigation; 2) by following the presumption in the case, if the doubt still remains.

181. **What does the presumption favor?**
Presumption favors 1) human liberty as long as it is not evidently restrained by the law of God; 2) it then favors the law until liberty is evidently freed again.

182. **What is the first obligation of conscience?**
The first obligation of conscience is to strive to form a true conscience.

183. **What hinders the formation of a true conscience?**
Ignorance, passion, and human respect hinder the formation of a true conscience.

184. **What is the result of acting with a right conscience?**
The result of acting with a right conscience is moral goodness or holiness.

The Ten Commandments

THE FIRST COMMANDMENT

185. **What is the first commandment?**
The first commandment is: I am the Lord thy God; thou shalt not have strange gods before me.

186. **What does the first commandment command?**

The first commandment commands us to worship God by acts of faith, hope, and charity; by prayer and sacrifice.

187. **What does the first commandment forbid?**

The first commandment forbids especially idolatry, false worship, superstition, neglect of prayer, all dealings with devils, spirit-mediums, and fortune tellers, and all sins against faith, hope, and charity.

188. **Which are the chief sins against faith?**

The chief sins against faith are: 1) willful religious ignorance; 2) willful religious indifference; 3) maliciously to deny God; 4) obstinately to refuse to believe his revelation; 5) not to profess the faith openly when circumstances require it.

189. **What leads to a loss of faith?**

A godless education, reading irreligious and immoral books, attending false worship, membership in un-Catholic societies, immorality, and intimate association with godless and immoral persons lead to a loss of faith.

190. **What are the sins against hope?**

The sins against hope are presumption and despair.

191. **Which sins offend against the love of God?**

All sins offend against the love of God, but especially hatred of God and holy things.

192. **Do transgressions against the first commandment constitute a grievous matter?**

Transgressions against the first commandment generally constitute a grievous matter.

THE SECOND COMMANDMENT

193. **What is the second commandment?**
The second commandment is: Thou shalt not take the name of the Lord thy God in vain.

194. **What does the second commandment command?**
The second commandment commands us: 1) to use the name of God reverently; 2) to speak with respect of God, holy persons, and holy things; 3) to keep our lawful oaths and vows.

195. **What does the second commandment forbid?**
The second commandment forbids the taking of God's name in vain, profane words, blasphemy, cursing, false and unjust oaths.

196. **Do transgressions against the second commandment constitute a light or a grievous matter?**
Blasphemy, cursing, and perjury constitute a grievous matter. Taking God's name in vain and profane words are ordinarily a light matter.

THE THIRD COMMANDMENT

197. **What is the third commandment?**
The third commandment is: Remember that thou keep holy the sabbath day.

198. **Which is the sabbath day?**
Saturday is the sabbath day.

199. **Why do we observe Sunday instead of Saturday?**
We observe Sunday instead of Saturday because the Catholic Church, in the Council of Laodicea (A.D. 336), transferred the solemnity from Saturday to Sunday.

200. **Why did the Catholic Church substitute Sunday for Saturday?**
The Church substituted Sunday for Saturday, because Christ rose from the dead on a Sunday, and the Holy Ghost descended upon the apostles on a Sunday.

201. **By what authority did the Church substitute Sunday for Saturday?**
The Church substituted Sunday for Saturday by the plenitude of that divine power which Jesus Christ bestowed upon her.

202. **What does the third commandment command?**
The third commandment commands us to sanctify Sunday as the Lord's day.

203. **What does the third commandment forbid?**
The third commandment forbids: 1) the omission of prayer and divine worship; 2) all unnecessary servile work; 3) whatever hinders the keeping of the Lord's day holy.

204. **Is the desecration of the Lord's day a grievous matter?**
The desecration of the Lord's day is a grievous matter in itself, though it admits of light matter.

THE FOURTH COMMANDMENT

205. **What is the fourth commandment?**
The fourth commandment is: Honor thy father and thy mother.

206. **What does the fourth commandment command?**
The fourth commandment commands: 1) children to love, honor, and obey their parents; 2) parents to provide for the temporal welfare of their children and give them a religious education; 3) it defines the duties of subjects and superiors.

207. **What reward did God promise to obedient children?**
God has promised a long and happy life to obedient children.

208. **What does the fourth commandment forbid?**
The fourth commandment forbids: 1) all disobedience, ill will, and contempt of parents, and other lawful superiors; 2) all neglect of duty in parents and other superiors.

209. **Is a transgression against the fourth commandment a grievous or a light matter?**
A transgression against the fourth commandment may be either a grievous or a light matter.

THE FIFTH COMMANDMENT

210. **What is the fifth commandment?**
The fifth commandment is: Thou shalt not kill.

211. **What does the fifth commandment command?**
The fifth commandment commands us to respect our neighbor's right to life, liberty, and heaven, and to consult our own temporal and spiritual welfare.

212. **What does the fifth commandment forbid?**
The fifth commandment forbids: 1) the injury of our neighbor's life and liberty, as hatred, revenge, angry and contemptuous words, blows, murder; 2) injury to our neighbor's soul, by scandal, leading him into sin, or cooperating in his sin; 3) all abuse of our own life and liberty, by excess in eating and drinking, or otherwise injuring our health, and suicide.

213. **Is a transgression against the fifth commandment a grievous or a light matter?**
A transgression against the fifth commandment may be either a grievous or a light matter.

THE SIXTH AND NINTH COMMANDMENTS

214. **What is the sixth commandment?**
The sixth commandment is: Thou shalt not commit adultery.

215. **What is the ninth commandment?**
The ninth commandment is: Thou shalt not covet thy neighbor's wife.

216. **What do the sixth and the ninth commandments command?**
The sixth and ninth commandments command us to be chaste in thought, desire, words, and actions.

217. **What does the sixth and ninth commandments forbid?**
The sixth and ninth commandments forbid all immodesty in thoughts, desires, words, and actions.

218. **Is a transgression against the sixth and ninth commandments a grievous matter?**
A direct transgression against the sixth and ninth commandments is always a grievous matter.

THE SEVENTH AND TENTH COMMANDMENTS

219. **What is the seventh commandment?**
The seventh commandment is: Thou shall not steal.

220. **What is the tenth commandment?**
The tenth commandment is: Thou shalt not covet thy neighbor's goods.

221. **What do the seventh and tenth commandments command?**
The seventh and tenth commandments command us to respect our neighbor's right to his property in desire and in action.

222. **What do the seventh and tenth commandments forbid?**
The seventh and tenth commandments forbid to desire, take, keep, or damage our neighbor's goods.

223. **What must he do who has willfully wronged his neighbor's right to his property?**
He who has willfully wronged his neighbor's right to his property must make restitution as soon as possible.

224. **Is a transgression against the seventh and tenth commandments a grievous or a light matter?**
A transgression against the seventh and tenth commandments may be either a grievous or a light matter.

THE EIGHTH COMMANDMENT

225. **What is the eighth commandment?**
The eighth commandment is: Thou shalt not bear false witness against thy neighbor.

226. **What does the eighth commandment command?**
The eighth commandment commands us to tell the truth and to be charitable in our words.

227. **What does the eighth commandment forbid?**
The eighth commandment forbids us to lie to our neighbor, or to injure him by calumnies, detractions, violations of secrecy, unjust suspicions, rash judgments, or unkind words.

228. **What must he do who has injured his neighbor's good name?**
He who has injured his neighbor's good name must undo the harm as soon as possible.

229. **Is a transgression against the eighth commandment a grievous or a light matter?**
A transgression against the eighth commandment may be either a grievous or a light matter.

The Six Precepts of the Church

230. **Which are the chief laws which the Church has made?**
The chief laws which the Church has made are the six precepts of the Church.

231. **Is a transgression of the precepts of the Church a grievous or a light matter?**
A transgression of the precepts of the Church is always a grievous matter.

232. **Why is a transgression of the precepts of the Church always a grievous matter?**
A transgression of the precepts of the Church is always a grievous matter because the precepts indicate the lowest standard consistent with Catholic practice.

THE FIRST PRECEPT

233. **What is the first precept?**
The first precept is: To hear Mass on Sundays and holy days of obligation.

234. **Why did the Church institute holy days?**
The Church instituted holy days to recall to our minds the great events in the life of our Lord and the saints.

235. **Which are the holy days of obligation in the United States?**
The holy days of obligation in the United States are:
1. The Circumcision of Our Lord, January 1st.
2. The Ascension of Our Lord, the fortieth day after Easter Sunday.
3. The Assumption of Our Lady, August 15th.
4. All Saints, November 1st.
5. The Immaculate Conception of Our Blessed Lady, December 8th.
6. The Birth of Our Lord, December 25th.

236. **How should we keep holy days of obligation?**
We should keep holy days of obligation as we should keep Sundays.

237. **Why is missing Mass on Sundays and holy days of obligation a grievous matter?**
Missing Mass on Sundays and holy days of obligation is a grievous matter because at least on these days we must unite ourselves to Jesus Christ, our mediator and high priest, to offer an acceptable sacrifice of adoration, thanksgiving, reparation, and petition to the eternal Father.

THE SECOND PRECEPT

238. **What is the second precept?**
The second precept is: To fast and abstain on days appointed.

239. **What are fast days?**
Fast days are days on which we are allowed but one full meal.

240. **What are days of abstinence?**
Days of abstinence are days on which the use of flesh meat is forbidden.

241. **Why are we commanded to fast and abstain?**
We are commanded to fast and abstain: 1) to practice self-denial and thereby bring the flesh under the dominion of the spirit; 2) to do penance for our sins.

242. **Why are we commanded to abstain from flesh meat on Fridays?**
We are commanded to abstain from flesh meat on Fridays: 1) as an act of gratitude to our Savior who died for us on Friday; 2) to do penance for our sins and thereby share in his merits.

243. **Who makes known to us the days and manner of fasting and abstinence?**
The bishop through our pastors makes known to us the days and manner of fasting and abstinence.

244. **Which are the fast days and days of abstinence in the United States?**
The fast days in the United States are: 1) The forty days of Lent; 2) the Vigils of Pentecost, the Assumption, All Saints, and Christmas; 3) the Ember days—these are the Wednesday, Friday, and Saturday, a) after the First Sunday in Lent, b) after Pentecost, c) after the fourteenth of September, d) after the Third Sunday in Advent; 4) the Fridays in Advent in the Provinces of Baltimore, Philadelphia, New York, and Boston.

The days of abstinence in the United States are: 1) all Fridays of the year, excepting when Christmas falls on a Friday; 2) all fast days.

245. **Who are dispensed from the fast prescribed by the Church?**
The sick, the infirm, and those who labor hard are dispensed from the fast prescribed by the Church.

246. **What should those do who have doubts about the law of fasting and abstinence?**
Those who have doubts about the laws of fasting and abstinence should consult their pastor or confessor.

THE THIRD PRECEPT

247. **What is the third precept?**
The third precept is: To confess our sins at least once a year.

248. **Why does the Church command us to confess at least once a year?**
The Church commands us to confess at least once a year: 1) to warn us against presuming on the mercy of God, which is a sin against the Holy Ghost; 2) to induce us to live Christian lives.

249. **At what age must parents prepare their children to go to confession?**
Parents must prepare their children for confession when the children learn to distinguish right from wrong, that is, when they are about seven years old.

THE FOURTH PRECEPT

250. **What is the fourth precept?**
The fourth precept is: To receive Holy Communion during Easter time.

251. **What is the Easter time in the United States?**
The Easter time in the United States begins with the First Sunday of Lent and ends with Trinity Sunday.

252. **Why does the Church command us to receive Holy Communion during Easter time?**
The Church commands us to receive Holy Communion at Easter time: 1) because Christ gave us a pledge of eternal life by his resurrection on Easter Sunday; 2) to warn us that we forfeit our claim to this pledge if we neglect to receive him during this time.

THE FIFTH PRECEPT

253. **What is the fifth precept?**
The fifth precept is: To contribute to the support of our Church, school, and pastor.

254. **What does the fifth precept command?**

The fifth precept commands us to contribute according to our means to the support of religion.

255. **Why should we contribute to the support of religion?**

We should contribute to the support of religion, because: 1) every society must supply its own want; 2) because religion is impossible without Church, school, and pastor; 3) because the school is the nursery of the parish; 4) because the laborer is worthy of his hire; 5) because the sacrifice of material offerings disposes us for spiritual blessings.

THE SIXTH PRECEPT: IMPEDIMENTS, DISPENSATIONS, DIVORCE, SEPARATION

Impediments to Marriage

256. **What is the sixth precept?**

The sixth precept is: Not to marry non-Catholics; nor to marry those who are related to us within the fourth degree of kinship; nor to solemnize marriage at forbidden times; and not to marry except in the presence of a duly appointed pastor and two witnesses.

257. **What does the sixth precept command?**

The sixth precept commands Catholics: 1) to marry Catholics; 2) who are not related to them within the fourth degree of kinship; 3) before their pastor and two witnesses; 4) during the open season of the year; 5) after the triple publication of the banns; 6) with the solemn blessing of the Church.

258. **What is a marriage impediment?**

A marriage impediment is a prohibition of God or his Church forbidding certain marriages.

259. **Why should Catholics marry Catholics?**
Catholics should marry Catholics to safeguard their own spiritual welfare and that of their children.

260. **Why should persons not marry near relatives?**
Persons should not marry near relatives because such marriages are unnatural and have a hurtful effect on the physical welfare of the children.

261. **Why must Catholics marry in the presence of their pastor and two witnesses?**
Catholics must marry in the presence of their pastor and two witnesses to safeguard the general welfare of religion.

262. **What is the open season for marriages?**
The open season for marriages extends from the seventh of January to Ash Wednesday, and from the First Sunday after Easter to the First Sunday in Advent.

263. **Why does the Church require a triple publication of the banns?**
The Church requires a triple publication of the banns to discover whether any impediments exist to the marriage.

264. **What is the marriage blessing?**
The marriage blessing is a most special blessing which the Church imparts only to Catholics who are married at a nuptial Mass.

265. **When does a Catholic contract an invalid marriage?**
A Catholic contracts an invalid marriage by marrying without the necessary dispensation: 1) a person not baptized; 2) a person related within the fourth degree of kinship; 3) by marrying otherwise than before the parish priest and two witnesses; 4) by marrying when any other invalidating impediment exists.

Dispensations

266. **What is a marriage dispensation?**
A marriage dispensation is an exemption to marry contrary to the laws of the Church.

267. **From whom must a marriage dispensation be obtained?**
A marriage dispensation must be obtained from the bishop of the diocese in which the parties live.

268. **Is a grave reason necessary to ask for a marriage dispensation?**
A grave reason is necessary to ask for a marriage dispensation.

Divorce, Separation

269. **What is divorce?**
Divorce is the dissolving of the marriage bond.

270. **Can man grant a divorce valid in the sight of God?**
No man can grant a divorce valid in the sight of God, for Christ said: "What God hath joined together, let no man put asunder."[39]

271. **What is a separation?**
A separation is a suspension of the actual marriage relation.

272. **What cause suffices for a temporary separation?**
Mutual consent for the sake of health, business, and the like, suffices for a temporary separation.

273. **What cause justifies a permanent separation?**
Infidelity, and grave danger of corporal or spiritual harm justifies a permanent separation.

[39] Mt 19:6

274. **Should Catholics consult their pastor before taking this extreme step?**
Catholics should consult their pastor before taking this extreme step.

275. **When may a Catholic have a permanent separation ratified by a civil divorce?**
A Catholic may have a permanent separation ratified by civil divorce when legal rights must be safeguarded.

276. **Is a Catholic in the United States bound to consult ecclesiastical authority before applying for a civil divorce?**
A Catholic in the United States is bound to consult ecclesiastical authority before applying for a civil divorce.[40]

277. **Dare Catholics ever regard a divorced person as eligible to marriage?**
Catholics dare not regard divorced persons as eligible to marriage unless their former marriage has been declared null and void by the ecclesiastical court.

The Evangelical Counsels, Vocation

The Evangelical Counsels

278. **What are the evangelical counsels?**
The evangelical counsels are our Savior's counsels to practice voluntary poverty, virginal chastity, and perfect obedience out of love for God.

279. **Why are they called "evangelical counsels"?**
They are called "evangelical counsels" because they are recorded by the evangelist.

[40] See the Third Plenary Council of Baltimore, n. 126.

280. **Does the practice of the evangelical counsels lead to the summit of Christian perfection?**
The practice of the evangelical counsels does lead to the summit of Christian perfection.

281. **How does the practice of the evangelical counsels lead to the summit of Christian perfection?**
The practice of the evangelical counsels leads to the summit of Christian perfection by remedying the three great sources of moral evil, which St. John calls the "concupiscence of the eyes, the concupiscence of the flesh, and the pride of life."[41]

282. **Who should embrace the evangelical counsels?**
Only those should embrace the evangelical counsels who have received a special vocation from God.

Vocation

283. **What are the general signs of a divine vocation to a particular state in life?**
The general signs of a divine vocation to a particular state in life are: 1) a constant desire to sanctify oneself in that state; 2) mental, moral, physical fitness; 3) the absence of impediments to that state.

284. **How many kinds of divine vocations are there?**
There are four kinds of divine vocations: 1) to the clerical state; 2) to the religious state; 3) to the life of virginity in the world; 4) to the married state.

285. **Which is nobler, the married state or virginity?**
Virginity is nobler than the married state.[42]

[41] 1 Jn 2:16
[42] See 1 Cor 7:1-40.

286. **What is a necessary and sure preparation for a divine vocation?**
A pure and devout life is a necessary and sure preparation for any vocation.

On Grace

287. **What can man do when left to his natural strength?**
When left to his natural strength, man can live only a natural, human life.

288. **What does man need to live the life of a child of God?**
To live the life of a child of God, man needs the grace of God.

289. **What is grace?**
Grace is a divine help given to man through the merits of Christ for his salvation.

290. **What claim has man on God's help?**
Man's only claim on God's help rests on the goodness and promises of God and the merits of his Savior.

291. **How may man dispose himself for the grace of God?**
Man disposes himself for the grace of God by observing the law of God as far as he knows it, and by practicing charity toward his neighbor.

292. **How is grace divided?**
Grace is divided into sanctifying and actual grace.

293. **What is sanctifying grace?**
Sanctifying grace is that grace which makes man holy and pleasing in the sight of God. It is also called "habitual grace," and "the grace of justification."

294. **How may man obtain sanctifying grace?**
Man may obtain sanctifying grace: 1) by receiving the sacraments of baptism and penance; 2) by perfect sorrow for his sins and ardent desire to do whatever God has ordained for his salvation.

295. **How does man lose sanctifying grace?**
Man loses sanctifying grace by committing any mortal sin.

296. **What is actual grace?**
Actual grace is a transient help of God, which enlightens the mind, and moves the will to perform virtuous actions.

297. **Can man neglect the grace of God?**
Man can, and unfortunately often does neglect the grace of God.

298. **What is the grace of perseverance?**
The grace of perseverance is a chain of actual graces which enables man to persevere in the friendship of God until death.

299. **How can man obtain the grace of God?**
Man can obtain the grace of God by prayer, the devout reception of the sacraments, and the pious use of the sacramentals.

The Sacraments

300. **What are the great means instituted by Christ to give grace?**
The great means instituted by Christ to give grace are the sacraments.

301. **What is a sacrament?**
A sacrament is an outward sign instituted by Christ to give grace.

302. **How many sacraments are there?**
There are seven sacraments.

303. **Which are the seven sacraments?**
The seven sacraments are: baptism, confirmation, Holy Eucharist, penance, extreme unction, holy orders, and matrimony.

304. **Why did Christ institute seven sacraments?**
Christ instituted seven sacraments to supply the seven spiritual wants of mankind.

305. **Which are the seven spiritual wants of mankind?**
The seven spiritual wants of mankind are: 1) spiritual life; 2) the perfection of spiritual life; 3) nourishment for the spiritual life; 4) a remedy for spiritual disease and death; 5) special provision for the journey to eternity; 6) power and strength to minister in the name of Christ; 7) special grace to bring up children for heaven.

306. **What graces do the sacraments give?**
Every sacrament gives a special grace, and all give, or increase, sanctifying grace.

307. **What special graces do the sacraments give?**
The special graces which the sacraments give is a right to those actual graces that are necessary to attain the end for which Christ instituted each particular sacrament. This special grace is called "sacramental grace."

308. **Which sacraments were instituted to give sanctifying grace?**
Baptism and penance were instituted to give sanctifying grace.

309. **Which sacraments were instituted to increase sanctifying grace?**
Confirmation, Holy Eucharist, extreme unction, holy orders, and matrimony were instituted to increase sanctifying grace.

310. **Which sacraments can be received but once?**
Baptism, confirmation, and holy orders can be received but once.

311. **Why can baptism, confirmation, and holy orders be received but once?**
Baptism, confirmation, and holy orders can be received but once, because these sacraments always attain their end by one reception, and therefore imprint a character on the soul that will last forever.

312. **How do the sacraments produce their effect?**
The sacraments produce their effect through the power of Christ, as long as we place no obstacle in the way.

313. **Which is the ordinary place for the administration and reception of the sacraments?**
The church is the ordinary place for the administration and reception of the sacraments.

314. **What sin is it to receive a sacrament unworthily?**
It is a sacrilege to receive a sacrament unworthily.

BAPTISM

315. **What is baptism?**
Baptism is a sacrament which frees us from original sin, makes us children of God, brethren of Christ, and coheirs with him of the kingdom of heaven.

316. **Does baptism ever remit actual sin?**
Baptism remits actual sin whenever the person baptized is guilty of any.

317. **Is baptism necessary for salvation?**
Baptism is necessary for salvation, for Christ says: "Unless a man be born again of water and the Holy Ghost, he shall not enter the kingdom of heaven."[43]

318. **Who can baptize?**
Any person having the use of reason can baptize.

319. **Who is the ordinary minister of baptism?**
The parish priest is the ordinary minister of baptism.

320. **When should a lay person baptize?**
A lay person should baptize when there is danger of death before a priest can arrive.

321. **How is baptism given?**
Baptism is given by pouring water on the head of the person to be baptized and saying whilst pouring: "I baptize you in the name of the Father, and of the Son, and of the Holy Ghost."[44]

322. **What should be done if a child that has received private baptism recovers?**
When a child that has received private baptism recovers, it should be brought to the church that the pastor may supply the canonical prayers and exorcisms.

323. **How can the baptism of water be supplied?**
The baptism of water can be supplied by the baptism of desire and the baptism of blood.

[43] Jn 3:5
[44] See Mt 28:19.

324. **What is the baptism of desire?**
The baptism of desire is the desire of baptism of water, which is included in an act of perfect love of God.

325. **What is the baptism of blood?**
The baptism of blood is the shedding of one's blood for Christ's sake, as many of the early martyrs did.

326. **What do we promise in baptism?**
In baptism, we promise: 1) to renounce Satan, all his works and pomps; 2) to be ever faithful to Jesus Christ and his Church.

327. **What are the works and pomps of Satan?**
The works and pomps of Satan are sin and its proximate occasions.

328. **Why are sponsors given in baptism?**
Sponsors are given in baptism: 1) that they may make the necessary promises when a child is baptized; 2) that they may watch over the spiritual welfare of the baptized person.

329. **What impediment to marriage is contracted by baptism?**
By baptism, the impediment of spiritual affinity is contracted, which forbids marriage between the sponsors and the person baptizing on the one side, and the person baptized and his parents on the other.

330. **Why is the name of a saint given in baptism?**
The name of a saint is given in baptism to place the person baptized under the special protection of that saint, and to encourage him to imitate the virtues of that saint.

CONFIRMATION

331. **What is confirmation?**

Confirmation is the sacrament which imparts to baptized persons the grace of the Holy Ghost to profess and practice their faith.

332. **Who is the ordinary minister of confirmation?**

The bishop is the ordinary minister of confirmation.

333. **How does the bishop administer confirmation?**

The bishop 1) extends his hands over all that are to be confirmed and prays that they may receive the Holy Ghost; 2) he then anoints the forehead of each with holy chrism in the form of a cross and says, "I sign thee with the sign of the cross, and I confirm thee with the chrism of salvation, in the name of the Father, and of the Son, and of the Holy Ghost"; 3) he gives those confirmed a slight blow on the cheek to remind them that they must be ready to suffer anything for the faith of Christ; 4) he concludes by imparting to them his episcopal blessing.

334. **How must confirmation be received?**

Confirmation must be received in the state of grace.

335. **What knowledge should a person to be confirmed possess?**

A person to be confirmed should know the mysteries of faith, the duties of a Christian, and the nature and effects of this sacrament.

336. **Is it a sin to neglect confirmation?**

It is a sin to neglect confirmation, especially now when faith and morals are exposed to so many and violent temptations.

337. **Which are the seven gifts of the Holy Ghost?**

The seven gifts of the Holy Ghost are: wisdom, understanding, counsel, fortitude, knowledge, piety, and fear of the Lord.

THE HOLY EUCHARIST

Its Institution

338. **What is the Holy Eucharist?**

The Holy Eucharist is: 1) the sacrament which contains the body and blood, soul and divinity of Jesus Christ, under the appearance of bread and wine; 2) the sacrifice of the new law.

339. **When did Christ promise the Holy Eucharist?**

Christ promised the Holy Eucharist after the miraculous multiplication of bread, about a year before he died. "I am the living bread which came down from heaven. If any man eat of this bread, he shall live for ever; and the bread that I will give is my flesh, for the life of the world."[45]

340. **When did Christ institute the Holy Eucharist?**

Christ instituted the Holy Eucharist at the last supper, the night before he died.

341. **Who were present when Christ instituted the Holy Eucharist?**

When Christ instituted the Holy Eucharist, the twelve apostles were present.

342. **How did Christ institute the Holy Eucharist?**

Christ took bread, blessed, broke, and gave to his disciples, saying: "Take ye and eat, this is my body." He then took a cup of wine and blessed it, saying: "Drink ye all of this: for this is my blood of the new testament, which shall be shed for many unto remission of sins...Do this in commemoration of me."[46]

[45] Jn 6:51-52

[46] Mt 26:26-28; Lk 22:19-20

343. **Why did Christ institute the Holy Eucharist?**
Christ instituted the Holy Eucharist: 1) as a token of his love, by abiding with us on our altars; 2) as food for our souls and as a pledge of our future glory in Holy Communion; 3) as a memorial of his death and the lasting sacrifice of the new law.

Transubstantiation, the Real Presence

344. **What is transubstantiation?**
Transubstantiation is the changing of the substance of bread and wine into the substance of the body and blood of Jesus Christ.

345. **When was the substance of bread and wine first changed into the substance of the body and blood of Christ?**
The substance of bread and wine was first changed into the substance of the body and blood of Jesus Christ at the last supper, when he said: "This is my body...This is my blood."

346. **How is transubstantiation effected?**
Transubstantiation is effected by the almighty power of Jesus Christ.

347. **What remained of the bread and wine after Christ said: "This is my body... This is my blood"?**
After Christ said: "This is my body...This is my blood," the accidents, or appearances, of bread and wine alone remained.

348. **What are the accidents, or appearances, of bread and wine?**
The accidents, or appearances, of bread and wine are whatever appears to the senses, as color, taste, shape, and the like.

349. **Is Christ whole and entire, both under the form of bread and under the form of wine?**
Christ is whole and entire, both under the form of bread and under the form of wine.

350. **Why is Christ whole and entire, both under the appearance of bread and under the appearance of wine?**
Christ is whole and entire both under the appearance of bread and under the appearance of wine, because in his living personality his body and blood are united.

351. **When did Christ make the apostles priests and give them the power to transubstantiate?**
Christ made his apostles priests and gave them the power to transubstantiate, when he said: "Do this in commemoration of me."[47]

352. **When does the priest today change bread and wine into the body and blood of Christ?**
The priest today changes bread and wine into the body and blood of Christ at the consecration of the Mass.

353. **Is the Holy Eucharist preserved on our altars?**
The Holy Eucharist is preserved on our altars.

354. **What do we call the Holy Eucharist when preserved on our altars?**
We call the Holy Eucharist, when preserved on our altars, "the real presence" or "the Blessed Sacrament."

355. **Why is the Blessed Sacrament kept on our altars?**
The Blessed Sacrament is kept on our altars: 1) to be adored by the faithful; 2) to be given in Holy Communion; 3) to be our Emmanuel or God-with-us to the end of the world.

[47] Lk 22:19

Holy Communion

356. **What is Holy Communion?**

Holy Communion is the receiving of Jesus Christ in the sacrament of the Holy Eucharist.

357. **How is Jesus Christ received in Holy Communion?**

In Holy Communion, Jesus Christ is received whole and entire: his body and his blood, his soul and his divinity.

358. **What are the chief benefits of Holy Communion?**

The chief benefits of Holy Communion are: 1) union with Jesus Christ in the sacrament of his love; 2) the reception of countless graces to enable us to avoid evil and to do good; 3) the cleansing of our nature from the dross of sin; 4) a pledge of a glorious resurrection and life everlasting.

359. **What must we do to receive Holy Communion worthily?**

To receive Holy Communion worthily, we must be in the state of grace and be fasting from midnight.

360. **How can we recover the grace of God, if we are in mortal sin?**

If we are in mortal sin, we can recover the grace of God by a good confession.

361. **What does the fast necessary for Holy Communion prescribe?**

The fast necessary for Holy Communion prescribes that we take nothing as food or drink from midnight to the time of Holy Communion.

362. **How long does the real presence remain with us in Holy Communion?**

The real presence remains with us in Holy Communion until the sacred species, or the appearances of bread and wine are destroyed.

363. **When is a Catholic allowed to receive Holy Communion when not fasting?**
A Catholic is allowed to receive Holy Communion when not fasting when he is in danger of death from sickness or accident.

364. **What is the dispensation in favor of those suffering from a lingering illness?**
The dispensation in favor of those suffering from a lingering illness is that they may receive Holy Communion occasionally when not fasting.

365. **What is required to receive Holy Communion daily?**
To receive Holy Communion daily, it is necessary: 1) to be in the state of grace; 2) to have a right intention; 3) to be guided by our father confessor.

366. **What should we do to receive plentifully the graces of Holy Communion?**
To receive plentifully the graces of Holy Communion, we should strive to overcome deliberate venial sins, perform acts of self-denial, and make acts of lively faith, firm hope, and of ardent love.

367. **How much time should we spend in adoration, petition, and thanksgiving after Holy Communion?**
After Holy Communion, we should spend at least a quarter of an hour in adoration, petition, and thanksgiving.

368. **When are we bound to receive Holy Communion under pain of mortal sin?**
We are bound to receive Holy Communion under pain of mortal sin during the Easter time and when we are in danger of death.

369. **Why does the Church give Communion to the laity only under the form of bread?**
The Church gives Communion to the laity only under the form of bread principally to emphasize the doctrine of the real presence of Jesus Christ, whole and entire, under each form.

The Sacrifice of the New Law

370. **How do we call the Holy Eucharist as the sacrifice of the new law?**
As the sacrifice of the new law, we call the Holy Eucharist "the Mass."

371. **What is the Mass?**
The Mass is the unbloody sacrifice of the body and blood of Christ.

372. **What is a sacrifice?**
A sacrifice is the offering of an object by a priest to God alone, and the destroying of it as the supreme act of adoration, thanksgiving, petition, and reparation.

373. **Is a sacrifice necessary to pay God man's debt of religion?**
A sacrifice is necessary to pay God man's debt of religion.

374. **When did Christ institute the Sacrifice of the Mass?**
Christ instituted the Sacrifice of the Mass at the last supper, when he said to the apostles: "Do this in commemoration of me."[48]

375. **How did the prophet Malachy foretell the Sacrifice of the Mass?**
The prophet Malachy foretold the Sacrifice of the Mass, when he said: "From the rising of the sun even to the going down, my name is great among the Gentiles, and in every place is sacrifice, and there is offered to my name a clean oblation."[49]

376. **What did the Hebrews understand by "clean oblation"?**
By "clean oblation," the Hebrews understood a sacrifice of bread and wine.

[48] Ibid.
[49] Mal 1:11

377. **Are the last supper, the sacrifice of the cross, and the Sacrifice of the Mass one and the same sacrifice?**

The last supper, the sacrifice of the cross, and the Sacrifice of the Mass are one and the same sacrifice.

378. **Why are the last supper, the sacrifice of the cross, and the Sacrifice of the Mass one and the same sacrifice?**

The last supper, the sacrifice of the cross, and the Sacrifice of the Mass are one and the same sacrifice, because the victim and the priest, Jesus Christ, is the same in all three.

379. **How do the sacrifice of the cross and the Sacrifice of the Mass differ?**

The sacrifice of the cross and the Sacrifice of the Mass differ in three ways. 1) The sacrifice of the cross was bloody; the Sacrifice of the Mass is an unbloody and commemorative sacrifice. 2) On the cross, Jesus Christ offered himself by himself; in the Mass, he offers himself by the hands of the ministering priest. 3) On the cross, Christ merited our salvation; in the Mass, he applies his merits to the faithful.

380. **Which is the best manner of assisting at Mass?**

The best manner of assisting at Mass is to offer it to God in union with the priest, to meditate on Christ's suffering and death, and to receive Holy Communion.

381. **Why are ceremonies used in divine worship?**

Ceremonies are used in divine worship, because: 1) they are prompted by the human heart; 2) they raise the mind and heart to God; 3) they are pleasing to God.

382. **Were the rites and ceremonies of the Mass instituted by Christ or by the Church?**

The rites and ceremonies of the Mass were instituted by the Church.

383. **What do the ceremonies of the Mass represent?**
The ceremonies of the Mass represent the details of the sacrifice of Calvary.[50]

PENANCE, THE FORGIVENESS OF SINS, THE POWER OF THE KEYS

384. **What is penance?**
Penance is the sacrament in which sins committed after baptism are forgiven.

385. **How does the sacrament of penance forgive sins?**
The sacrament of penance forgives sins through the absolution of the priest.

386. **When did Jesus Christ give the priest the power of forgiving sins?**
Jesus Christ gave the priest the power of forgiving sins when he said: "Whose sins you shall forgive, they are forgiven them; and whose sins you shall retain, they are retained."[51]

387. **Why did Christ delegate the power of forgiving sins?**
Christ delegated the power of forgiving sins, because: 1) he is infinitely merciful; 2) he, knowing the weakness of human nature, and the temptations and allurements to sin, saw that sins would be committed after the reception of baptism; 3) he wished to give every repentant sinner an occasion of reconciliation and the certainty of divine pardon.

388. **What consolation does the sacrament of penance give to a repentant soul?**
The sacrament of penance: 1) gives divine certainty to the repentant soul that past sins are forgiven; 2) it gives peace and joy in reconciling the soul to God; 3) it infuses courage and hope to serve God faithfully in the future.

[50] For an explanation of the ceremonies of the Mass, see "The Mission Remembrance," p. 39-79.

[51] Jn 20:23

389. **Why is the power of forgiving sins called "the power of the keys"?**
The power of forgiving sins is called "the power of the keys" because, when promising it, Christ said to St. Peter: "I will give to thee the keys of the kingdom of heaven."[52]

AURICULAR CONFESSION

390. **What is confession?**
Confession is the telling of our sins to the priest of God to obtain forgiveness.

391. **What testimony have we that auricular confession was practiced in the early Church?**
We have the testimony of the fathers of the Church that auricular confession was always practiced in the early Church, for example: 1) St. John + 101: "If we confess our sins, he is faithful and just, to forgive us our sins, and to cleanse us from iniquity."[53] 2) St. Cyprian + 257: "Let each confess his sins, and the satisfaction and remission made through the priest are pleasing before the Lord."[54] "Confession is made with inquiry into the life of him who is doing penance, nor may anyone come to Communion, except the hand shall have been imposed on him by the clergy." 3) St. Athanasius + 373: "He who confesses in penance receives through the priest, by the grace of Christ, the remission of his sins." 4) St. Ambrose + 397: "The poison is sin; confession is the remedy." "God promised mercy to all and granted his priests permission to loose all without exception."[55]

392. **What must the penitent do to obtain forgiveness?**
To obtain forgiveness, the penitent must: 1) examine his conscience; 2) be sorry for his sins; 3) resolve nevermore to offend God; 4) confess his sins to the priest; 5) perform the penance that the priest imposes.

[52] Mt 16:19
[53] 1 Jn 1:9
[54] Cyprian, *On the Lapsed*, n. 29
[55] Ambrose, *On Repentance*, Bk. 1, Ch. 3, n. 10

393. **How can the penitent easily examine his conscience?**
The penitent can easily examine his conscience by consulting the examination of conscience in his prayer book.[56]

394. **What motives may prompt the sinner to true repentance?**
The motives that may prompt a sinner to true repentance are the fear of God and the love of God.

395. **What does the fear of God do?**
The fear of God moves the sinner to turn from sin because he dreads the pains of hell and the loss of heaven. This sorrow is called "imperfect contrition."

396. **What does the love of God do?**
The love of God prompts the sinner to return to God because God is infinitely good and deserving of all love. This sorrow is called "perfect contrition."

397. **May perfect contrition remit mortal sin?**
Perfect contrition, united with the resolution of going to confession, remits mortal sin.

398. **Why must the penitent detest sin more than any other evil?**
The sinner must detest sin more than any other evil because sin is the greatest evil.

399. **Must the penitent feel his sorrow?**
It is not necessary for the penitent to feel his sorrow, because contrition is essentially an act of the will.

[56] See "The Mission Remembrance," p. 269, 271, 275.

400. **How is a soul moved to sorrow for sin?**

A soul is moved to sorrow for sin by reflecting on the shortness of life, the certainty of death, the transient gratification of sin, the joys of heaven, the torments of hell, the mercy of God, and the price of sin paid by the Savior on the cross.

401. **In what does the purpose of amendment consist?**

The purpose of amendment consists in a fixed determination to avoid at least all mortal sin and its proximate occasion, and to use the necessary means to persevere in the friendship of God.

402. **What is the proximate occasion of sin?**

The proximate occasion of sin is any person, place, or thing that easily leads us into sin.

403. **What sins must the penitent confess?**

The penitent must confess all his mortal sins, their number and the circumstances which change their nature.

404. **If without his fault a person forgets a mortal sin in confession, is it forgiven?**

If without his fault a person forgets a mortal sin in confession, the sin is forgiven, but must be confessed later if it comes to mind.

405. **What sin is it willfully to conceal a mortal sin in confession?**

Willfully to conceal a mortal sin in confession is a sacrilege, or an abuse of the sacrament, which renders the confession worthless.

406. **How can a bad confession be remedied?**

A bad confession can be remedied only by a general confession, or the repetition of all the confessions that have been made since the last worthy confession.

407. **Is it well to include some past sins when we have only venial sins to confess?**
It is well to include some past sins, for which we are sorry, when we have only venial sins to confess, so that we receive the benefit of absolution.

408. **What should we do on entering the confessional?**
On entering the confessional, we should kneel, make the sign of the cross, and say: "Bless me, Father. It is (state length of time) since my last confession. Since then I have (mention the sins). I also include in this confession all my past sins, and especially... I humbly ask pardon of God and you, my spiritual Father."

409. **Has a priest ever revealed the confession of anyone?**
No priest has ever revealed the confession of anyone. He is bound to silence, and God watches over this sacrament of his mercy by his special providence.

410. **What penance does a priest give in confession?**
As penance, the priest usually prescribes the recitation of some prayers or the performance of some good work.

INDULGENCES

411. **What is an indulgence?**
An indulgence is the remission of the temporal punishment due to sin.

412. **How are the indulgences divided?**
Indulgences are divided into plenary and partial.

413. **What is a plenary indulgence?**
A plenary indulgence is the full remission of the temporal punishment due to sin.

414. **What is a partial indulgence?**

A partial indulgence is the remission in part of the temporal punishment due to sin.

415. **Why can the Church grant an indulgence?**

The Church can grant an indulgence because Christ gave her the power to forgive sin and the punishment due to sin.

416. **How does the Church grant an indulgence?**

The Church grants an indulgence by applying to the faithful the merits of Jesus Christ outside of the sacraments.

417. **What must a person do to gain an indulgence?**

To gain an indulgence, a person must be in a state of grace and perform the works prescribed.

EXTREME UNCTION

418. **What is extreme unction?**

Extreme unction is the sacrament which gives grace and sometimes restores health to those who are in danger of death from sickness.

419. **Who is the minister of extreme unction?**

The priest is the minister of extreme unction.

420. **How does the priest give extreme unction?**

The priest gives extreme unction by praying over the sick and anointing them in the name of the Lord.

421. **When should the priest be called to a sick person?**

A priest should be called to a sick person when the illness has become serious.

422. **What are the effects of extreme unction?**

The effects of extreme unction are: 1) an increase of grace; 2) resignation to God's will; 3) comfort in pain; 4) strength in temptation; 5) remission of venial sin; 6) remission of mortal sins, if the sick person be sorry for them; 7) the restoration of health if God sees fit.

HOLY ORDERS

423. **What is holy orders?**

Holy orders is the sacrament by which the ministers of the Church are ordained and receive the power and grace to perform their sacred duties.

424. **What is necessary to receive holy orders worthily?**

To receive holy orders worthily, it is necessary to be in the state of grace, to have the necessary knowledge, and the divine vocation for this sacred office.

425. **Is it a source of blessing to have a priest in the family?**

It is a source of countless blessings to have a priest in the family.

MATRIMONY

426. **What is matrimony?**

Matrimony is a sacrament which unites and sanctifies the Christian man and woman in lawful marriage.

427. **How can the bond of Christian marriage be dissolved?**

The bond of a Christian marriage can be broken only by the death of husband or wife.

428. **What are the effects of the sacrament of matrimony?**

The effects of the sacrament of matrimony are: 1) to sanctify the love of husband and wife; 2) it gives them the strength to bear up with each other's weaknesses; 3) to enable them to bring up their children in the fear and love of God.

429. **How should those called to the marriage state prepare themselves for this sacrament?**
Those called to the married state should prepare themselves for this sacrament by living a life of practical faith and holy purity, by consulting the parents, and by notifying their pastor about a month before the marriage.

430. **What is an ideal Catholic wedding?**
An ideal Catholic wedding is one in which: 1) the contracting parties are both practical Catholics; 2) the bonds of marriage have been published on three successive Sundays; and 3) the contracting parties are married at a nuptial Mass and receive Holy Communion.

Prayer; Devotion to Mary; Intercession of the Saints; Veneration of Saints, Relics, and Images; Prayers for the Dead

Prayer

431. **What is prayer?**
Prayer is asking God's help.

432. **Is prayer necessary to salvation?**
For those who have reached the use of reason, prayer is necessary for salvation.

433. **Why is prayer necessary to salvation for those who have reached the use of reason?**

Prayer is necessary to salvation for those who have reached the use of reason, because God will not give them the grace to avoid evil and do good, unless they submit themselves to the influence of his grace of their own free will.

434. **How do we pray always?**

We pray always: 1) by reciting vocal prayers at stated times; 2) by renewing our good intention frequently; 3) and by keeping our minds busied with spiritual things while performing our daily work.

Devotion to Mary, Intercession of the Saints

435. **Why do Catholics honor and love Mary?**

Catholics honor and love Mary, because: 1) God honors her above all other creatures; 2) Mary has given us spiritual life in the Person of her divine Son.

436. **What is the communion of saints?**

The communion of saints is the union of charity and good will that unites all God's friends in heaven, on earth, and in purgatory.

437. **Why can the saints pray for us?**

The saints can pray for us, because they have influence with God, who makes our wants known to them.

Veneration of Saints, Relics, and Images

438. **Is it lawful to honor the saints?**

It is lawful to honor the saints, because we thereby honor God whose grace has made them saints.

439. **Do Catholics adore relics and images of saints?**
Catholics adore God alone. They honor the relics and images of the saints as precious souvenirs of the champions of the faith and friends of God.

Prayers for the Dead

440. **Is it good and useful to pray for the dead?**
"It is a holy and wholesome thought to pray for the dead that they may be loosed from their sins."[57]

The Sacramentals, Blessings of the Church, Articles of Devotion, Catholic Devotions

The Sacramentals

441. **What is a sacramental?**
A sacramental is an external act of religion, established by the Church, to draw God's blessings on the faithful.

442. **How many kinds of sacramentals are there?**
There are four kinds of sacramentals: 1) the rites and ceremonies used in the administration of the sacraments; 2) blessings and exorcisms used independently of the sacraments; 3) the use of sacred names, signs, and things, such as the name of Jesus, the sign of the cross, the use of blessed articles; 4) the use of pious exercises, as the recitation of the Lord's Prayer, praying in a consecrated church, giving alms prescribed by the Church, and many others.

[57] 2 Mc 12:46

443. **What benefits are derived from the devout use of the sacramentals?**
The benefits derived from the devout use of the sacramentals are five: 1) they excite good thoughts and increase devotion; 2) they remit venial sin by inspiring one with sorrow for the same; 3) they remit temporal punishments as acts of satisfaction; 4) they strengthen us against temptations and put the powers of darkness to flight; 5) they sometimes effect health of body and other temporal favors.

444. **Whence do the sacramentals derive their power?**
The sacramentals derive their power from the institution and prayer of the Church, which is always pleasing to God.

Blessings of the Church

445. **What is a blessing?**
A blessing, as a sacramental, is a religious ceremony, which draws the protection of God on a person, or on a thing and those who use it devoutly.

Articles of Devotion, Catholic Devotions

446. **What is an article of devotion?**
An article of devotion is anything withdrawn from profane use and devoted to the exercise of religion.

447. **Which are the principal articles of devotion in use among Catholics?**
The principal articles of devotion in use among Catholics are: the crucifix, holy pictures, rosary beads, medals, scapulars, candles, holy water, and blessed palms and ashes.

448. **What is a Catholic devotion?**
A Catholic devotion is a pious practice approved by the Church.

449. **Name the principal devotions approved by the Church.**

The principal devotions approved by the Church are: devotion to the Blessed Sacrament, frequent Communion, devotion to the Sacred Heart, the way of the cross, devotion to the Blessed Virgin, the rosary, the scapulars, besides various other devotions in honor of St. Joseph and other saints and angels.

APPENDIX

Prayers, Devotions, and Good Works

Sign of the Cross

The sign of the cross is made by putting the right hand to the forehead, then to the breast, then to the left and right shoulders, saying: "In the name of the Father, and of the Son, and of the Holy Ghost. Amen."

The sign of the cross is a profession of faith in the chief mysteries of the true religion. The words, "In the name," express the unity of God. The words that follow, "of the Father, and of the Son, and of the Holy Ghost," express the mystery of the Trinity. The making of the sign of the cross expresses the mystery of the incarnation and redemption, by reminding us that the Son of God came down from heaven, suffered, and died on the cross, to save us from perdition and bring us to salvation.

The Our Father

Our Father, who art in heaven, hallowed be thy name. Thy kingdom come. Thy will be done on earth as it is in heaven. Give us this day our daily bread, and forgive us our trespasses as we forgive them who trespass against us. And lead us not into temptation. But deliver us from evil. Amen.[58]

[58] Cf. Mt 6:9-13

Hail Mary

Hail Mary, full of grace, the Lord is with thee: blessed art thou among women,[59] and blessed is the fruit of thy womb,[60] Jesus. Holy Mary, Mother of God, pray for us sinners, now and at the hour of our death. Amen.[61]

The Apostles' Creed

I believe in God, the Father Almighty, the Creator of heaven and earth; and in Jesus Christ, his only Son, our Lord; who was conceived by the Holy Ghost, born of the Virgin Mary, suffered under Pontius Pilate, was crucified, died, and was buried. He descended into hell: the third day he arose again from the dead: he ascended into heaven, sitteth at the right hand of God the Father Almighty; from thence he shall come to judge the living and the dead. I believe in the Holy Ghost, the holy Catholic Church, the communion of saints, the forgiveness of sins, the resurrection of the body, and in life everlasting. Amen.

THE CHRISTIAN ACTS

An Act of Faith

O my God, I firmly believe that thou art one God in three divine Persons, the Father, the Son, and Holy Ghost. I believe that thy divine Son became man and died for our sins, and that he will come to judge the living and the dead. I believe these and all the truths which the holy Catholic Church teaches, because thou hast revealed them, who canst neither deceive nor be deceived.

[59] Cf. Lk 1:28
[60] Cf. Lk 1:42
[61] Cf. Council of Ephesus

An Act of Hope

O my God, relying on thy infinite goodness and thy promises, I hope to obtain pardon of my sins, the help of thy grace, and life everlasting, through the merits of Jesus Christ, my Lord and Redeemer.

An Act of Love

O my God, I love thee above all things, with my whole heart and soul, because thou art all good and worthy of all love. I love my neighbor as myself for the love of thee. I forgive all who have injured me, and ask pardon of all whom I have injured.

An Act of Contrition

O my God, I am heartily sorry for having offended thee, and I detest all my sins, because I dread the loss of heaven and the pains of hell, but most of all because they offend thee, my God, who art all good and deserving of all my love. I firmly resolve with the help of thy grace, to confess my sins, to do penance, and to amend my life.

The Confiteor

I confess to Almighty God, to the Blessed Mary ever Virgin, to the blessed Michael the archangel, to blessed John the Baptist, to the holy apostles, Peter and Paul, and to all the saints that I have sinned exceedingly, in thought, word, and deed, through my fault, through my fault, through my most grievous fault. Therefore I beseech thee, Blessed Mary ever Virgin, blessed Michael the archangel, blessed John the Baptist, the holy apostles, Peter and Paul, and all the saints, to pray to the Lord our God for me.—May the Almighty God have mercy on me and forgive me my sins, and bring me to everlasting life. May the Almighty and merciful Lord grant me pardon, absolution, and remission of all my sins. Amen.

The Blessing before Meals

+ Bless us, O Lord, and these thy gifts, which we are about to receive from thy bounty, through Christ our Lord. Amen.

Grace after Meals

+ We give thanks for all thy benefits, O Almighty God, who livest and reignest forever; and may the souls of the faithful departed, through the mercy of God, rest in peace. Amen.

The Angelus

1. The angel of the Lord declared unto Mary:
And she conceived by the Holy Ghost.
Hail Mary! etc.
2. Behold the handmaid of the Lord:
Be it done unto me according to thy Word.
Hail Mary! etc.
3. And the Word was made flesh:
And dwelt amongst us.
Hail Mary! etc.

Pray for us, O holy Mother of God:
That we may be made worthy of the promises of Christ.
Let us pray.

Pour forth, we beseech thee, O Lord, thy grace into our hearts, that we, to whom the incarnation of Christ, thy Son, was made known by the message of an angel, may, by his passion and cross, be brought to the glory of his resurrection, through the same Jesus Christ our Lord. Amen.

May the divine assistance remain always with us.

And may the souls of the faithful departed, through the mercy of God, rest in peace. Amen.

MYSTERIES OF THE HOLY ROSARY

The Five Joyful Mysteries

1. The annunciation by the archangel Gabriel.
2. The visit of the Blessed Virgin to her cousin, Saint Elizabeth.
3. The birth of our Savior.
4. The presentation of the Infant Jesus in the Temple.
5. The finding of the Child Jesus in the Temple amidst the doctors.

The Five Sorrowful Mysteries

1. The agony in the garden.
2. The scourging at the pillar.
3. The crowning with thorns.
4. The carrying of the cross.
5. The crucifixion and death of our Savior.

The Five Glorious Mysteries

1. The resurrection of our Lord.
2. The ascension into heaven.
3. The coming down of the Holy Ghost.
4. The assumption of our Blessed Lady into heaven.
5. The crowning of the most Blessed Virgin Mary in heaven.

The Three Chief Good Works

The three chief good works are: prayer, fasting, and almsgiving.

The Evangelical Counsels

The evangelical counsels are: voluntary poverty, perpetual chastity, and entire obedience.

The Eight Beatitudes

1. Blessed are the poor in spirit; for theirs is the kingdom of heaven.
2. Blessed are the meek; for they shall possess the land.
3. Blessed are they that mourn; for they shall be comforted.
4. Blessed are they that hunger and thirst after justice; for they shall be filled.
5. Blessed are the merciful; for they shall obtain mercy.
6. Blessed are the clean of heart; for they shall see God.
7. Blessed are the peacemakers; for they shall be called the children of God.
8. Blessed are they that suffer persecution for justice's sake; for theirs is the kingdom of heaven.[62]

The Spiritual Works of Mercy

1. To give counsel to the doubtful.
2. To instruct the ignorant.
3. To admonish sinners.
4. To comfort the afflicted.
5. To forgive offenses.
6. To bear patiently the troublesome.
7. To pray for the living and the dead.

The Corporal Works of Mercy

1. To feed the hungry.
2. To give drink to the thirsty.
3. To clothe the naked.
4. To harbor the harborless.
5. To visit the sick.
6. To visit the imprisoned.
7. To bury the dead.

[62] Cf. Mt 5

Obligations

The Ten Commandments

1. I am the Lord thy God, thou shalt not have strange gods before me.
2. Thou shalt not take the name of the Lord thy God in vain.
3. Remember thou keep holy the sabbath day.
4. Honor thy father and thy mother.
5. Thou shalt not kill.
6. Thou shalt not commit adultery.
7. Thou shalt not steal.
8. Thou shalt not bear false witness against thy neighbor.
9. Thou shalt not covet thy neighbor's wife.
10. Thou shalt not covet thy neighbor's goods.

The Precepts

1. Hear Mass on Sundays and holy days of obligation.
2. Fast and abstain on the days appointed.
3. Confess at least once a year.
4. Receive the Holy Eucharist during the Easter time.
5. Contribute to the support of the pastor, church, and school.
6. Not to marry non-Catholics, nor relatives within the fourth degree of kindred. Not to marry privately without pastor and two witnesses, nor to solemnize marriage at forbidden times.

Days of Obligation in the United States

1. All Sundays of the year.
2. The Circumcision of Our Lord, January 1.
3. Ascension day, fortieth day after Easter.
4. Assumption of the Blessed Virgin, August 15.

5. All Saints' day, November 1.
6. The Immaculate Conception of the Blessed Virgin Mary, December 8.
7. Nativity of Our Lord, December 25.

Abstinence Days

All Fridays of the year, except when Christmas falls on a Friday, and all fast days.

Fast Days

1. The Fridays of Advent in the Provinces of Baltimore, Philadelphia, New York, and Boston.
2. Every day in Lent, except Sundays.
3. Ember days, namely: the Wednesdays, Fridays, and Saturdays following a) the First Sunday of Lent; b) Whitsunday; c) the fourteenth of September; d) the Third Sunday in Advent.
4. Vigils of Whitsunday, of the Assumption, of All Saints, and of Christmas.

Note.—1) When a fast day falls on a Sunday, it is kept on the Saturday before. 2) The dispensations from fasting and abstinence granted to the faithful are annually explained by the pastors.

Reception of a Convert

The Profession of Faith

I, N., having before my eyes the holy gospels, which I touch with my hands, and knowing that no one can be saved without that faith which the holy, Catholic, apostolic, Roman Church holds, believes, and teaches, against which I agree that I have greatly erred, inasmuch as I have held and believed doctrines opposed to her teaching,

I now, with grief and contrition for my past errors, profess that I believe the holy, Catholic, apostolic, Roman Church to be the only and true Church established on earth by Jesus Christ, to which I submit myself with my whole heart. I believe all the articles that she proposes to my belief, and I reject and condemn all that she rejects and condemns, and I am ready to observe all that she commands me. And especially I profess that I believe: one only God in three divine Persons, distinct from and equal to each other—that is to say, the Father, the Son, and the Holy Ghost; the Catholic doctrine of the incarnation, passion, death, and resurrection of our Lord Jesus Christ; and the personal union of the two natures, the divine and the human; the divine maternity of the most holy Mary, together with her most spotless virginity;

The true, real, and substantial presence of the body and blood, together with the soul and divinity of our Lord Jesus Christ, in the most Holy Sacrament of the Eucharist;

The seven sacraments instituted by Jesus Christ for the salvation of mankind; that is to say: baptism, confirmation, Eucharist, penance, extreme unction, order, matrimony;

Purgatory, the resurrection of the dead, everlasting life;

The primacy, not only of honor, but also of jurisdiction of the Roman pontiff, successor of St. Peter, prince of the apostles, vicar of Jesus Christ; the veneration of the saints and of their images; the authority of the apostolic and ecclesiastical traditions, and of the holy scriptures, which we must interpret and understand only in the sense which our holy mother the Catholic Church has held and does hold; and everything else that has been defined and declared by the sacred canons and by the general councils, and particularly by the holy Council of Trent, and delivered, defined, and declared by the General Council of the Vatican, especially concerning the primacy of the Roman pontiff and his infallible teaching authority.

With a sincere heart, therefore, and with unfeigned faith, I detest and abjure every error, heresy, and sect opposed to the said holy Catholic and apostolic Roman Church. So help me God and these holy gospels, which I touch with my hand.

Ceremonies of Baptism

Only sincere, exemplary Catholics should be taken as sponsors.

The candidate is given a saint's name. He should come to the baptismal font with the collar or clothing about the neck arranged in such a way that it can be easily removed when the priest is about to anoint the lower part of the neck, above the breast and between the shoulders.

The priest begins: "N., what dost thou ask of the Church of God?"

The candidate answers: "Faith."

"What doth faith give thee?"

Answer: "Life everlasting."

The priest then prays over the candidate and breathes upon him three times, saying: "Depart from him, thou unclean spirit, and make way for the Holy Ghost, the Comforter."

The sign of the cross is made on the forehead and breast, as a sign that the Christian belongs to the crucified Savior. A small quantity of salt is placed in the candidate's mouth, with the words: "Receive the salt of Wisdom." Salt is a symbol of Christian wisdom and a protection from the foulness of sin. Through repeated prayers, blessings, and the imposition of hands upon the head, the priest shows the conquest of grace over Satan, and the change of the sinner into a child of God. The Apostles' Creed and the Lord's Prayer are recited aloud by the candidate as a profession of faith. The priest, after the example of Jesus, touches with spittle the ears and nose of the person to be baptized, saying: "Be thou opened." Man's spiritual sense is opened by baptism to receive heavenly truths.

Satan with all his works and pomps must be renounced. The candidate declares, when questioned: "I do renounce him. I do renounce them."

Next comes the anointing of the breast and shoulders with holy oil. Anointing with holy oils in holy scriptures and in the traditions of the Church is a sign of spiritual strength, and also of consecration to the service of God.

To the three questions, "Dost thou believe," etc., the candidate answers, "I do believe." "Wilt thou be baptized?" Answer: "I will."

When the priest pours the water on the head, the sponsors hold their right hands on the shoulders of the candidate.

After baptism, the head is anointed with chrism, because the person baptized is to take his place among Christians; he is of Christ's anointed. A white cloth is placed upon the head to admonish the Christian to lead a pure and holy life. The lighted candle, which is placed in the hand, signifies the light of Christian faith, hope, and charity.

After conditional baptism, the convert goes to the confessional to confess his sins and receive conditional absolution.

Catechism

for

First Communicants

Revised Edition

Frederick Pustet Co., Inc.

52 Barclay Street
New York, N. Y.

436 Main Street
Cincinnati, O.

Catechism

for

First Communicants

Revised Edition

Frederick Pustet Co., Inc.

52 Barclay Street
New York, N. Y.

436 Main Street
Cincinnati, O.

NIHIL OBSTAT
Remigius Lafort, S. T. L.
Censor.

IMPRIMATUR
+ John M. Farley,
Archbishop of New York.

New York, March 20, 1911.

Extract from Decree of S. Congre. S. S. on First Holy Communion, August 8, 1910

1. "The age of discretion required both for confession and Communion is the time when the child begins to reason; that is, about the seventh year, more or less. From this time on, the obligation of satisfying the precept of both confession and Communion begins.

2. "Both for first confession and first Communion, a complete and perfect knowledge of Christian doctrine is not necessary. The child will, however, be obliged to gradually learn the whole catechism according to its ability."

Things Necessary to Be Known by Little Children before First Communion

3. "The knowledge of Christian doctrine required in children in order to be properly prepared for first Communion is that they understand, according to their capacity, those mysteries of faith which are necessary as a means of salvation—that they be able to distinguish the Eucharist from common and material bread—and also approach the sacred table with the devotion becoming their age."

(Decree Aug. 8, 1910.)

Catechism for First Communicants

On the Mysteries of Faith, the Knowledge of Which Is Necessary for Salvation

On the Existence and Nature of God

1. **Who made us and the whole world?**
God made us and the whole world, heaven and earth, and all things.

2. **Who is God?**
God is the Lord and Maker of heaven and earth and all things.

3. **Is there more than one God?**
No, there is but one God.

4. **Had God a beginning?**
No, God had no beginning; God is eternal, that is, God always was and always will be.

On the Most Blessed Trinity

5. **Is there more than one Person in God?**
Yes, in God there are three Persons: the Father, the Son, and the Holy Ghost.

6. **Is each of these three Persons true God?**
Yes, each of these three Persons is true God.

7. **Is there, then, more than one God?**
No, there is but one God.

8. **What do we call the three divine Persons in one divine nature?**
The three divine Persons in one divine nature are called the most Blessed Trinity.

The Incarnation

9. **Is one of the three divine Persons become man?**
Yes, the Son of God is become man.

10. **How is the Son of God become man?**
The Son of God is become man by being conceived by the Holy Ghost and being born of the Blessed Virgin Mary.

11. **Why is the Son of God become man?**
The Son of God is become man in order to redeem us from eternal damnation.

12. **How did the Son of God redeem us from eternal damnation?**
The Son of God redeemed us from eternal damnation by his suffering and dying for us on the cross.

13. **How do we call the Son of God as man?**
As man, we call the Son of God "Jesus Christ, our Lord."

On the Everlasting Reward and Punishment

14. **How does God repay man for his works?**
God repays man for his works by rewarding the good and punishing the bad.

15. **Does God repay man only in this life?**
No, God metes out his reward and his punishment also after death.

16. **Then the soul does not die with the body?**
No, it is impossible for the soul to die.

17. **How does God reward the souls of the just?**
God rewards the souls of the just by taking them into heaven.

18. **How does God punish the souls of the wicked?**
God punishes the souls of the wicked by sending them into hell.

19. **What is heaven?**
Heaven is everlasting happiness with God.

20. **What is hell?**
Hell is everlasting suffering away from God.

On Holy Communion

The Real Presence

21. **What do we receive in Holy Communion?**
In Holy Communion, we receive the true body and the true blood of our Lord Jesus Christ.

22. **Is, then, the sacred host no longer bread?**
No; but the sacred host is the true body and the true blood of our Lord Jesus Christ.

23. **How is the bread changed into the true flesh and blood of Jesus Christ?**
The bread is changed into the true flesh and blood of Jesus Christ by the word of Jesus Christ.

24. **When is the bread changed into the true flesh and blood of Jesus Christ?**
The bread is changed into the true flesh and blood of Jesus Christ at the consecration of the Mass.

25. **Does the sacred host not appear to be bread?**
Yes, the sacred host appears to be bread, because even after the consecration the appearances of bread remain.

26. **What, then, is changed at the consecration?**
At the consecration, the substance of the bread is changed into the substance of the true and living Savior.

Preparation for Holy Communion

27. **Must we be free from sin at Holy Communion?**
Yes, at Holy Communion we must be free at least from all grievous or mortal sin.

28. **Are we allowed to eat or drink before Holy Communion?**
No, at Holy Communion we must be absolutely fasting from all food and drink from midnight.

On Frequent Communion

29. **Should we often receive Holy Communion?**
Yes, we should often receive Holy Communion; if possible, every day.

30. **Must we go to confession every time we wish to go to Holy Communion?**
No, it is not necessary to go to confession every time we wish to go to Holy Communion, unless we have committed a mortal sin.

31. **May we go to Holy Communion even if we have committed some little fault after confession?**
Yes, even if we have committed some little fault after confession, we may go to Holy Communion; but it is good to be sorry for that fault.

32. **Whom should we ask for advice about frequent Communion?**
We should ask our confessor for advice about frequent Communion.

33. **Why should we often go to Holy Communion?**
We should often go to Holy Communion, because it pleases God and assists us to lead a holy life.

On the Sacrament of Penance

On Recalling Our Sins

34. **How can we recall our sins to memory?**
We can recall our sins to memory by earnestly inquiring into our past life.

35. **What must we do before we begin to recall our sins?**
Before we begin to recall our sins, we must pray to God to help us know and understand our sins.

On Contrition

36. **Must we be sorry for our sins?**
Yes, at least at confession we must be sorry for our sins.

37. **How are we sorry for our sins?**
We are sorry for our sins by hating them and sincerely wishing that we had not done them.

38. **Why must we be sorry for our sins?**
We must be sorry for our sins, because they offend God.

39. **Make an act of contrition.**
O my God, I am really sorry for all my sins; I hate and detest them with all my heart because they displease thee, my good God, and I firmly purpose, with thy help, never to commit sin again.

On the Purpose of Amendment

40. **Must we also purpose to avoid sin after confession?**
Yes, we must firmly purpose to remain good after confession.

41. **Can we avoid sin without the help of God?**
No; without the help of God no one can remain good to the end.

42. **How can we obtain the help of God?**
We can obtain the help of God by prayer and other works of piety.

43. **What else, then, must we do to keep from sin?**
To keep from sin, we must at all times do our duty, resist temptation, and avoid bad companions.

On Confession

44. **What must we do before Holy Communion if we have committed a mortal sin?**
If we have committed a mortal sin, we must go to confession before going to Holy Communion.

45. **How do we make a good confession?**
We make a good confession by sorrowfully telling our sins to the priest.

46. **Must we tell all our sins in confession?**
Yes, in confession we must tell all our sins, at least all our mortal sins.

47. **Can the priest forgive us our sins?**
Yes, the priest can forgive us our sins by the power of God.

48. **Is it a sin if we conceal a mortal sin in confession?**
Yes, it is a new and grievous sin, a sacrilege, to conceal a mortal sin in confession.

49. **Are any sins at all forgiven by a bad confession?**
No, by a bad confession, no sins at all are forgiven.

On Penance, or Satisfaction

50. **Can we make satisfaction to God for our sins?**
Yes, after confession we can make satisfaction to God for our sins by doing penance.

51. **What is "doing penance"?**
"Doing penance" is saying the prayers, or performing the good works, which our confessor imposes upon us.

52. **Should we be satisfied with the penance imposed upon us?**
No, we should not be satisfied with the penance imposed upon us, but of our own accord practice piety to remain good.

On Confirmation

53. **What is confirmation?**
Confirmation is a sacrament by which the Holy Ghost is given to us.

54. **Why is the Holy Ghost given to us?**
The Holy Ghost is given to us that he may strengthen our faith and adorn our soul.

55. **Can we be confirmed more than once?**
No, we can be confirmed only once, because confirmation imprints an indelible mark upon our souls.

56. **Who can give confirmation?**
By virtue of his office, the bishop alone gives confirmation.

57. **Must we be free from mortal sin at confirmation?**
Yes, at confirmation we must be free from all mortal sins, lest we commit a sacrilege.

Prayers

The Sign of the Cross

In the name of the Father, and of the Son, and of the Holy Ghost. Amen.

The Lord's Prayer

Our Father, who art in heaven, hallowed be thy name; thy kingdom come; thy will be done on earth as it is in heaven. Give us this day our daily bread; and forgive us our trespasses as we forgive those who trespass against us; and lead us not into temptation, but deliver us from evil. Amen.

The Angelical Salutation

Hail Mary, full of grace, the Lord is with thee; blessed art thou amongst women, and blessed is the fruit of thy womb, Jesus. Holy Mary, Mother of God, pray for us sinners, now and at the hour of our death. Amen.

The Apostles' Creed

I believe in God, the Father Almighty, Creator of heaven and earth, and in Jesus Christ, his only Son, our Lord; who was conceived by the Holy Ghost, born of the Virgin Mary, suffered under Pontius Pilate, was crucified, died, and was buried. He descended into hell; the third day he arose again from the dead: he ascended into heaven, sitteth at the right hand of God, the Father Almighty; from thence he shall come to judge the living and the dead. I believe in the Holy Ghost, the holy Catholic Church, the communion of saints, the forgiveness of sins, the resurrection of the body, and the life everlasting. Amen.

The Ten Commandments

1. I am the Lord thy God; thou shalt not have strange gods before me.
2. Thou shalt not take the name of the Lord thy God in vain.
3. Remember thou keep holy the Lord's day.
4. Honor thy father and thy mother.
5. Thou shalt not kill.
6. Thou shalt not commit adultery.
7. Thou shalt not steal.

8. Thou shalt not bear false witness against thy neighbor.
9. Thou shalt not covet thy neighbor's wife.
10. Thou shalt not covet thy neighbor's goods.

The Seven Sacraments

1. Baptism.
2. Confirmation.
3. Holy Eucharist.
4. Penance.
5. Extreme unction.
6. Holy orders.
7. Matrimony.

The Three Theological Virtues

Faith. O my God, I believe in thee, and I firmly believe all thou hast revealed and proposest through thy holy Catholic Church for my belief; because thou, the eternal and infallible truth, hast said it.

Hope. O my God, I hope in thee, and I hope to obtain, through the merits of Jesus Christ, the remission of my sins, thy grace, and life everlasting; because thou, the Almighty, merciful, and faithful God hast promised it.

Charity. O my God, I love thee with my whole heart and above all things; because thou art my loving Father, the supreme and most amiable good. For thy sake, I also love my neighbor, friend or enemy, as myself.

Blessing before Meals

+ Bless us, O Lord! and these thy gifts, which we are about to receive from thy bounty, through Christ our Lord. Amen.

Grace after Meals

+ We give thee thanks for all thy benefits, O Almighty God, who livest and reignest forever; and may the souls of the faithful departed, through the mercy of God, rest in peace. Amen.

Morning Prayer

In the name of the Father, etc.

O God, I give thee thanks for having so graciously preserved me this night from a sudden and unprovided-for death. Grant that I may nevermore offend thee by sin. Our Father, etc. Amen.

Evening Prayers

In the name of the Father, etc.

Save us, O Lord, when awake, and watch over us when asleep, that we may watch with Christ and rest in comfort.

Merciful God, I thank thee for all the gifts of body and soul thou hast this day bestowed upon me; protect me this night in thy infinite mercy from all the snares of the devil, from all evils of body and soul, especially from a sudden and unforeseen death. Amen.

(Here make a short examination of conscience, to find out the sins you have committed during the day; then make an act of contrition.)

O my God, I am, etc.[1]

In the name of my crucified Redeemer, I go to rest. May he protect me now and ever, and lead me to everlasting life. Amen.

We fly to thy patronage, O holy Mother of God. Despise not our petitions in our necessities, but deliver us from all dangers, O ever glorious and Blessed Virgin.

Jesus, Mary, and Joseph, I give you my heart, and my soul!

Jesus, Mary, and Joseph, assist me in my last agony!

Jesus, Mary, and Joseph, may I breathe forth my soul in peace with you!

[1] Same as on p. 103, "Contrition."

O angel of God, whom God hath appointed to be my guardian, enlighten, protect, direct, and govern me.

Our Father, etc. Hail Mary, etc. I believe in God, etc.

When Taking Holy Water Say:

May the Almighty and merciful God, the Father, the Son, and the Holy Ghost bless me. Amen.

THE CATECHISM SIMPLY EXPLAINED

BY H. CANON CAFFERATA

NEW REVISED AND ENLARGED EDITION

B. HERDER BOOK COMPANY
15 & 17 SOUTH BROADWAY
ST. LOUIS, MO.

THE CATECHISM SIMPLY EXPLAINED

BY H. CANON CAFFERATA

NEW REVISED AND ENLARGED EDITION

B. HERDER BOOK COMPANY
15 & 17 SOUTH BROADWAY
ST. LOUIS, MO.

NIHIL OBSTAT
Eduardus J. Mahoney, S. Th. D.,
Censor Deputatus.

IMPRIMATUR
+ Josephus Butt,
Vicarius Generalis.

Westmonasterii,
Die 21 Iulii, 1932.

St. George's Cathedral,
Southwark, S.E.
March 19, 1897.

We wish this work every blessing, and a very large circulation among the faithful and those desiring instruction in the doctrines of the Church, to all of whom it may be of the greatest service.

+ JOHN, Bishop of Southwark.
+ FRANCIS, Bishop of Epiphania, Coadjutor.

Bishop's House,
Southwark.

We cordially bless the second edition of this work, and trust that it will continue to do the good which has so largely resulted from it in the past.

+ FRANCIS, Bishop of Southwark.
Feast of St. George, 1899.

AUTHOR'S INTRODUCTION

I have long felt the want of a book of instruction for converts that would put the Catholic doctrine before them in a simple and plain way. There exist already a goodly number of manuals of instruction, but they are for the most part too long and too expensive; moreover, they do not all follow the order of the catechism, and this is generally made the textbook for converts.

It frequently happens that we come across non-Catholics who seem well disposed toward the Church, but who have very little knowledge of its teaching; and we wish we had some short, practical book to put in their hands that would give them an accurate account of the faith. The bishops' catechism may do something but not very much toward removing their difficulties and putting matters before them in a true light.

Moreover, a priest's time is so taken up with various duties that it would be a great boon to him if he could enlist the services of efficient secular helpers to lay the groundwork of the instruction of converts. Lay workers could do this if they had a simple manual explanatory of the catechism. This book will, I hope, supply the wants mentioned.

Again, I have frequently noticed that, during the course of their instructions, converts are liable to forget the explanations that have already been given to them. This is not surprising when one takes into account the amount of ground that has to be covered, but still it involves a repetition of what has already been explained, and this necessarily lengthens the time of instruction.

With this book in hand there will be no difficulty in reading over at home what has already been explained, and in keeping it fresh in the mind. Any point that has been forgotten can easily be found in the index, and the explanation referred to.

I have aimed throughout at extreme simplicity of language and style, using as nearly as possible the very words an instructor would employ in teaching.

With the exception of the texts used in the catechism, the quotations from the sacred scriptures are taken mostly from the protestant revised version. Many outside the Church think that the Catholic and protestant versions of the Bible are very different from each other, and that, though it may not be difficult to prove the Catholic doctrines from the Catholic version, there might be considerable difficulty in proving them from the protestant version.

I have made use from time to time of the *Book of Common Prayer*, the official prayer book of the Church of England. Many protestants are unaware that it contains several of the doctrines taught by the Catholic Church.

— H. T. C.

The Catechism Simply Explained

Faith

1. **Who made you?**

God made me.

There is no doubt about this, for the ninety-ninth Psalm of holy David says, "He made us and not we ourselves."[1] Some people do, indeed, deny the existence of God; but to do this is to act against reason, for they thereby make their own existence a greater mystery than that which they deny.

2. **Why did God make you?**

God made me to know him, love him and serve him in this world, and to be happy with him forever in the next.

Here we are face-to-face with the greatest problem of our existence—viz., why we are here. God never does anything, even the most minute thing, without having some end in view; and surely when he created man, the noblest work of his hands, he must have had some very special object in creating him. The catechism tells us that he made man for himself.

First, to know him. Now we can, and do, know a great deal about God, even though we have never seen him: 1) from the old testament, where God revealed himself to the patriarchs and prophets; 2) from the new testament, where God has made known to us much about himself and the next world through Jesus Christ, his only Son.

[1] Ps 99:3

Secondly, we are made to love God. The more we know about him the more we see his infinite beauty and goodness, and thus we are induced to love him; for even in this world, we love what is beautiful and good.

Lastly, we are made to serve God. The way we show our love for God is by serving him, by doing his will. He himself has said, "If you love me, keep my commandments."[2] The reward of all this — viz., of trying to know all we can about God, of loving and of serving him — is to be the possession of heaven, that happy place to which everyone is anxious to go. God has promised this, so we cannot doubt it.

So you understand now why you were made, why you are here: not to make a great name for yourself, not to get rich, not to enjoy yourself as you like, but simply to serve the God who made you. You are one of his creatures; you depend entirely upon him for everything. As your Creator, God has his rights over you, and the greatest of these rights is that you should know and love and serve him.

3. **In whose image and likeness did God make you?**
God made me in his own image and likeness.

We are composed of body and soul; and there are within us two kinds of life: the life of the body and the life of the soul. The image of God is in the soul, not in the body. God has not a body as we have, he is a Spirit; he has made our souls spirits like to himself. This is what the catechism means when it asks:

4. **Is this likeness to God in your body or in your soul?**
This likeness to God is chiefly in my soul.

We are then asked:

5. **How is your soul like to God?**
My soul is like to God because it is a spirit, and is immortal.

A spirit is something that we cannot see, but which really lives and exists, like God himself or the angels. We know for certain that each one

[2] Jn 14:15

has a soul living in him, but we cannot see it. If you have ever seen a person die, you knew that the soul had left and gone out of the body; but you could not see it go, because it was a spirit. God is the great Spirit, and we are, as it were, spirits of a lower order or kind; but because we are spirits, we are like to God. Again, the catechism says my soul is immortal. Now, God is immortal—that is, he cannot die; and he has made my soul immortal like himself. My soul can never die now; it must live as long as God lives, either with him in heaven or apart from him in hell. That is the reason why heaven and hell are eternal.

6. **What do you mean when you say that your soul is immortal?**
When I say that my soul is immortal, I mean that my soul can never die.

This has just been explained. Next comes a most important question:

7. **Of which must you take most care, of your body or of your soul?**
I must take most care of my soul; for Christ has said, "What doth it profit a man, if he gain the whole world, and suffer the loss of his own soul?"[3]

When we die, our bodies are in a short time placed in a coffin and buried deep in the earth; but what has become of the soul? It has appeared before God, and has been judged by him according to the life it led upon earth. Then, at least, shall we understand why God has made us. It will not matter much to us then what has become of our body, but it will matter to us what becomes of our soul. If I were to say to you, "Do you want to save your soul? Do you really want to make it safe for the next world?" Of course you would say, "Yes"; but perhaps your difficulty may be that you do not know how to go about it. That is why the catechism next asks:

8. **What must you do to save your soul?**
To save my soul I must worship God by faith, hope, and charity; that is, I must believe in him, I must hope in him, and I must love him with my whole heart.

[3] Mt 16:26

So you see you have to do three things. You must believe in God—that is, you must believe that there is a God; and you must believe everything that God has said, whether you understand it or not, and whether you like it or not, for God has made known to us some things which are very unpleasant to think about; for instance, the eternity of hell. Then you must hope in God—that means you must trust in his word and promise to save you and to take you to heaven, on condition that you do what he wants you to do here in this life. It is not always easy to do all that God requires of us; for example, we have to keep his commandments and to keep out of sin, and this is sometimes very hard; but God's promise of heaven supports us and helps us to do it. Moreover, he does not leave us to do it all by ourselves. He helps us by his grace to do these hard and difficult things. This he has promised always to do; but we must ask him for his help and grace, and this is why, in the chapter on hope,[4] the catechism speaks to us about prayer and how we ought to pray. Lastly, we must love him with our whole hearts, more than all persons or things on this earth; and we must always wish and seek to please him. People who commit sins love themselves and their pleasures more than God. This is why our Lord has told us to keep his commandments as a proof that we really love him. The chapter on charity, or the love of God,[5] teaches us about the commandments.

9. **What is faith?**

Faith is a supernatural gift of God which enables us to believe, without doubting, whatever God has revealed.

Faith means belief: to have faith means to believe, and to believe means to take as true something that is said to you, because you consider that the person who says it knows all about it, and would not deceive you or tell you a lie. It does not mean that you know all about it yourself, or that you quite understand what he says; but you believe him because he knows and he understands.

[4] See q. 135-140, below.

[5] See q. 169-227, below.

There are two kinds of faith—human faith and divine faith; faith in man's word and faith in God's word. Now, what do I mean by *human faith*? Supposing you told me that you had seen a great fire in the city today; naturally, thinking you to be a truthful, honest man, I should at once believe you, because you had seen the fire and knew all about it (I had not seen it, nor did I understand or know how it had been caused). Then I should have human faith—that is, I should believe on the authority of a man. Of course, you could deceive me, and might, indeed, be actually deceiving me for some purpose of your own; so, human faith is not absolutely to be depended on. If, instead of believing you at once, I were to say, "Well, of course you may be quite correct in what you say, but I did not see that fire, and I do not believe it," this would pain you very much, and you would naturally consider yourself insulted by having your word doubted.

Now let us take faith in God's word, or *divine faith*. This means believing things which God has said, and believing them on his word, because he has said them. God, we know, is the very truth. He cannot be deceived as we can nor can he himself deceive; therefore, whatever he says must be true. There are, of course, many things that he has said which we cannot understand because they are above our reason; but God knows all about them, and because he cannot deceive us, we at once believe him. This is divine faith, or having faith in God's word. If I doubt God's word or say that I do not believe him, this would be a great sin: it would be accusing God of telling me a lie, and would insult him very much.

The catechism says that faith is a gift of God. It is he who gives us the power and the good will to believe. We receive the gift of faith in baptism. It is a supernatural gift, because it is given to us to believe truths about God and the next world. Human faith is a natural gift, because it is only used for believing what concerns us in this world. The catechism asks:

10. **Why must you believe whatever God has revealed?**

I must believe whatever God has revealed, because God is the very truth and can neither deceive nor be deceived.

This, I think, you can easily understand; but a great difficulty will at once occur to you—viz.:

11. **How are you to know what God has revealed?**

I am to know what God has revealed by the testimony, teaching, and authority of the Catholic Church.

But why the Catholic Church? Where does the Catholic Church get the authority and the power to teach me? Show me that clearly, and I will at once submit my mind to it, and believe whatever it teaches me. If it is the Church founded by Jesus Christ, I must of course believe all it says. This will be proved later on.[6]

12. **Who gave the Catholic Church divine authority to teach?**

Jesus Christ gave the Catholic Church divine authority to teach when he said, "Go ye and teach all nations."[7]

Yes, it was Jesus Christ who came down upon earth to die for us and to teach us how to get to heaven, who chose twelve men (called the twelve apostles) and taught them during his lifetime all the truths that people had to know and believe in order to save their souls. These twelve men he sent to teach his truths to the world. Before they commenced their teaching, they put all these truths together, so that they should all teach the same thing, and this collection of truths, which we are now going to explain, is called the Apostles' Creed.

The Apostles' Creed

13. **What are the chief things which God has revealed?**

The chief things which God has revealed are contained in the Apostles' Creed.

[6] See q. 84ff, below.

[7] Mt 28:19

14. **Say the Apostles' Creed.**

I believe in God the Father Almighty, Creator of heaven and earth; and in Jesus Christ his only Son our Lord; who was conceived by the Holy Ghost, born of the Virgin Mary; suffered under Pontius Pilate, was crucified, dead, and buried; he descended into hell; the third day he rose again from the dead; he ascended into heaven, sitteth at the right hand of God the Father Almighty; from thence he shall come to judge the living and the dead; I believe in the Holy Ghost; the holy Catholic Church; the communion of saints; the forgiveness of sins; the resurrection of the body; and life everlasting. Amen.

This Apostles' Creed contains all the truths which you must believe in order to be saved; and once you have had them explained to you, and you have believed them, and you try to put them in practice in your daily life, you need not have any anxiety about your salvation, for Jesus Christ has said, "He that believeth and is baptized shall be saved."[8]

15. **How is the Apostles' Creed divided?**

The Apostles' Creed is divided into twelve parts or articles.

The first eight articles tell us about the three Persons of the Blessed Trinity; the ninth about the Church founded by Jesus Christ, about the three parts of the Church and how they are in communion with each other; the tenth about sin and how it is forgiven in this world; the eleventh about the resurrection of the body; and the last about heaven and hell.

EXPLANATION OF THE CREED

The First Article

16. **What is the first article of the Creed?**

The first article of the Creed is: "I believe in God the Father Almighty, Creator of heaven and earth."

[8] Mk 16:16

17. **What is God?**

God is the supreme Spirit, who alone exists of himself, and is infinite in all perfections.

God is the great Spirit, the greatest one, the supreme, the highest Spirit, whom nobody made. He alone was never created, he always existed; this eternity of God is a thing we cannot understand. Go back millions of ages, and still God existed. He never commenced to exist as we did; some time ago we did not exist except in God's mind; he drew us out of non-existence, out of nothingness. We exist now, and our souls, being immortal, will always exist; they can never die, they will live as long as God lives—that is, forever—for God made them immortal like himself.

God is infinite in all his perfections—that is, his perfections are without bounds or limits.

The perfections of God are his omnipotence, by which we mean that he can do all things, for he is the Almighty God; his holiness, his justice, his mercy, his knowledge, and so on. God is perfectly powerful, perfectly holy, perfectly just, etc., and we are only imperfectly powerful, imperfectly holy, imperfectly just, etc.

18. **Why is God called "Almighty"?**

God is called "Almighty," because he can do all things: "With God all things are possible."[9]

Except one thing: God cannot commit a sin or do anything wrong or against reason, such as making a round square.

19. **Why is God called "Creator of heaven and earth"?**

God is called "Creator of heaven and earth," because he made heaven and earth and all things out of nothing by his Word.

This we learn from the first book of the Bible, which is called "Genesis," where the creation of the world is described. The six days of creation do not mean six days of twenty-four hours each, but six periods of time; each period may have been millions of years.

[9] Mt 19:26

20. **Had God any beginning?**

God had no beginning, he always was, he is, and he always will be.

This we have already explained in Question 17. There is a great, or rather, an infinite difference between God and us in this: that God was never made nor had he any beginning as we had. But there is this likeness between us and God: that we now exist as truly as God exists, and that we, too, shall always exist—that is, we shall live forever in the next world, either in heaven or hell.

21. **Where is God?**

God is everywhere.

There is no place wherein we can hide from God.

22. **Does God know and see all things?**

God knows and sees all things, even our most secret thoughts.

So that there is nothing hidden from God; there is no darkness for God; all is light before him. Sometimes people commit sins in secret, but God can see them. Again, God does not forget sins which we have forgotten all about. There is no past nor future with God: all past things and all future things are present to him. He knows everything that will happen till the end of the world and for all eternity. He sees it all before him at this present moment.

23. **Has God any body?**

God has no body; he is a Spirit.

We are made of body and soul (or spirit), but God has no body; he is a Spirit only.

24. **Is there only one God?**

There is only one God.

All Christians believe this. Some people, such as pagans, idolaters, heathens, etc., believe either that there is no God, or that there are more gods than one.

25. **Are there three Persons in God?**
There are three Persons in God—God the Father, God the Son, and God the Holy Ghost.

26. **Are these three Persons three Gods?**
These three Persons are not three Gods; the Father, the Son, and the Holy Ghost are all one and the same God.

27. **What is the mystery of the three Persons in one God called?**
The mystery of the three Persons in one God is called "the mystery of the Blessed Trinity."

28. **What do you mean by *a mystery*?**
By *a mystery*, I mean a truth which is above reason, but revealed by God.

I have grouped these four questions together in order that you may understand them better. God has made known to us that there is only one true, living God, and that in this one God there are three distinct divine Persons—the Father, the Son, the Holy Ghost. These are not separate Persons, because they exist in one God, but they are distinct from one another; the Father is really God, the Son is really God, and the Holy Ghost is really God, but they are not three Gods, but only one God. How three Persons can be in one God is a mystery—that is, it is something hidden from our understanding, something that our minds cannot grasp; it is called "the mystery of the Blessed Trinity," because it is the mystery of three Persons in one God. It cannot be against reason or contrary to reason, otherwise it would not be true. God cannot reveal anything that is not true, for he is the very truth itself, and he has revealed, or made known to us, that this mystery is true.

29. **Is there any likeness to the Blessed Trinity in your soul?**
There is this likeness to the Blessed Trinity in my soul: that, as in one God there are three Persons, so in my one soul there are three powers.

30. **Which are the three powers of your soul?**

The three powers of my soul are my memory, my understanding, and my will.

Although God has concealed the understanding of this mystery from us, there are, nevertheless, several things in nature which illustrate it. I do not mean explain it, but they show us how it is possible. Tell me, how many souls have you got? "Only one," you will answer. And how many things can that soul do? How many powers or operations or faculties does that soul possess? The catechism tells us that it has three—the power of understanding, the power of memory, and the power of will. These are three distinct, not different, powers, for they all exist together in one soul. To show you that they are distinct—tell me, what power of your soul are you using whilst you are reading these lines? The understanding, of course, because you are trying to understand what you are reading, but it is not the memory nor the will; these are, as it were, lying idle for the time being. Again, if I were to ask you what you were doing yesterday, you would begin to use your memory, and more or less leave the understanding alone; and, lastly, if I ask you what makes you act and do things, you would say, "My will," because you wish or will to do them. You have not three souls within you, one to understand with, one to remember with, and one to will with, but all these three distinct powers reside or exist in one soul, as the three distinct Persons of the Blessed Trinity exist in one God.

The Second Article

31. **What is the second article of the Creed?**

The second article of the Creed is: "And in Jesus Christ, his only Son, our Lord."

That is, "I believe in Jesus Christ, our Lord."

32. **Who is Jesus Christ?**

Jesus Christ is God the Son, made man for us.

He is the second Person of the Blessed Trinity who came down from heaven and became man to redeem us and to teach us how to save our souls.

33. **Is Jesus Christ truly God?**
Jesus Christ is truly God.

34. **Why is Jesus Christ truly God?**
Jesus Christ is truly God because he has one and the same nature with God the Father.

Yes, he is really God, because he is one of the three Persons of the Blessed Trinity, and each divine Person is really and truly God.

35. **Was Jesus Christ always God?**
Jesus Christ was always God, born of the Father from all eternity.

This does not mean that God the Father existed before God the Son, for we have already seen that the Father and Son are equal in all things, and therefore in the eternity of their existence as well as in everything else.

36. **Which Person of the Blessed Trinity is Jesus Christ?**
Jesus Christ is the second Person of the Blessed Trinity.

This you must keep well in your mind. It was not God the Father nor God the Holy Ghost that became man, but God the Son, the second Person of the Blessed Trinity.

37. **Is Jesus Christ truly man?**
Jesus Christ is truly man.

38. **Why is Jesus Christ truly man?**
Jesus Christ is truly man because he has the nature of man, having a body and soul like ours.

Jesus Christ, besides being truly God, is also truly or really man—that is to say, he has a real body and soul as we have, and, when on earth, he did all the things we do, except, of course, committing sin. He was hungry and thirsty and weary, and he walked and spoke and slept and suffered, just as we do.

39. Was Jesus Christ always man?

Jesus Christ was not always man; he has been man only from the time of his incarnation.

His human life commenced when he was conceived in his Mother's womb. He was always God, but he was not always man.

40. What do you mean by *the incarnation*?

I mean by *the incarnation* that God the Son took to himself the nature of man: "The Word was made flesh."[10]

The word *incarnation* is a Latin word. It means "becoming man," and hence the act of our Lord in becoming man or taking a human nature to himself, which he made his own, is called "the incarnation."

41. How many natures are there in Jesus Christ?

There are two natures in Jesus Christ—the nature of God and the nature of man.

That is to say, that he was really God and really man. We have only one nature—the nature of man, or human nature; but our Lord has two natures—the divine nature and the human nature, because he was really God and really man.

Now, how can we show by a very simple argument that he was really God and really man at the same time? Because he did the things that God only can do, and he also did the things that man does. For instance, he raised the dead to life, he cured all kinds of diseases, he performed all manner of miracles to prove that he was really God, the greatest of these being that on the day of the resurrection, he raised himself to life. These are things that God only can do; and at the same time this same Person, Jesus Christ, did all the things that we do and endured those things that happen to us. He was born, he labored and toiled, he suffered, and he died.

42. Is there only one Person in Jesus Christ?

There is only one Person in Jesus Christ, which is the Person of God the Son.

[10] Jn 1:14

Though there are two natures in our Lord—the nature of God and the nature of man—there is but one Person in him, or rather he is one Person, the Person of God the Son, but he acts in his two natures. Whatever he did as God, it was, of course, God who did it; and also, whatever he did as man, it was God who did it; that is why we say that God died for us, though it was only his human nature that died, because God died in his human nature.

43. **Why was God the Son made man?**

God the Son was made man to redeem us from sin and hell and to teach us the way to heaven.

This is a most important answer, and you must try to get the meaning of it well into your mind, for it is the key to the mystery of the incarnation. Once we understand this answer, we shall understand a great deal about Jesus Christ and his love for us.

Let us go back for a moment to the creation of the world. You can read all about it in Genesis, the first book of the Bible. After God had made the world and all that is in it, he made our first parents, Adam and Eve, and placed them in the garden of paradise. God told them to till it and to keep it in order. He gave them only one commandment to keep, and that was that they should not eat of the fruit of a certain tree which stood in the midst of paradise. The name of the tree was "the tree of the knowledge of good and evil." God told Adam and Eve that if they broke this commandment and ate of this forbidden fruit, they should "surely die"; so they had plenty of warning from God of the punishment they would receive if they disobeyed him.

"But why," you may ask me, "did God give them this commandment?" Because it was to be their trial. God intended them to go to heaven, and you must know that God never allows anybody to go to heaven without a trial; that is the reason why we have crosses and troubles and temptations in this world, for we are all on our trial now; life is the time of our trial, and the world is the place of our trial. If we are faithful to God and bear our trials patiently, and fight against our temptations and keep out of sin, then God will reward us in heaven for our faithfulness; but if we do not serve God by doing his will, but give way to temptation and commit sin, then, when we die, God cannot reward us, but he must and will punish us because we have not been faithful to him; we could have kept out of sin if we had liked.

But you may ask me, "Had the angels any trial? They are, of course, in heaven now. Did God place them there without making them go through any trial?" Well, this is a very natural question to ask, for I had said that no one gets to heaven without having been tried. My answer is that even the angels—bright, beautiful spirits that they are—had to undergo a very severe trial or temptation before they secured the happiness of heaven for eternity. Of course, I am supposing that you know that there was a time when not even the angels existed; when God alone—that is, the Blessed Trinity only—existed; and that a time came when God created the angels to praise, love, and serve him. God could have done without them; they were not necessary for his happiness in any way. He created them, too, as he created us to make them happy with him in heaven for all eternity; but he had to try them to see if they would really be faithful to him.

So God gave them a trial, and it is generally believed to have been this: God revealed or made known to them that a time would come when God the Son, the second Person of the Blessed Trinity, would become man—that is to say, that he would take upon himself a nature lower than the angels' nature—for you must know that the angels' nature is much higher and more exalted than ours. And then God called upon Lucifer, who was the chief angel, and all his companions to adore the sacred human nature of God the Son. This Lucifer and a great many of the angels refused to do. This was a terrible sin of pride and revolt against God; and God was so angry that he at once made hell, and cast into it all the rebel angels. These angels are the bad angels or devils who tempt us now to commit sin. They hate God; but as they cannot hurt him in any way, they vent their rage and hatred upon us, because they see in us the image of God. They are terribly jealous of us and of the happiness which God has in store for us, for we were created to take their places in heaven; and God allows them to tempt us to sin, but only so far as he sees we can bear it. He never allows us to be tempted beyond our strength; so, if we give way to temptation, we must not blame God but ourselves, for we can resist it if we make use of the help which God gives us.

Now these temptations to sin which come from the devil are our trial. If we resist them and refuse to commit the sins to which we are tempted, God will reward us in heaven for being faithful to his law; but if we willfully, of our own free consent and knowing that we are doing wrong, give way to these temptations and rebel against God's law as the angels did, and die in this state, we, too, shall go to hell as they did. We must always bear in mind, however, that hell was not created for us, but only for the rebel angels. God has said so distinctly in the words of condemnation which he will say to the wicked at the end of the world: "Depart from me ye cursed into everlasting fire which was prepared for the devil and his angels."[11] Whereas, on the contrary, he will say to the just: "Come, ye blessed of my Father, possess ye the kingdom prepared for you."[12] Heaven, therefore, was made for us, not hell.

When Adam and Eve disobeyed God, it was a very great sin; so great that God cursed the earth and all that was in it, and closed the gates of heaven against the human race, so that no one could ever get in. Adam and Eve were driven out of paradise to be wanderers upon the earth; but God, who is infinite in his mercy, did not abandon them; he determined to save the human race by sending his only-begotten Son to redeem it. But why did not Adam and Eve ask God's forgiveness for their sin and get it forgiven at once, as we do? Try to understand the answer to this, for it is very important.

The sin which they committed was in some respects one of infinite malice, and therefore God's justice demanded from them a satisfaction proportionate to their crime. Now, what does that mean? Supposing you met a person in the street, and without any just reason you insulted him and struck him; this would be an offense against the laws of the land, and you would be punished for it by having to pay a fine or by spending a certain time in prison. When the fine was paid or the imprisonment was over,

[11] Mt 25:41
[12] Mt 25:34

you would be considered to have done enough to have fully compensated the person for the injury you had inflicted upon him. Proper satisfaction can always be made by one man to another; but when it is a question of an insult offered to God, it is a very different matter indeed. God is the Creator, and we are only the creatures; God is infinite, and we are only finite creatures; and, therefore, if we offer any insult to God or commit a sin against him, it is an infinite offense, because it is committed against an infinite being. Hence we cannot give any proper satisfaction to him of ourselves, because we are not infinite like God, and God demands an infinite satisfaction. This is why it was necessary for an infinite being to come down from heaven and to offer this infinite satisfaction for us. This is what Jesus Christ did. He was God, and he alone could make satisfaction for our sins—only an infinite being like God can make proper satisfaction to God for sin. Hence we call our Lord "our Savior" because he saved us from sin and hell, and we call him "our Redeemer" because he redeemed us from the power of the devil. You must, therefore, love Jesus Christ very much, for if it had not been for him, you would have had no right to go to heaven.

44. **What does the holy name of Jesus mean?**
The holy name of Jesus means "Savior."

The word *Jesus* is really a Greek word, which means "Savior"; and it was given to our Lord because he was to save us from sin and hell. Catholics have the pious habit of bowing the head every time they mention or hear the name of Jesus. They do it out of respect for that holy name.

45. **What does the name *Christ* mean?**
The name *Christ* means "anointed."

The word *Christ* is also a Greek word, which means "anointed," because our Lord is our anointed King, and we are his subjects. He conquered the devil and ransomed us from his slavery, so that we owe Christ allegiance, and we are bound to obey him as all loyal subjects obey the king who rules over the land in which they live. If we do not obey him, we are rebels, and he will punish us in the next world for our rebellion as he punished the wicked angels.

46. **Where is Jesus Christ?**
As God, Jesus Christ is everywhere. As God made man, he is in heaven, and in the Blessed Sacrament of the altar.

You will remember that we explained[13] that Jesus Christ was both God and man. Because he is God, and God is everywhere, therefore Jesus Christ in his divine nature is everywhere; but as man, or in his human nature, he is not everywhere. As God made man he is in heaven, sitting on the right hand of God the Father Almighty, as the Creed says; and he is also in every Catholic church or chapel in the world where the Blessed Sacrament is kept. When you enter a Catholic church, you will always see a light burning in front of the altar, which is a sign that the Blessed Sacrament is in the tabernacle on the altar, and that Jesus Christ is really there, though you cannot see him. All this will be explained later on.

The Third Article

47. **What is the third article of the Creed?**
The third article of the Creed is: "Who was conceived by the Holy Ghost, born of the Virgin Mary."

48. **What does the third article mean?**
The third article means that God the Son took a body and soul like ours, in the womb of the Blessed Virgin Mary, by the power of the Holy Ghost.

From this third article we learn that God the Son, the second Person of the Blessed Trinity, became man for us, and that he had a real Mother as we have had, but he had no man for his father on earth; his sacred body was created in Mary's womb by the Holy Ghost, "conceived by the Holy Ghost," as the Creed says; but Mary was really his Mother.

[13] See q. 33-40, above.

49. **Had Jesus Christ any father on earth?**
Jesus Christ had no father on earth; St. Joseph was only his guardian or foster-father.

St. Joseph is called "the father of Jesus" in the sacred scripture, though he was only his foster-father—that is to say, he acted as a father to him; he took care of the Child Jesus and of our Blessed Lady. Our Lord must have loved him very much for this, and this is the reason why we Catholics have a great devotion to him; we believe that, now that he is in heaven, our Lord has given him great power to help us, in return for the care he took of him when he was a child upon earth. There is a little book called "Who is St. Joseph?" which will tell you much about this great saint. You can get this and the other books mentioned in this explanatory catechism from the publishers of this work.

50. **Where was our Savior born?**
Our Savior was born in a stable at Bethlehem.

51. **On what day was our Savior born?**
Our Savior was born on Christmas day.

All this every good Christian knows and believes.

The Fourth Article

52. **What is the fourth article of the Creed?**
The fourth article of the Creed is: "Suffered under Pontius Pilate, was crucified, dead, and buried."

53. **What were the chief sufferings of Christ?**
The chief sufferings of Christ were: first, his agony and his sweat of blood in the garden; secondly, his being scourged at the pillar and crowned with thorns; and, thirdly, his carrying his cross, his crucifixion, and his death between two thieves.

You can read the account of our Lord's sufferings and death in your Bible. Begin at the twenty-sixth chapter of St. Matthew's gospel and read carefully to the end of chapter twenty-seven. There is also a little book called "The Love and Passion of Jesus Christ," which will help you very much to understand our Lord's sufferings.

54. **What are the chief sufferings of our Lord called?**
The chief sufferings of our Lord are called "the passion of Jesus Christ."

The word *passion* means "suffering," from the Latin word *passio*; when we speak of passion, we generally mean great anger. We say, "So-and-so was in a great passion," meaning that he was very angry; but when we speak of our Lord's passion, we mean his sufferings and death.

55. **Why did our Savior suffer?**
Our Savior suffered to atone for our sins and to purchase for us eternal life.

This answer has been sufficiently explained in Question 43.

56. **Why is Jesus Christ called "our Redeemer"?**
Jesus Christ is called "our Redeemer" because his precious blood is the price by which we were ransomed.

The word *Redeemer* means "one who buys back"; we were slaves, under the power of the devil, and our Lord bought us back from that slavery; he did not pay gold or silver for us, but he gave his life on the cross. We really, therefore, belong to him; he is our master, and we should faithfully serve him by leading good lives and keeping his commandments.

57. **On what day did our Savior die?**
Our Savior died on Good Friday.

58. **Where did our Savior die?**
Our Savior died on Mount Calvary.

59. **Why do we make the sign of the cross?**
We make the sign of the cross: first, to put us in mind of the Blessed Trinity; and, secondly, to remind us that God the Son died for us on the cross.

This is an act of devotion which is practiced by Catholics of all countries and to a great extent by those who belong to the High Church section of the Church of England, but which is looked upon as rank superstition by protestants in general. The sign of the cross consists of two things—an outward sign and a form of words. The sign of the cross is made by placing the fingers of the right hand on the forehead (saying at the same time, "In the name of the Father"), then upon the breast (saying, "and of the Son") then upon the left shoulder (saying, "and of the Holy Ghost") and lastly upon the right shoulder (saying, "Amen"). Some people prefer to say "Holy" on the left shoulder and "Ghost" on the right, and say "Amen" with the hands closed.

The sign of the cross has been used from the earliest ages. Writing in the year 195, Tertullian says, "In all our travels and movements, in all our coming in and going out, in putting on our clothes and shoes, at the bath, at the table, in lighting our lamps, in lying down, in sitting down, whatever employment occupies us, we mark our forehead with the sign of the cross."[14]

Now, far from it being an act of superstition, the sign of the cross is a wonderful act of religion, for it is an outward act of faith in the two greatest mysteries of the Christian religion—the mystery of the Blessed Trinity and that of the incarnation of the Son of God.

60. In making the sign of the cross, how are we reminded of the Blessed Trinity?

In making the sign of the cross, we are reminded of the Blessed Trinity by the words, "In the name of the Father, and of the Son, and of the Holy Ghost."

In other words, we profess to believe in the one name of God: of Father, Son, and Holy Ghost.

[14] Tertullian, *De Corona Militis*, Ch. 3

61. **In making the sign of the cross, how are we reminded that Christ died for us on the cross?**
In making the sign of the cross, we are reminded that Christ died for us on the cross by the very form of the cross which we make upon ourselves.

If you notice, you make the real shape of the cross upon yourself. From the forehead to the breast is the long, upright part of the cross; from shoulder to shoulder forms the arms. We make the sign of the cross before and after our prayers, before and after our meals, when we enter the church (and then it is made with holy water as an act of purification, for we are entering the presence of God), and, lastly, in time of temptation, for it is a very powerful means of driving away the devil. He hates the cross; it is the sign of our Lord's triumph over sin, and he cannot hurt those who are armed with the sign, for our Lord protects them.

The Fifth Article

62. **What is the fifth article of the Creed?**
The fifth article of the Creed is: "He descended into hell, the third day he rose again from the dead."

63. **What do you mean by the words, "He descended into hell"?**
By the words, "He descended into hell," I mean that, as soon as Christ was dead, his blessed soul went down into that part of hell called limbo.

This is a most important article to understand, because it tells us about the existence of a third state in the next world. Protestants, you know, say that there are only two places or states in the next world—heaven and hell—and, therefore, when a person dies, I suppose they must believe that his soul goes either straight to heaven or straight to hell. We Catholics believe that there are three places or states in the next world—heaven, hell, and purgatory. Of purgatory proper we shall speak later on. Here we have to consider the existence of some third state before the time of our Lord's coming on earth.

You will remember that I spoke to you about the fall of Adam and Eve. After their fall, the gates of heaven were closed against them and their posterity, and were only opened again by the death of Jesus Christ upon the cross. This, as we all know, happened many thousands of years after the creation of our first parents, and of course many, many millions of people lived and died during those years. The wicked were lost in hell; but where did the good go to? God could not send them to hell, and you must remember the gates of heaven were closed, so they must of necessity have gone to some other place where God kept them until our Lord came to redeem them. This place was limbo, and it was into this place that our Lord's blessed soul descended immediately after his death on the cross. He went there to comfort the souls of the just, and to tell them that they were redeemed. Besides, our Lord himself spoke of this third state or place. When the good thief said to him, as he was dying on the cross, "Lord, remember me when thou comest into thy kingdom," he answered, "Amen, I say to thee, this day thou shalt be with me in paradise."[15] That *paradise* could not mean heaven, for our Lord did not ascend there till the day of the ascension; it must, therefore, have meant the place whither Jesus descended immediately after his death. You will now be able to understand the two next questions of the catechism.

64. **What do you mean by *limbo*?**

By *limbo*, I mean a place of rest, where the souls of the just who died before Christ were detained.

The word *limbo* means a "border" or "fringe," here it means some place or state on the outside or outskirts of hell.

65. **Why were the souls of the just detained in limbo?**

The souls of the just were detained in limbo because they could not go up to the kingdom of heaven until Christ had opened it for them.

So you see that from the time of Adam's fall there were three distinct places or states of souls in the next world. If this third place was a reality,

[15] Lk 23:42-43

then why cannot it be a reality now if there is a necessity for it? We shall see later on that there is.[16]

66. **What do you mean by the words, "The third day he rose again from the dead"?**
By the words, "The third day he rose again from the dead," I mean that after Christ had been dead and buried part of three days, he raised his blessed body to life again on the third day.

Our Lord died at three o'clock on Good Friday afternoon; his body was taken down from the cross at six o'clock and placed in the tomb; there it remained all Good Friday night, all Holy Saturday, and it rose from the dead on Easter Sunday morning—that is, on the morning of the third day.

67. **On what day did Christ rise again from the dead?**
Christ rose again from the dead on Easter Sunday.

Easter Sunday is a glorious day for all Christians, for our Savior rose from the dead on that day to prove that he was God.

The Sixth Article

68. **What is the sixth article of the Creed?**
The sixth article of the Creed is: "He ascended into heaven, sitteth at the right hand of God the Father Almighty."

69. **What do you mean by the words, "He ascended into heaven"?**
By the words, "He ascended into heaven," I mean that our Savior went up body and soul into heaven on Ascension day, forty days after his resurrection.

Our Lord went up into heaven by his own power, and thus he gave another proof of his divinity. During the forty days which elapsed between his rising from the dead on Easter Sunday and his going into heaven on Ascension day, the holy scripture tells us that our Lord often appeared to

[16] See q. 107 and 115, below.

his apostles, "speaking of the kingdom of God."[17] It was during these days that he gave the apostles further and more complete instructions about how they were to act, and how they were to govern the Church after he had left them. He gave them the power to forgive sins[18] and to preach and baptize,[19] and prepared them for the work they had to do amongst men.

70. **What do you mean by the words, "sitteth at the right hand of God the Father Almighty"?**

By the words, "sitteth at the right hand of God the Father Almighty," I do not mean that God the Father has hands, for he is a Spirit; but I mean that Christ, as God, is equal to the Father, and, as man, is in the highest place in heaven.

You must remember always that Jesus Christ is both God and man. As God he is in all ways equal to his Father in power, in dignity, in eternity, in Godhead; but as man he is not equal to God, because a man cannot be equal to God, so as man he takes the next place to God in heaven. When we speak of God's "right hand," we do not of course mean that God the Father has hands like we have, or that he has a body like Jesus Christ had, but the expression "at the right hand of God" must be taken figuratively to mean the highest place next to God. Supposing you had a very intimate and dear friend, and you were to invite him to dinner at your house, you would place him at your right hand at the dinner table, because that is considered to be the place of honor.

The Seventh Article

71. **What is the seventh article of the Creed?**

The seventh article of the Creed is: "From thence he shall come to judge the living and the dead."

From thence—that is to say, "from heaven."

[17] Acts 1:3
[18] Cf. Jn 20:23
[19] Cf. Mt 28:19

72. **When will Christ come again?**

Christ will come again from heaven at the last day, to judge all mankind.

Our Lord, therefore, will come again at the last day to judge the world. He came at his incarnation to save it; at his second coming he comes to judge it.

73. **What are the things Christ will judge?**

Christ will judge our thoughts, words, works, and omissions.

Our Lord will examine and judge all our good and bad thoughts, our good and bad words, our good and bad works, and the omission of our duties. We can commit sins, therefore, in four ways:

1. *By thinking of what is wrong.* Many people imagine that merely thinking about a thing which is wrong is not a sin in itself, provided you do not do the action; but this is a mistake. If God has forbidden us to do a certain thing, he has thereby certainly forbidden us to think of doing it. For instance, everybody knows it is wrong to steal. God has said so: "Thou shalt not steal";[20] but he has also forbidden us to make up our minds to steal, or even to entertain the thought of taking what does not belong to us. He has said: "Thou shalt not covet thy neighbor's goods"[21]—that is, wish to get hold of them by dishonest means. Supposing you knew where there was some money, and you made up your mind to steal it, but you did not get the chance, would you have committed a sin? Certainly, just as great a sin before God as if you had really stolen it. The sin would not take place when you actually put out your hand to steal it, but when you made up your mind to steal it, only, of course, as you did not actually take the money you would not be bound to any restitution. In the same way, it was not when the murderer pulled the trigger of the revolver to murder his victim that the sin of murder was committed, but when he bought the revolver and made up his mind to murder the person.

I do not, of course, mean to say that all wicked thoughts that come into our heads are sins. We cannot help many of them—the devil puts

[20] Ex 20:15

[21] Cf. Ex 20:17

them there; but we can put them out of our minds and refuse to think of them, and pray to God to help us to get rid of them. If we do this, we cannot commit a sin by thought; but if we are aware that a bad thought is in our minds, and we do not pray, and do not try to put it away, but go on thinking of it purposely, then we commit a sin by thought. If the thought is a very wicked one, then the sin is a great one; but it is only a small sin if the thought is not very bad, or if we give only a kind of half consent to it, even though it be very wicked in itself.

2. *By word*—that is, by saying things we are forbidden to say, viz., words of anger, words against our neighbor's character, lies, curses, unlawful oaths, etc.

3. *By deed*—viz., doing anything wrong, such as stealing, striking a person in anger, getting drunk, etc.

4. *By omission*—that is, by omitting to do what we are commanded to do. God has not only forbidden us to do certain things, but he has also commanded us to do certain things; and if we fail to do them, this is a sin of omission, because it is omitting to do our duty. If a father drinks and wastes his wages, and thus neglects his home and children, he is omitting to do his duty as a father. Again, if a person stays in bed on Sunday instead of going to Mass, he commits a sin of omission, because he is omitting to hear Mass through his own fault; if a person does not pay his debts, he is guilty of omitting the duty of justice.

74. **What will Christ say to the wicked?**

Christ will say to the wicked, "Depart from me, ye cursed, into everlasting fire which was prepared for the devil and his angels."[22]

These words come in St. Matthew's gospel. Our Lord does not say that hell was prepared for us, but for the devil and his angels. Heaven was prepared for us, not hell; if we go to hell, it will be through our own fault. God is not himself the author of a soul's condemnation: the soul condemns itself by willfully leading a wicked life. No soul goes to hell by accident; only those souls go there who have really deserved such a punishment

[22] Mt 25:41

through their own fault. We have all got a conscience which tells us what is right and what is wrong. We all know, too, that there is a God who has promised to reward us if we are good, and has threatened to punish us if we are wicked. We have a free will to do as we like; we can offend God or serve him, just as we like, only we must remember the consequences. Some people think that God is unjust and cruel to keep a soul in hell for all eternity, and that hell must end someday. But they forget that God has made the soul immortal, that is, it can never die.[23] It is not that hell is of itself eternal, and that when an unfortunate soul gets there, it cannot get out because hell keeps it there; no, but the soul is eternal, and, because it is eternal, it drags the eternity of hell along with it. Hell must last forever, because the soul must last forever. God cannot punish a soul one bit more than it deserves. God is infinitely just; he would not be God if he were not. He rewards us beyond what we deserve, but never punishes us beyond what we deserve. However, it is not of much use to discuss whether hell is eternal or not; the great thing is for us to lead good lives, and to make sure that we do not go there.

75. **What will Christ say to the just?**

Christ will say to the just, "Come, ye blessed of my Father, possess ye the kingdom prepared for you."[24]

You see, our Lord says distinctly that heaven was prepared for us—not hell. Heaven is the happy home where we are to be with God for eternity, but in the same way that no one goes to hell without having richly deserved it, so no one can get to heaven without having worked for it. There is only one way of getting to heaven, and that is the way laid down and pointed out by our Lord, not the way that we think is right or that we have invented for ourselves, or that any man has invented for us.

[23] See q. 6, above.

[24] Mt 25:34

76. **Will everyone be judged at death, as well as at the last day?**
Everyone will be judged at death, as well as at the last day: "It is appointed unto men once to die, and after this the judgment."[25]

There are two judgments for us in the next world—one takes place immediately after death, and is called the "private" or "particular judgment," because it takes place between God and the soul alone, and upon this judgment all our eternity will depend. The last moment of our life is the most important one of the whole of our existence. If the soul is then in a state of grace and pleasing to God, we are safe for eternity. If not, then all is lost. Moreover, we are judged not only at the moment after death, but wherever we are when we die; there in that very spot we are judged, there Jesus Christ stands ready to judge us. Oh! how we ought to think about that awful moment and prepare well for it during our lifetime.

The second judgment, which will take place at the end of the world, is called the "general judgment." All the human race will assemble somewhere at the last day, and everyone will be judged publicly before the whole world; everyone's secret sins will be known to the whole world if they are not repented of and forgiven in this life. How ashamed sinners will feel then, when everybody else knows and sees clearly all the secret sins and crimes of their lives.

The Eighth Article

77. **What is the eighth article of the Creed?**
The eighth article of the Creed is: "I believe in the Holy Ghost."

78. **Who is the Holy Ghost?**
The Holy Ghost is the third Person of the Blessed Trinity.[26]

79. **From whom does the Holy Ghost proceed?**
The Holy Ghost proceeds from the Father and the Son.

[25] Heb 9:27

[26] This we have already seen and explained in q. 25-28.

That does not mean that the Holy Ghost is in any way inferior to God the Father and God the Son because he proceeds or comes forth from them, or because he is the third Person; nor does it mean that he ceases to be divinely united to them, for he is equally God with them.

80. **Is the Holy Ghost equal to the Father and to the Son?**
The Holy Ghost is equal to the Father and to the Son, for he is the same Lord and God as they are.

Hence, there can be no inferiority amongst these three divine Persons, for they are all equally God.

81. **When did the Holy Ghost come down on the apostles?**
The Holy Ghost came down on the apostles on Whitsunday in the form of "parted tongues as it were of fire."[27]

Before our Lord went up into heaven on Ascension day, he told his apostles that he would send the Holy Ghost down upon them. He fulfilled this promise on Whitsunday, or Pentecost Sunday, as we learn from the Acts of the Apostles.[28] The Holy Ghost appeared in the form of parted tongues of fire. He took that shape, or appearance, to show that the apostles were to go and preach. That is the reason of the appearance of the tongues (for we speak with the tongue), and the tongues were, as it were, of fire, to show that the apostles were to enkindle the fire of God's love in the people's hearts; and, lastly, the tongues were parted, or divided, to signify that the apostles received the gift of tongues—that is, that though they preached in their own native language yet all who heard them could understand them whether they knew the apostles' language or not.

82. **Why did the Holy Ghost come down on the apostles?**
The Holy Ghost came down on the apostles to confirm their faith, to sanctify them, and to enable them to found the Church.

[27] Acts 2:3
[28] Cf. Acts 2:1-4

The Holy Ghost came down upon the apostles to strengthen them in their faith, for they would have to encounter all kinds of temptations and sufferings and even death in defense of it; secondly, to make them good and holy, and thus to fit them for the duty of making others good like themselves; and, lastly, to help them in the great work our Lord had given them to do—namely, to spread his holy religion.

The Ninth Article

83. **What is the ninth article of the Creed?**
The ninth article of the Creed is: "The holy Catholic Church; the communion of saints."

84. **What is the Catholic Church?**
The Catholic Church is the union of all the faithful under one head.

We now come to the most important part of the Creed. The ninth article says, "I believe in the holy Catholic Church"—that is to say, I believe that the holy Catholic Church is the one true Church founded by Jesus Christ, and to that Church I must belong if I intend to be saved. I think we all agree about that. The question is: Where is the Catholic Church? Which is it? Some protestants say that they are the Catholic Church, or, at least, they are a branch of it. They no longer like the name of *protestant*—it seems to insult them if you call them by that name; even the poor in the workhouses have dropped the name and are "Church" or "Church of England." Of course, you know what *protestant* means—it means "one who protests," for at the Reformation, the makers of the new religion protested against the old faith of England. Unless they had something of their own to put in its place, mere protesting could scarcely be called a religion. Protestantism is not, and cannot be, a religion, because it is simply a denial of, or a protestation against, a religion which already existed. It is a system which teaches a certain number of the truths revealed by Jesus Christ, but rejects others.

The true Catholic Church was founded by our Lord Jesus Christ when he was upon earth; it exists now and it will exist till the end of the world.

The catechism says, "It is the union of all the faithful under one head."

The Church of Jesus Christ is a society formed of men, women, and children who believe all the doctrines taught by him to the world (*faithful* means "people who believe"). This society exists here on earth, and numbers about 320,000,000 members at the present day; all of these members believe exactly the same doctrine, and worship God in exactly the same way. Now, every society must have a head to guide and rule it; if it has no head, it will soon come to naught, because everybody will want to have his own way, and union will no longer be possible. So the catechism asks:

85. **Who is the head of the Catholic Church?**

The head of the Catholic Church is Jesus Christ our Lord.

Naturally, because he founded it. But where is Jesus Christ? He is no longer visible on earth; he is in heaven, whither he ascended on Ascension day, so that in case of necessity or difficulty his Church cannot speak to him or consult him. The apostles could speak to him when he was on earth with them, but this is no longer possible to the successors of the apostles. Our Lord foresaw this and wisely arranged that there should always be someone on earth to represent him, to take his place and to act and speak for him. So the catechism asks:

86. **Has the Church a visible head on earth?**

The Church has a visible head on earth, the bishop of Rome, who is the vicar of Christ.

Visible means "someone that we can see and speak to," so the bishop of Rome is the visible head of Christ's Church on earth.

But you will naturally say, "How do you make that out? We have always been taught that the pope is a very wicked man, that he is Antichrist. How can he be the vicar of Christ?" Yes, I daresay you have been taught so, but does it always follow that what people teach is the truth, especially when they are speaking about persons whom they hate and detest? At any rate, you must admit that you may have been taught wrong, and you must also remember that while there are a few evil-minded people who say this about the pope, there are about 320,000,000 of people in the world, of all nations and races, who say just the contrary, and who believe most firmly that the pope is really the representative of Christ upon earth. Surely, if what you say is true, it speaks very badly for the wisdom and common sense of this enormous number of people. There must be some mistake somewhere, so let us go on and see.

87. **Why is the bishop of Rome the head of the Church?**
The bishop of Rome is the head of the Church because he is the successor of St. Peter, whom Christ appointed to be head of the Church.

I suppose we shall all be right if we take the Bible, and see what it has to say about the matter, and therefore the catechism asks where we get our information from that Christ did really appoint some man to be the head of his Church in his place, and who that man was. It asks that question, because if it can be proved that Christ really did appoint some man, there certainly must be a successor to that man somewhere on the earth now, as the Church of Christ was not to last merely during the life of one person, but to the end of time, to the end of the world.

88. **How do you know that Christ appointed St. Peter to be the head of the Church?**
I know that Christ appointed St. Peter to be the head of the Church, because Christ said to him: "Thou art Peter, and upon this rock I will build my church, and the gates of hell shall not prevail against it. And to thee I will give the keys of the kingdom of heaven."[29]

We do not quite get the force of Christ's words from the English text, because in English *Peter* and *rock* are practically two different words, or at least seem to be so; so we must try and find out from the original words of Christ if there is anything that will make things clearer to us. Just take your Bible and open it at the first chapter of St. John's gospel and the forty-second verse, and you will find these words: "He brought him unto Jesus...Jesus looked upon him and said, 'Thou art Simon the son of John, thou shalt be called Cephas' (which is by interpretation, *Peter*)," and you

[29] Mt 16:18-19

will also find in the Revised Version of the Bible a marginal note which tells you what *Peter* means; the note says, "that is, 'rock' or 'stone.'" So that when our divine Lord said, "Thou art Peter, and upon this rock," etc., he said, "Thou art Cephas, and upon this Cephas" (that is, "upon thee, Peter") "I will build my church"; so that our Lord told St. Peter that he should be the foundation stone of his Church, the principal part of it, the head of his Church; and we must bear in mind who it is that is speaking. It is Christ, the Son of the living God. He calls it his Church. "My church"; it is therefore the Church of God, and Peter was to be its first head on earth. And then comes a most remarkable promise from the lips of Jesus Christ: "And the gates of hell shall not prevail against it"—that is, against "my church." The *gates of hell* mean "the powers of darkness, error, falsehood"; these shall not prevail against or destroy his Church, the Church which he founded upon St. Peter; so that the Church of which St. Peter was to be the head could never fall into error or teach false doctrines. If it could, it stands to reason that the promises of Christ would fail; this, of course, is impossible.

And there is something else very striking which our Lord said to St. Peter: "And to thee (Peter) I will give the keys of the kingdom of heaven." These words need a little explanation. To have the keys of a place means to have absolute power over that place. If you have a cupboard or a desk and you have the keys of it, you are practically master of it, you can put things in or take them out just as you please. Our Lord therefore promises to give to St. Peter a power, an absolute power, and over what? "The kingdom of heaven." These words mean the kingdom of God on earth, or the Church. Our Lord often spoke of the Church as the kingdom of heaven. He compares it to a net gathering fishes of every kind;[30] to the sower;[31] to a grain of mustard seed.[32] If you read these parables, you will see that they refer to the Church on earth. So that our Lord in this text promises to give to St. Peter an absolute power to rule the Church.

[30] Cf. Mt 13:47
[31] Cf. Mt 13:24
[32] Cf. Mt 13:31

After our Lord ascended into heaven, St. Peter took his position as head of the Church, and remained at Antioch for seven years; then he went to Rome, which was the center of civilization, and there he lived for twenty-five years, ruling and governing the Church. He was put to death for his faith by the emperor Nero in the year A.D. 67. After his death, another bishop of Rome was chosen in his place; he, of course, became head of the Church in St. Peter's place. The new bishop's name was St. Linus. He was put to death in the same year, and was succeeded by St. Cletus, who was martyred in the year A.D. 78. At his death, another successor was chosen, and so it has gone on to the present time. Altogether there have been 260 bishops of Rome, or popes as they are called, one succeeding another from the days of St. Peter down to Pope Pius XI, the present bishop of Rome, who is the 259th direct successor of St. Peter. That Church, therefore, over which Pius XI rules, and of which he is the head, is the Church of St. Peter and that Church which was founded by Jesus Christ, and of which St. Peter was made the first head. This is the Roman Catholic Church, and none other. It is the only true Church because it alone can show, through its long unbroken line of pontiffs, its direct origin from Christ.

89. **What is the bishop of Rome called?**

The bishop of Rome is called "the pope" which word signifies "father."

The Latin word for *pope* is *papa.* You often hear children call their father "papa"; this means "father."

90. **Is the pope the spiritual father of all Christians?**

The pope is the spiritual father of all Christians. He is the head of the Christian Church; he has to rule and guide them.

91. **Is the pope the shepherd and teacher of all Christians?**

The pope is the shepherd and teacher of all Christians because Christ made St. Peter the shepherd of the whole flock when he said: "Feed my lambs; feed my sheep."[33] He also prayed that his "faith" might never fail, and commanded him to "confirm" his brethren.[34]

Whatever powers and privileges our Lord gave to St. Peter as head of the Church were not merely for himself, but were to be possessed afterward by all those who succeeded him as head of the Church. Our Lord gave St. Peter power to rule the Church, to feed his lambs and his sheep, and this same power has descended to all St. Peter's successors. Again, our Lord gave a very special privilege to St. Peter. Open your Bible at the twentysecond chapter of St. Luke's gospel (verse thirty-one) and you will read these words: "Simon, Simon, behold Satan asked to have you that he might sift you as wheat, but I have made supplication for thee that thy faith fail not, and do thou, when thou hast turned again, stablish thy brethren." Now, I must explain these words and the circumstances in which they were spoken. It was just after the last supper: our Lord was speaking to his apostles. He turns to Simon Peter and says the above words. Of course, in speaking to Peter, he was really addressing them all, as the plural word *you* shows. He tells them all that Satan has asked permission from God to tempt them in their faith (to "sift as wheat," meaning "to tempt"), but there is one about whom he is particularly anxious. "I have prayed for thee (Peter) that thy faith fail not." If the faith of the others failed, Peter's was never to fail, because he was to be the future head of the Church, and if his faith failed, if he could believe or teach false doctrine, the Church over which he was to rule would fail too. Hence there was a very special reason why Peter's faith should never fail. Moreover, he had to "stablish his brethren" in the faith, to confirm them in the faith if ever they failed in it: "Thou being converted, confirm thy brethren," as the Catholic Bible says.

This "stablishing" or "confirming" power was contained in the words, "Feed my lambs; feed my sheep"—that is, "my whole flock." The *sheep* represented the apostles and their successors in the ministry; the *lambs* the faithful, the people of the Church; so St. Peter's power was to feed by doctrine and to rule by authority over the whole Church.

[33] Cf. Jn 21:15-17
[34] Cf. Lk 22:32

92. **Is the pope infallible?**

The pope is infallible.

93. **What do you mean when you say the pope is infallible?**

When I say that the pope is infallible, I mean that the pope cannot err when, as shepherd and teacher of all Christians, he defines a doctrine concerning faith or morals to be held by the whole Church.

How is this to be explained? What does this word *infallible* mean? Does it mean that the pope cannot commit a sin? Certainly not; for he is liable to fall like anyone else. Does it mean that whatever he says or writes about science or history must necessarily be true, and cannot possibly be false? Certainly not. Supposing I were to write to him and ask his opinion about anything the Church teaches, would his answer to me be considered infallible? No, because he would be writing to me privately, simply as an ordinary bishop of the Church. Or if he came to preach in any church in England, would his words be necessarily infallible? No, because he would be preaching not as the head of the Church, but merely as an ordinary preacher who might make a mistake; but when the pope, as the catechism says, speaks as the head shepherd and teacher of the whole Church of Christ, and declares what is the faith revealed by Christ to the Church on any given point, then, and only then, does Jesus Christ preserve him from declaring what is contrary to faith. God does not inspire the pope what to teach, but simply prevents him from giving forth a wrong decision about any article of faith; otherwise we should not know for certain what we had to believe as true, and what we had to reject as false. Inspiration is much higher and greater than infallibility. The apostles were inspired, but the pope is not.

There is one remark I should like to make to those who, without really knowing what infallibility means, cry out against it, and say that to claim it is an act of presumption on the part of the pope. Whenever a protestant or any dissenter reads the Bible, he claims to read it as the word of God, and, what is more, he claims a power to understand it as the word of God; he believes that God really inspires him to understand it as the word of God. Does not this look as if he really claimed more than infallibility? The pope does not claim inspiration from God, but only a divine protection preventing him from teaching false doctrine. So that, really, protestants claim a great deal more for themselves than the pope does, and yet they cry out against him, though he really claims less than they do.

Now let us see how infallibility works, and when it is used. Let us take a practical illustration of it from the proclamation of the dogma of the immaculate conception of the Blessed Virgin.[35] Up to the year 1854, it was a controverted point as to whether the Blessed Virgin was immaculate from the first moment of her conception or from some later period. In 1854, the Church asked to have the matter definitely settled. It appealed to Rome, to Pius IX, the then pope. Pius IX summoned a great number of the Catholic bishops of the world to Rome, and instructed them to examine the question—that is, to see what had been the general belief of the Catholic Church from the very beginning of Christianity concerning it. You must know that we possess the writings of many of the earliest Christians, principally of bishops or men who were the champions of the faith in those days. When these writings speak of a certain doctrine as universally believed by all Christians in those times, it is perhaps the surest sign we could have that that doctrine was revealed by Christ to his apostles, and that it is, of course, of divine faith.

The council of bishops examined these writings carefully, and also all that the Bible said about the question of the immaculate conception, and they came to the unanimous conclusion that this doctrine had been made known or revealed by our Lord to his apostles as a divine truth, and therefore that it formed part of the Christian faith. When it was clearly proved that this doctrine was taught in scripture, and had always been believed from the earliest ages of Christianity as part of the revelation of Christ to his apostles, the pope, speaking as head and teacher of the Church of God, solemnly proclaimed that this doctrine was amongst those revealed by Jesus Christ, and therefore all Christians were bound to believe it as part of their faith. The pope did not make a new doctrine—no man could do that; but he simply declared what was Christ's doctrine to the apostles.

[35] See q. 117, below.

Let me take another example to illustrate my meaning. All such examples are, of course, very imperfect, but perhaps the following one may throw some light on the subject. Suppose some important case comes before the courts and they cannot agree about it—one judge takes one view about it and another a different one. The case comes at last, in due course before the House of Lords and is decided. This decision is for all practical purposes final—that is, it finally disposes of the case and lays down a principle on which the lower courts are supposed to act. It is not infallible, because, later on, the same court may reconsider the principle on which it decided, and in some other case act on a different one; but still the decision is quite authoritative enough for human affairs. When, however, we come to matters of faith, we must have an absolute certainty, and therefore, the pope, in deciding a matter of faith, exactly follows the practice of the House of Lords in discussing the case, and taking into account the opinions of inferior tribunals; but he does not decide, as an ordinary court must do, relying simply on his own judgment and the wisdom of men, but he trusts to the supernatural guidance which has been distinctly promised by our Lord to St. Peter and his successors.[36] A judgment given by divine authority can never be altered or reversed, and, therefore, the pope's authority in matters of faith is not only practically infallible as being the superior court, but actually infallible because it rests on the promises of God. It is God who helps him to decide and who prevents him from making a mistake.

94. **Has the Church any marks by which we may know her?**
The Church of Christ has four marks by which we may know her. She is one; she is holy; she is catholic; she is apostolic.

There are at least three hundred various religious sects in England and America, each sect maintaining, I suppose, that it alone has the true faith of Christ, and yet they cannot all be true. There is but one true religion, and all the others must be false. Which, then, is the true one? Our Lord must have known that there would exist false religions; indeed, he

[36] See q. 91, above.

foretold it: "Many false prophets shall arise, and shall lead many astray."[37] He cannot therefore have left us without some means of finding out the true religion. It must have certain marks or signs about it which other religions have not, and which at once show it to be true. You will find these marks in the Nicene Creed. "I believe in...one, holy, catholic, and apostolic Church." These, then, are the marks of the Church of Christ; any Church which does not possess these cannot be the true one.

95. **How is the Church one?**

The Church is one, because all her members agree in one faith, have all the same sacrifice and sacraments, and are all united under one head.

This is the greatest and most certain sign of truth: that unity should exist in everything in the true Church. Our Lord himself has specially spoken of it: "And other sheep I have which are not of this fold; them also I must bring, that they shall hear my voice and they shall become one flock, one shepherd."[38]

1. *The Church must be one in faith.* All her members must believe the same truths—not any truths they like, passing over unpleasant or unintelligible truths, but believing all that our Lord has taught. "Go ye, therefore, and teach all nations,...teaching them to observe all things whatsoever I have commanded you," etc.[39] Go where you like, all over the world, you will find every Catholic bishop and priest teaching, and every one of the faithful believing, exactly the same doctrine; there is no High Church, Broad Church, or Low Church party amongst us. Turn for a moment to the Protestant Church, and see how little unity exists there, some clergymen teaching nearly every Catholic doctrine, such as the Mass, confession, prayers for the dead, and prayers to the saints; other clergymen of the same Church saying that all these practices were condemned at the Reformation, and are, therefore, wicked; "the Mass is a blasphemous fable"; "confession is the invention of man"; "there is no purgatory, and therefore no need of praying for the dead," etc. Surely a Church in which such disunion exists

[37] Mt 24:11

[38] Jn 10:16

[39] Mt 28:19-20

on such important doctrines cannot claim to have the first mark of Christ's Church—namely, unity.

2. *The Church must be one in worship.* You find the same Mass and the same seven sacraments all over the world in the Catholic Church.

3. *It must be one in government.* All the 320,000,000 of Catholics unite in obeying one head—the pope, the vicar of Christ on earth.

96. **How is the Church holy?**

The Church is holy, because she teaches a holy doctrine, offers to all the means of holiness, and is distinguished by the eminent holiness of so many thousands of her children.

The doctrine she teaches is our Lord's doctrine, the doctrine of the God of holiness, and therefore it must be holy. Whatever she teaches tends to make her people lead holy lives, and she puts before them the most powerful reasons to induce them to become holy.

The Catholic Church offers to all the means of holiness. If a Catholic lives up to the teaching of his religion, he must lead a good life; he cannot help it. If ever you come across Catholics who are leading bad lives, this is simply because they do not attend to their religion. It has in its teaching all that is necessary for the life of a saint. The Catholic Church is distinguished by the holiness of so many thousands of her children. These are the saints. All the canonized saints belong to the Catholic Church. They are her saints; they were all Catholics. The Protestant Church has not made a saint yet: take her founders, for instance. Would you say, "St. Luther," or "St. Henry VIII," or "St. Elizabeth, Queen of England, pray for us"? I don't think you would go so far, and yet these were the people who founded and fostered protestantism. Protestants omit the word *holy* in the Nicene Creed.

97. **What does the word catholic mean?**

The word *catholic* means "universal."

98. **How is the Church catholic or universal?**

The Church is catholic or universal, because she subsists in all ages, teaches all nations, and is the one ark of salvation for all.

Anglicans know full well the value of the word *catholic*, hence they call themselves "English Catholics," or "Anglo-Catholics," but calling themselves "Catholic" does not make them so; nobody else calls them by that name, and besides that, the majority of Anglicans call themselves "protestants"; it is only a section of the community that speak of themselves as "Catholics," and that only amongst themselves. Ask the first policeman you meet to show you the way to the nearest Catholic Church; would he send you to a High Church? Or ask him where the priest lives; I doubt very much if he would send you to a High Church clergy-house.

Well, the real Church of Christ must be catholic, or universal; it must be universal in point of time—that is, it must have always existed since the days of our Lord. We claim to be universal in point of time, and everybody knows that we are the old Church. It must also be universal in place. The Catholic Church is everywhere; its enormous number of believers shows this; and, lastly, it must be universal in doctrine. It must teach all that Christ taught; it must teach all that the Apostles' Creed teaches, and it is the only Church that does teach it all.

She is the one ark of salvation. Protestants look upon us as very bigoted because we say that no one outside the Catholic Church can be saved. But this is nevertheless quite true. A person must be baptized to be saved.[40] If a person has been really baptized—it matters not by whom[41]—that person belongs to the Catholic Church, which is the true Church of Christ. Now, if that person never willfully denies what he knows to be the truth of God, and, moreover, never willfully breaks any of the great commandments of God, that person will be saved, no matter what denomination he may have belonged to, because, by his baptism, he has become a child of God, and therefore belongs to the Catholic Church, and he has never willfully lost God's grace and love by willful heresy and mortal sin.

[40] Baptism can either be by water, blood, i.e. martyrdom, or desire, for which an act of perfect contrition is essential.

[41] See q. 258, below.

99. **How is the Church apostolic?**

The Church is apostolic, because she holds the doctrines and traditions of the apostles, and because, through the unbroken succession of her pastors, she derives her orders and her mission from them.

She is apostolic—that is, she is the Church of the apostles; she holds and teaches their doctrines (the Apostles' Creed) and their traditions—that is, what they have handed down to us by word of mouth, and through the long line of her popes she can trace her origin back to our blessed Lord. Her priests' orders are real and valid, her commission to teach is divine, because, again, both have come down from Christ through her long line of successors of St. Peter.

100. **Can the Church err in what she teaches?**

The Church cannot err in what she teaches as to faith or morals, for she is our infallible guide in both.

I think enough has already been said on this point.[42]

101. **How do you know that the Church cannot err in what she teaches?**

I know that the Church cannot err in what she teaches, because Christ promised that the gates of hell shall not prevail against his Church,[43] that the Holy Ghost shall teach her all things,[44] and that he himself will be with her all days even to the consummation of the world.[45]

Surely these promises of our Lord are proof enough that the Catholic Church is guided and protected by divine assistance, that she cannot teach a false doctrine, and that, therefore, if we want to make sure that we belong to the true Church we must belong to her.

[42] See q. 84-93, above.
[43] Cf. Mt 16:18
[44] Cf. Jn 14:16-26
[45] Cf. Mt 28:20

102. **What do you mean by "the communion of saints"?**

By "the communion of saints," I mean that all the members of the Church in heaven, on earth, and in purgatory are in communion with each other as being one body in Jesus Christ.

The Church of Christ is composed of three parts. 1) *The saints in heaven, or the Church triumphant.* This consists of those who have been here on this earth, who have had the same battle to fight as we have, the same temptations to overcome as we have; they have been faithful to God here, and now they are in possession of that happiness which God has promised to all who love and serve him. 2) *The Church on earth, or the Church militant.* This is composed of all those baptized Christians on earth who are, or ought to be, leading good lives, in order to get to heaven hereafter. 3) *The Church in purgatory, or the Church suffering.* This part of the Church comprises all those souls who at death were not found worthy to enter heaven at once owing to the presence of some venial sins upon their souls, or because they had not done sufficient penance for their sins in this life. This will be explained later on. The communion of saints means that all these three parts of the Church, the Church triumphant, militant, and suffering, are joined together by a bond of union as being one body in Jesus Christ.

103. **How are the faithful on earth in communion with each other?**

The faithful on earth are in communion with each other by professing the same faith, obeying the same authority, and assisting each other with their prayers and good works.

All Catholics throughout the world believe the same faith and obey the same ecclesiastical authority; they pray for each other, and assist each other by their works of charity. All this makes a common bond of union amongst them.

104. **How are we in communion with the saints in heaven?**

We are in communion with the saints in heaven by honoring them as the glorified members of the Church, and also by our praying to them and by their praying for us.

This answer will need some explanation, for it contains one of the articles of faith against which the authors of the Reformation protested. The twenty-second article of the protestant religion says, "The Romish doctrine concerning...invocation of saints is a fond thing vainly invented, and founded upon no warranty of scripture, but rather repugnant to the word of God." The Catholic doctrine teaches that "the saints reigning together with Christ are to be honored and invoked, and that they offer prayers to God for us."

Now let us see which of these doctrines is the right one. I suppose everybody believes in the existence of the devil, the enemy of mankind. Most people unfortunately have had practical experience of his existence from having yielded at some time of their life to his evil suggestions.

The devil tempts us like he tempted Adam and Eve. God gives him permission to do so—it is our trial here. If we are faithful to God and resist temptation, we shall be rewarded in heaven; if we give way to temptation and die in mortal sin, we shall be punished in hell. I suppose all Christians believe this. Now, I argue, if God allows the devil, the evil spirit, to tempt us and try to get us to do wrong, surely he gives the good angels power to try and help us to do right. He cannot give the devils a greater power than he gives his own blessed spirits, to those who were faithful to him in their time of trial.[46] Again, if the devils are always seeking our destruction, will not the good angels be working for our salvation? Lastly, may we not drive the devil away by speaking to him, and telling him to go behind us and not to molest us? So in like manner may we not ask the angels and saints to come near and help us? Did you ever read the history of Dives and Lazarus in St. Luke's gospel?[47] Our Lord himself tells us how the rich man (Dives), when buried in hell, cried out to Father Abraham to send Lazarus, that he might dip his finger in water and cool his tongue. Here we have an instance of a soul in hell praying to a saint, and asking him to send another saint to relieve his torment, and when he was told that this could not be done, he asked the saintly Abraham to send Lazarus to his father's house on earth

[46] See q. 43, above.

[47] Cf. Lk 16:19

(for he had five brothers alive) to warn them, lest they also should come into that place of torment. So here a soul in hell prays for his brethren on earth, and asks the saints to use their influence to prevent them from being lost. Our Lord himself tells us the parable. Can there be any harm, therefore, in our asking the saints to help us, or to help our friends?

Lastly, we know for certain, from the words of Jesus Christ, that the angels and saints know distinctly what is passing on earth, and that they take a deep, practical interest in our eternal salvation. "So I say to you, there is joy before the angels of God upon one sinner doing penance."[48] This shows that the angels know when we repent, and, moreover, that they are glad and rejoice when they see us repent.

I have often wondered why, as protestants do not believe that we may ask the angels and saints to help us, they directly ask that they may be succored and defended by the ministering spirits. In the collect appointed to be said on the feast of St. Michael and all angels, in the *Book of Common Prayer*, we read thus: "O everlasting God, who hast ordained and constituted the services of angels and of men in a wonderful order, mercifully grant that as thy holy angels always do thee service in heaven, so by thy appointment they may succor and defend us on earth." This looks as if they did believe that God had appointed the angels to succor and defend us on earth.

One objection commonly made against praying to the angels and saints is that it is an injury to the mediation of Christ, that it interferes with Christ as our mediator; but this objection really comes from a misunderstanding. Jesus Christ alone has a right to ask and obtain for us whatever he pleases from his heavenly Father; neither we nor the angels have any such right—it is only through the infinite merits of our Savior that we or they can obtain anything from God. We do not, therefore, ask them to help us of their own power, but simply to use on our behalf the power which Christ has given to them. May not we on earth pray for each other? How often do we not ask our friends on earth to pray for us when we are in trouble or sorrow? Surely this does not take away from the mediation

[48] Lk 15:10

of Christ! St. John[49] prayed for grace and peace from the seven spirits who stand before the throne of God and from Jesus Christ who is the faithful witness. It was not wrong, or St. John would not have done it. St. Paul frequently asked the prayers of the people. He writes to the Philippians: "I know that this shall turn to my salvation through your supplication."[50] God told Job's friends to go to him (Job) and Job should pray for them, and God would accept his prayers and would not punish them.[51] God often spared the Israelites at the prayer of Moses.

The next question in the catechism refers to the prayers for the dead or prayers for the souls in purgatory; so, perhaps, we had better speak about purgatory first.

105. **What is purgatory?**

Purgatory is a place where souls suffer for a time after death on account of their sins.

The Catholic Church teaches us that "there is a purgatory, and that the souls therein detained are helped by the suffrages of the faithful." Protestantism teaches that "the Romish doctrine of purgatory is a fond thing vainly invented, and grounded upon no warranty of scripture, but rather repugnant to the word of God." According to this protestant teaching, there are only two places in the next world, heaven and hell; and all those who die must go straight either to heaven or to hell. Supposing I asked you this question: "Think for a moment of those who are dead whom you have known in life; of how many of these could you safely say that their lives were so absolutely holy and pure and innocent and sinless that they must have gone straight to heaven?" For remember that "there shall in no wise enter into it (heaven) anything unclean (sinful)."[52] The slightest stain of sin is enough to prevent us going to heaven. I am afraid you would be forced to admit that very few indeed had led such perfect lives. Then, if there is no third state, you must admit that if they have not

[49] Cf. Apoc 1:4-5

[50] Phil 1:19

[51] Cf. Jb 42:8

[52] Apoc 21.27

gone straight to heaven, they must have gone straight to hell. There is no alternative. What a cold, cruel, heartless doctrine this is! and what scanty hope it holds out to poor sinners! How charitable and consoling, on the other hand, is the Catholic doctrine which teaches that, although the soul may not have gone straight to heaven (its life may not have deserved that), yet it may have escaped hell; it has another chance—God keeps it in a third or middle state, where it has the opportunity of expiating whatever may still be preventing it from going to heaven.

You will remember[53] that, when I was explaining the fifth article, I spoke about a third state existing in the next world before the coming of Christ. If that state once existed, why should it not exist now, especially when there are such reasons for it? These reasons we will now speak of.

106. **What souls go to purgatory?**

Those souls go to purgatory that depart this life in venial sin, or that have not fully paid the debt of temporal punishment due to those sins of which the guilt has been forgiven.

107. **What is temporal punishment?**

Temporal punishment is punishment that will have an end either in this world or in the world to come.

According to the teaching of the Church, two kinds or classes of souls go to purgatory. 1) Those who go before God stained with venial sin. Let us deal with these first. In the tenth article, we shall explain more about sin and its various kinds. And perhaps it would be well for you to turn to Question 127 first and read what is said about venial sin. This sin is of much less malice and gravity than mortal sin, and does not deserve the eternal punishment which mortal sin deserves. Now, supposing a soul dies in venial sin, where will that soul go to? Protestants must say to hell at once; it cannot get into heaven in that state, and it must go to hell for eternity, simply because it has committed a trifling offense against God! I think that you yourself would say that it would be unjust

[53] See q. 63, above.

on the part of God to condemn that soul to eternal punishment for a trifling sin. The Catholic Church teaches that though that soul could not enter heaven at once, it is, nevertheless, saved, and that God will give it the means of expiating that sin somewhere in the next world and of thus getting sometime into heaven—that "somewhere" is purgatory, which really means a place of cleansing. Now, besides this, a person may die who has led a bad life, but who, through God's mercy and grace, repented either during his lifetime or immediately before death—his sins were forgiven by absolution, and he goes sinless into the presence of God. One might be tempted to say, "Well, at any rate that soul is safe, for there is nothing to stop its entrance into heaven. But just let us see if really all is right with that soul." 2) This will bring us to the second class of souls that go to purgatory—viz., those that have not fully paid the debt of temporal punishment due to those sins of which the guilt has been forgiven.

We must distinguish two things in sin—viz., its guilt and its punishment. When God forgives a sin, he does not thereby take away all the punishment which was due for that sin; the eternal punishment (hell) is taken away because the guilt has been pardoned; but God changes that eternal punishment into a temporal one—in other words, though God forgives us our sins, we always have to do penance for them somewhere, either in this world, or in the next if we die before having done it all here. This is called "temporal punishment." Let me give you one or two instances of God's way of acting in this matter. Take Adam and Eve; they offended God grievously by disobeying him. God forgave them by promising them a Redeemer; and yet, though he forgave them, he drove them out of paradise, and their lives were lives of penance and punishment for that one sin. Again, take the example of David: this is a very striking one. David had committed a great sin, and God sent Nathan the prophet to him. "David said unto Nathan, 'I have sinned against the Lord.' And Nathan said unto David, 'The Lord also hath put away thy sin; thou shalt not die. Howbeit, because by this deed thou hast given great occasion to the enemies of the

Lord to blaspheme, the child also that is born unto thee shall surely die.'"[54] Here we see that God had forgiven David's sin, but yet he punishes him by letting the child die.

One more example. You remember the incident narrated in Numbers[55] of Moses striking the rock to get water for the people: he struck the rock twice. It was an act of want of confidence in God; and although God forgave him and allowed him still to lead the people, he would not allow him to enter the promised land. And so it is with us. Although God forgives us our sins by the means he himself has appointed, yet there is always some punishment left for us to do. Now, supposing we die before we have done all that punishment. Take the case of a man who is pardoned on his deathbed and has no time in this life to undergo the temporal punishment due to his sins. He must suffer it somewhere in the next world. He cannot do it in heaven; he has escaped hell. There must be some other place to do it in, and that place is purgatory. So, you see that, because some people die in venial sin, and others die without having fully paid the debt of temporal punishment due to their sins, there must be a third place in the next world where these sins can be expiated and this punishment completed.

108. **How are we in communion with the souls in purgatory?**
We are in communion with the souls in purgatory by helping them with our prayers and good works. "It is a holy and wholesome thought to pray for the dead, that they may be loosed from sins."[56]

The Catholic Church teaches that we can assist the souls in purgatory (that is, the suffering Church) by praying to God for them, asking him in his mercy to release them from their sufferings, and also by offering our good works for them. You can understand praying for them, but perhaps you may be a little puzzled by my saying that we can offer our good works for them. Well, let me try to explain this.

Supposing you give an alms to a poor person for the love of Jesus Christ—not out of vanity or any evil or indifferent motive, but purely to

[54] 2 Sam 12:13; Catholic version, 2 Kgs 12:13

[55] Cf. Nm 20:7

[56] 2 Mc 12:46

please our Lord and in satisfaction for your sins—you, of course, merit the reward which God has promised to every good act done out of charity.[57] The merit of this good act you cannot make over to anyone else, but the satisfaction you may have made to God for your sins you may ask God to apply to someone else. The Church teaches us that we may offer to God all our good works, insofar as they are satisfying for sin, for the souls in purgatory; and that God will, if he sees it expedient to do so, apply them to those souls for whom we particularly pray as part of the debt due from them to his justice. You see how this doctrine makes us here on earth try to lead good lives and do good works. If a man is in a state of sin against God, he cannot help these suffering souls, for God will not listen to the prayers of one who is in rebellion against him, except to give him grace to repent himself. No prayers on our part, either for the living or the dead, are of any use to them unless we are living in a state of grace.

109. **How do you prove that there is a purgatory?**

I prove that there is a purgatory from the constant teaching of the Church and from the doctrine of holy scripture which declares that God will render to every man according to his works;[58] that nothing defiled shall enter heaven;[59] and that some will be saved, "yet so as by fire."[60]

I have already given sufficient proof of the necessity of the existence of purgatory from reason, but there are other proofs of more consequence than this. First, the Church has taught this truth from the beginning. We know it also from the writings of the early Christians; they wrote about it as the faith of their day. Moreover, we must remember that the Jews, before our Lord came, used to pray for the dead. We know this from the second book of Machabees,[61] where it is said: "It is a holy and wholesome thought to pray for the dead, that they may be loosed from sins." Protestants do not admit the books of the Machabees to be part of the

[57] Cf. Mt 10:42
[58] Cf. Mt 16:27
[59] Cf. Apoc 21:27
[60] 1 Cor 3:15
[61] Cf. 2 Mc 12:39-46

scripture; the reformers rejected them because they taught prayers for the dead. This was rather an easy way of getting rid of those parts of the Bible that did not agree with their views; but, even supposing that these books were not inspired—though they had formed part of the Bible from its beginning—nevertheless, they are historical, and show us, as a matter of history, that it was the custom of the Jews to pray for their dead, and this they do even to the present day. Now, we know our Lord used to attend the services of the Jewish synagogue. He must, therefore, have been present when the sacrifices were being offered for the souls of the dead; and yet we never read that he spoke against the custom, though he never spared the high priests if he found them doing anything contrary to the book of the law.

We know from St. Matthew's gospel that there are sins which are forgiven in the next world. "Whosoever shall speak a word against the Son of man, it shall be forgiven him; but whosoever shall speak against the Holy Ghost, it shall not be forgiven him, neither in this world nor in the world to come."[62] It follows from these words that there are some sins which are forgiven in the world to come. This cannot mean "hell," for no sins are forgiven there—in hell, there is no redemption—and it cannot mean "heaven," for there nothing sinful can enter; it must mean, therefore, a third place, and that is purgatory.

St. Paul, in his first epistle to the Corinthians, says, "If any man's work shall be burned, he shall suffer loss; but he himself shall be saved, yet so as through fire."[63] Our Lord is speaking of how every man's work shall be made manifest at the judgment; for the day of the Lord shall declare it. What fire is this that will save the man though it burns his bad works? It cannot be hell fire, for that cannot save us. It must be the fire of purgatory, which burns away our sins and failings, and then we are admitted to heaven, or saved by it. Does all this look as if the doctrine of purgatory were repugnant to the word of God? Or, rather, does it not seem to agree with it?

[62] Mt 12:32
[63] 1 Cor 3:15

The Tenth Article

110. **What is the tenth article of the Creed?**

The tenth article of the Creed is: "The forgiveness of sins."

111. **What do you mean by "the forgiveness of sins"?**

By "the forgiveness of sins," I mean that Christ has left the power of forgiving sins to the pastors of his Church.[64]

We now come to another doctrine of the Catholic Church which, like those I have already explained, presents a good deal of difficulty to a protestant who has been taught from early childhood that no man can forgive sins on earth, and that confession to a priest is anything but the right thing. Now, first, have you ever read that part of the *Book of Common Prayer* called the "Ordering of Priests"? Just look at it. Toward the end of the service, you will read certain words which the bishop has to say to the person he is ordaining. These words are: "Receive the Holy Ghost for the office and work of a priest in the Church of God...Whose sins thou dost forgive, they are forgiven; and whose sins thou dost retain, they are retained." Does that not look like giving a man power to forgive sins? Again, open the book at the Communion Service, at the exhortation commencing "Dearly beloved, on...day next I purpose," etc., and toward the end of the exhortation you will read these words: "If there be any of you who by these means [confessing to God] cannot quiet his own conscience, herein...let him come to me [the clergyman] or to some other discreet or learned minister of God's word, and open his grief [this looks very like confession, does it not?] that by the ministry of God's holy word he may receive the benefit of absolution" (that is, the forgiveness of his sins).

Let me again ask you to turn to the "Order for the Visitation of the Sick," and here you will find something which will, I think, rather astonish you if you have never seen it before. About halfway through the prayers, you will find the following: "Here shall the sick person be moved to make a special confession of his sins, if he feel his conscience troubled with any

[64] This question should be compared with Question 293.

weighty matter; after which confession, the priest [the protestant clergyman, of course] shall absolve him, if he humbly and heartily desire it, after this sort: 'Our Lord Jesus Christ, who hath left power to his Church to absolve all sinners who truly repent and believe in him, of his great mercy forgive thee thine offenses: And by his [God's] authority committed to me, I [the clergyman] absolve thee from all thy sins, in the name of the Father, and of the Son, and of the Holy Ghost.'" Surely this looks very like confession and the forgiveness of sins! If it is not intended to be so, a deathbed is scarcely the place or time to go through an empty ceremony.

There is, perhaps, no doctrine or practice of the Catholic Church that frightens protestants more than that of confession, and yet they are taught in their own prayer book that it is a thing that ought to be done at the time of death—they are to be moved to make a special confession of their sins. If it is a good thing to prepare one's soul for eternity by confession at the approach of death, is it not a much better thing to do it during one's lifetime, and thus to keep the soul ready?—for death sometimes comes very suddenly, and does not leave a person time to send for a clergyman, or even to make an act of contrition.

The Catholic Church, then, teaches that Christ left power on earth to forgive sins. He gave this power to his apostles on the day of his resurrection, as you can read in St. John's gospel. It was the occasion of Christ's first appearance to his apostles after his resurrection. "Jesus therefore said to them again, 'Peace be unto you: as the Father has sent me, even so send I you.' And when he had said this, he breathed on them, and saith to them, 'Receive ye the Holy Ghost: whosesoever sins ye forgive, they are forgiven unto them; whosesoever sins ye retain, they are retained.'"[65] In these words, besides giving his apostles power to forgive sin, Christ gives them a power to retain sin, so that the people had no other means of obtaining forgiveness of their sins except by applying to the apostles for it. Supposing one of the early Christians confessed his sins to one of the apostles, and the apostle, judging that he was not sorry for them, refused to forgive him (or retained his sins), God himself retained them, God refused

[65] Jn 20:21-23

to forgive them. Go where he might, God would not forgive him until he had received absolution from one to whom Christ had given the power to absolve. So that it was only through the ministry of the apostles that God would forgive the people's sins. Of course, this extraordinary power was not meant for the apostles only; it was not to die with them, but it had to last in the Church till the end of time, and had to be possessed and exercised by every lawfully and validly ordained priest of the Church of God.

112. **By what means are sins forgiven?**
Sins are forgiven principally by the sacraments of baptism and penance.

113. **How many kinds of sin are there?**
There are two kinds of sin—original sin and actual sin.

Christ instituted a particular sacrament for the forgiveness of each of these kinds of sin.

114. **What is original sin?**
Original sin is that guilt and stain of sin which we inherit from Adam, who was the origin and head of all mankind.

115. **What was the sin committed by Adam?**
The sin committed by Adam was the sin of disobedience when he ate the forbidden fruit.

When a child is born, it comes into the world having the stain of Adam's sin upon it. A Christian mother takes her child as soon as possible to have it baptized—that is, to have the stain of Adam's sin removed from the child's soul, Christ having instituted baptism for that purpose. If a child dies unbaptized, it cannot get to heaven owing to the original sin upon it, for Christ has distinctly said: "Except a man be born of water and of the spirit, he cannot enter into the kingdom of God."[66] Now, what becomes of that child's soul? The Church has not distinctly told us. It certainly does not go to heaven, nor does it go to hell or to purgatory, for it has not

[66] Jn 3:5

committed any sin of its own. It must, of course, go somewhere, and we generally believe that God places it in some state of natural happiness in the next world, where it enjoys all the happiness it can in its present state, but it does not suffer. May I here remark that this makes a fourth state in the next world. There is heaven, hell, purgatory, and this state of the unbaptized. So far as we know, there may be forty millions of states. In heaven itself, there are many states: "In my Father's house are many mansions," says our Lord.[67] If in heaven, why not outside heaven too?

So the child is taken to be baptized, and baptism, if properly conferred, takes original sin from its soul. Now, who baptizes? A human being, a man; so that here again we see how a man has received power from God to remit or remove or forgive sin. He who baptizes says, "I...baptize thee," etc. He does not say, "God baptizes thee," but "I do it." Therefore, he takes the sin away in God's name.

116. **Have all mankind contracted the guilt and stain of original sin?**
All mankind have contracted the guilt and stain of original sin, except the Blessed Virgin, who, through the merits of her divine Son, was conceived without the least guilt or stain of original sin.

117. **What is this privilege of the Blessed Virgin called?**
This privilege of the Blessed Virgin is called "the immaculate conception."

Before we go on to explain the second kind of sin, there is one question connected with original sin that we must speak of. I mean the immaculate conception of the Blessed Virgin. This does not mean, as some people have absurdly supposed, that the Blessed Virgin was conceived in some miraculous way like our Lord was, for she had a father and mother (St. Joachim and St. Anne) like any other human being; but it means that when God created her soul, he did not allow it to be stained with original sin. She is the only one of the human race since the fall of our first parents who has escaped this penalty. Christ redeemed her as he redeemed us. He cleansed us from original sin, but he prevented Mary from being stained by it, and

[67] Jn 14:2

this through the merits of his death and passion. Now, on what grounds does the Church base this belief? for it is an article of our faith. Turn for a moment to the first book of the Bible—I mean the book of Genesis.[68] You will read how God spoke to the devil and cursed him for what he had done, and then, continuing to speak to him, he says, "I will put enmity between thee [the devil] and the woman, and between thy seed and her seed." Here God, in the first prophecy ever recorded, says that he will put enmity—that is to say, perpetual and complete enmity—between the devil and the woman; so deep and absolute an enmity as must exist between her seed (Jesus Christ) and the seed of the devil—viz., sin. Now, who is this woman? It cannot be Eve, for she had just placed herself under the devil's power by consenting to the temptation; it must be some other woman not yet born, for God speaks of the future, "I will put." And whose seed was Jesus Christ to be? "Everyone," says a protestant bishop (Bull), "now knows that the seed here spoken of is Christ, and consequently that the individual woman whose immediate seed he was to be is the Virgin Mary." Therefore, there was never to be anything in common between Mary and the devil; he was never to have any power over her, so that there never could have been any sin, either original or actual, on Mary's soul, even for one instant. This has been the belief of the Catholic Church from the very beginning.

Immaculate conception means "conceived without stain of original sin."

118. **What is actual sin?**

Actual sin is every sin which we ourselves commit.

119. **What is sin?**

Sin is an offense against God by any thought, word, deed, or omission against the law of God.

I am afraid few people realize or understand what sin really is. They say a thing "is wrong," "not the proper thing to do," "not right," etc., but no words of this kind bring home to our minds the real malice of sin as "an

[68] Cf. Gn 3:14-15

offense against God." To have some idea of it, we must call to mind what some sins have done.

Take the fall of the angels. For one single sin of thought, one single sin of pride, God created hell, and cast into it, for all eternity, myriads of those once blessed spirits whom he had made to be happy with him for all eternity. Again, the human race suffered, does suffer, and will suffer to the end of time for that one sin of Adam and Eve. No one can number the souls that have been lost in consequence of that one sin. Again, look at the crucifix; who is it that is hanging there, his hands and feet nailed to the cross, dying in agony and shame? It is Jesus Christ our Savior, who died to save us from hell, the penalty of sin; and when we commit a mortal sin, when we willfully and deliberately violate one of God's great commandments, is it enough to say, "Of course I know it is wrong," or, "I know it is not right"? Is that all the crucifix says to you? Try to realize the awful malice of sin, and make a resolution before God never to commit a great sin deliberately.

Now, what is sin? Any thought, word, deed, or omission against the law of God. So, we can commit sin in four ways. (This I have explained in Question 73 in the seventh article of the Creed.)

120. **How is actual sin divided?**

Actual sin is divided into mortal sin and venial sin.

121. **What is mortal sin?**

Mortal sin is a grievous offense against God.

This is the sin we must avoid at any cost. It is the greatest act of rebellion we can commit against God. There are three things necessary to make a sin mortal:

1) The thing that is thought of or said or done must be something very serious, like real hatred, revenge, cursing, drunkenness, murder, or robbery; for you cannot make mortal sin out of little things, such as a little lie, impatience, etc., unless you have what is called a false conscience. 2) You must know quite well that it is a serious sin at the time of committing it, and that if you do it, and die with that sin on your soul, you will go to hell. 3) You must do it deliberately—that is, you must be free to do it or not

as you like. Therefore, a grievous matter, full knowledge, and full consent are necessary to make a sin mortal. A man who would thus willfully defy his God must be a monster indeed.

122. **Why is it called "mortal sin"?**

It is called "mortal sin," because it kills the soul and deserves hell.

The word *mortal* comes from the Latin word *mors*, which means "death"; *mortal* means "deadly," or, "something that causes death." We say a man received a mortal wound—that is, one that will cause his death.

123. **How does mortal sin kill the soul?**

Mortal sin kills the soul by depriving it of sanctifying grace, which is the supernatural life of the soul.

In the beginning of the catechism, you will remember we saw that the soul is immortal—that is, that it can never die—and here we are told that mortal sin kills the soul. Of course, *killing* here does not mean "crushing out of existence" so that the soul does not exist anymore, but it means "taking away from that soul its real life," which is the love of God. When a soul is in a state of mortal sin, it has lost God's love and God's favor, and is dead in his sight; just like a bad son who will not obey his father is sometimes turned out of his house and home, the father saying to him, "Go away, you are no longer my son, you are dead to me now." Of course, the son would still be alive, but the father would look upon him as dead to him, because he would not obey him.

124. **Is it a great evil to fall into mortal sin?**

It is the greatest of all evils to fall into mortal sin.

We were made to be happy with God in heaven for all eternity; to lose heaven, therefore, would be the greatest calamity that could possibly befall us. There is only one thing in this world that can take heaven from us, and that is mortal sin; neither poverty, nor sickness, nor suffering, nor death can take it from us, only mortal sin.

125. **Where will they go who die in mortal sin?**

They who die in mortal sin will go to hell for all eternity.

To lose heaven would be bad enough, but there is something still more terrible awaiting those who die in mortal sin: I mean the fire of hell for all eternity. You will sometimes hear people talk as though it were not just or fair on the part of God to send a soul to hell forever; but these people have probably never thought of, or realized, the enormity of a mortal sin. Jesus died on the cross to expiate it, to get it forgiven, and we go and deliberately do it again, knowing how it offends him and what its punishment must be. Besides, God came to save us, not to condemn us; if we go to hell, we go there of our own free accord; we are not obliged to commit mortal sin, it is our own fault, it is our own doing; we choose to do it knowing what the consequences will and must be; we cannot, therefore, blame God for it. Hell was prepared for the devil and his angels, not for us; the kingdom of heaven was prepared for us; if we lose it, it is our own fault. God does not send a soul to hell, the soul sends itself there by deliberately doing what it knows will deserve hell.

126. **What is venial sin?**

Venial sin is an offense which does not kill the soul, yet displeases God, and often leads to mortal sin.

127. **Why is it called "venial sin"?**

It is called "venial sin," because it is more easily pardoned than mortal sin.

The word *venial* comes from the Latin word *venia*, which means "pardon," because God pardons small sins more easily than great ones. To get mortal sin forgiven, we are bound to go to confession and receive absolution from a priest, or, in case of necessity, to make an act of perfect contrition, having at the same time a desire to go to confession,[69] but if we make an act of sorrow for venial or small sins, God forgives us at once, and no confession or absolution is necessary; we are not bound to confess small sins. The difference between a mortal and venial sin comes from

[69] See q. 294, below.

the seriousness or importance of what we do, and also from the amount of deliberation and knowledge with which we do it. If the thing we do is not of serious consequence, or, as we generally say, a little sin, it is venial, but to make it a sin you must know and think that it is a sin, and then commit it in spite of this knowledge. Supposing a person is tempted to tell a lie; he knows it is a sin and that he ought not to do it, but he does not care, it will get him out of a bother, and he deliberately tells it—that is a venial sin. Of course, if that lie were to destroy his neighbor's character, and make him lose his situation, when he was quite innocent of the charge brought against him, that lie would become a mortal sin, because it would be a serious matter.

Sometimes people say, "Oh, it is only a little sin, it does not matter much." They who say this have no real love for God. No sin is really little before God; all sin strikes at his infinite goodness and sanctity. It is true God does not punish venial sin in hell, but he must punish it somewhere, either in this world or in the next in purgatory. What would you think of a son who, it is true, kept from violating any serious command of his father, but was constantly disobeying him in smaller things? Would you say that that son had any real love for his father? This is how we act against God when we commit venial sin.

The Eleventh Article

128. **What is the eleventh article of the Creed?**
The eleventh article of the Creed is: "The resurrection of the body."

129. **What do you mean by "the resurrection of the body"?**
By "the resurrection of the body," I mean that we shall all rise again with the same bodies at the day of judgment.

When we die, the body and soul are separated for a time; the soul goes to be judged by God, and is rewarded or punished according to its works; the body is buried, and in course of time falls away into dust. "Dust thou art and unto dust thou shalt return."[70] At the end of the world, the body and soul are united together again, the body rises and comes to life when the soul enters into it. It will be the same body that we have had on earth, but a spiritualized body like our Lord had after his resurrection from the dead. When the soul is admitted into heaven, it is happy, but, as it is not in its natural state, it is not so happy as it will be when it is joined again to the body at the last day; then both body and soul, being in their natural state (because God made them to be united together), will receive an increase of happiness from seeing God as God made them. In the same way, the lost souls will have an increase of punishment in hell, when their bodies are joined to them at the last day, for then both body and soul will be punished together.

The Twelfth Article

130. **What is the twelfth article of the Creed?**
The twelfth article of the Creed is: "Life everlasting."

131. **What does life everlasting mean?**
Life everlasting means that the good shall live forever in the glory and happiness of heaven.

We believe, as Christians, that there is a future life after the one in this world, a place of reward or punishment according to the life we have led here.

The hope of a future reward helps and supports us here in the fearful struggle we have to endure in battling against temptation and sin. Reason itself convinces us that there must be some reward for all this, but we have a greater certainty than reason — viz., our faith in the word of God, for he has revealed to us this consoling truth, and we know his words are true.

132. **What is the glory and happiness of heaven?**
The glory and happiness of heaven is to see, love, and enjoy God forever.

[70] Gn 3:19

133. **What does the scripture say of the happiness of heaven?**

The scripture says of the happiness of heaven that "eye hath not seen, nor ear heard, neither hath it entered into the heart of man, what things God hath prepared for them that love him."[71]

No one can realize what the happiness of heaven will be; we are not capable of understanding it here, but we know that it will be the possession and sight of God and of his infinite beauty for all eternity, and, moreover, everlasting, eternal peace and rest, no more sorrow or pain or suffering; all that will be over, never to return.

134. **Shall not the wicked also live forever?**

The wicked also shall live and be punished forever in the fire of hell.

The thought of hell is an awful thought. The souls of the damned have seen God at their judgment. The sight of God's beauty and the thought that it would have been so easy to have been saved will haunt them for all eternity. Moreover, they are punished by fire; God has said so: "Depart… into everlasting fire."[72] God grant we may escape this doom! It will be our own fault if we are lost, for we have in the Catholic religion the means that Christ has established of saving our souls.

Hope

135. **Will faith alone save us?**

Faith alone will not save us without good works; we must also have hope and charity.

Some people believe that it is sufficient to have faith in order to be saved; so it is, if they understand what having faith really means. It does not mean merely that you must believe there is a God, but also that you

[71] 1 Cor 2:9
[72] Mt 25:41

must believe all that that God has said and taught you, and further, that you must do all that he has told you to do. It means that you must believe that he has established a religion which you must practice; that he has founded a Church whose duty it is to teach you how to save your soul, and that you must belong to and obey that Church and its teaching. Faith teaches you that God is your Creator, and that he has a Creator's right over you. As you depend upon him completely, he requires that you should show this dependence by prayer, by asking him for what you want, for all things must come to you from him. Then, again, God has given you certain laws, which he has called his commandments. You are bound to observe these laws, and thereby to testify your love for your Creator. To pray to him, therefore, and to love him are duties quite as necessary as believing in him.

136. **What is hope?**

Hope is a supernatural gift of God, by which we firmly trust that God will give us eternal life and all the means necessary to obtain it if we do what he requires of us.

In sending us into this world, God has made a contract with us. He promises to give us heaven for all eternity and all the means necessary to get there on condition that we do what he requires of us here.

I know it is indeed difficult to lead a good life, for there are so many temptations around us; but our Lord knew that would be the case, and that is why he established his holy religion, in order to give us the help we should need to overcome sin. When we practice this religion, and do all that it teaches us, we thereby do all that God requires of us, we do our part; and then we have a right, a just right, to expect that God will do for us all that he has promised. This is what we call making an act of hope, for we expect with confidence that God will keep his word to us.

In the same way that a master engages a workman to do so much work for him and promises him a certain amount of money for his work when completed, and the workman toils on, putting up with all the inconveniences the work may cause him because he has the prospect of his pay before him; so we Christians struggle on in this life, bearing all our crosses patiently, avoiding sin and its pleasures, and look forward with confidence to the day when our divine master will more than amply reward us for our fidelity.

137. **Why must we hope in God?**

We must hope in God because he is infinitely good, infinitely powerful, and faithful to his promises.

God is infinitely good—that is, he loves us, and, because of his love, we firmly trust that he will do everything that he has promised to do. He is infinitely powerful, therefore he can do all that he has promised. Lastly, God cannot fail in his promises, and this is a source of perfect confidence to us.

138. **Can we do any good work of ourselves toward our salvation?**

We can do no good work of ourselves toward our salvation; we need the help of God's grace.

A person may do things that are good in themselves, like giving something to the poor, etc.; but these naturally good acts will not help him to get to heaven unless they are done out of love for God or for God's sake in some way or another. God must help us to do them, if they are to be rewarded by him. He helps us by giving us his grace. "I am the vine, ye are the branches. He that abideth in me and I in him, the same beareth much fruit, for apart from me ye can do nothing," says Jesus Christ.[73]

139. **What is grace?**

Grace is a supernatural gift of God, freely bestowed upon us for our sanctification and salvation.

By "a supernatural gift" is meant something that God gives to us which is not at all due to us. Grace is a divine quality which God gives to the soul, and which cleanses it from all stains of sin and makes it beautiful and pleasing to him. It is called "grace," because it is a free gift of God to us through the merits of Christ. Grace is also a help from God which enables us to avoid evil and to do good.

[73] Jn 15:5

There are two kinds of grace: sanctifying (or habitual) and actual grace.

Sanctifying grace is a communication which God makes of himself to our souls, and by which our sins are washed away and we are made holy and pleasing in his sight. St. Peter calls it "a partaking in the divine nature."[74]

If you pick up a piece of iron, you will find it of a darkish color, cold and hard; put it in a furnace and it becomes bright and shining like the fire itself. So when a soul is in a state of sin, it is hateful in the sight of God, cold and tepid toward all that is good, and hard in its evil ways; but when God communicates himself to that soul by sanctifying grace, all its sinful ugliness is washed away, and it becomes bright and beautiful before him, partaking in his divine nature. When we have no mortal sin upon our souls, we are "in a state of grace"—that is, pleasing to God. If we commit mortal sin, we "lose the grace of God," and if we die in that state, we are lost forever. We can regain the state of grace by repentance.

When we are already in a state of grace and our souls are holy and pleasing to God, any further increase of sanctifying grace makes us still more holy and pleasing to him; we should therefore increase it as much as possible by prayer and the frequent reception of the sacraments, and guard it as our greatest treasure.

Actual grace is a supernatural help which God gives to the soul to enable it to avoid evil and to do good. It is a kind of passing inspiration to us from God; it enlightens our mind and moves our will, and also strengthens it to induce us to do some good work, or to keep some commandment, or to overcome a temptation. Good thoughts that come across our minds to love and serve God better, to repent of our sins, to forgive injuries, to be kind to the poor, etc., are all examples of actual grace.

140. **How must we obtain God's grace?**

We must obtain God's grace chiefly by prayer and the holy sacraments.

[74] Cf. 2 Pt 1:4

Prayer and the sacraments[75] are the means appointed by God himself for obtaining his grace. We must pray for it; this is why prayer is such a necessity. We cannot be saved unless we pray. Heaven is filled with people who prayed; hell is filled with people who did not and would not pray. Then, again, we must receive the sacraments, principally the sacraments of penance and Holy Communion, for these were instituted by Christ specially to give us the grace to lead good lives.

Prayer

141. **What is prayer?**

Prayer is the raising up of the mind and heart to God.

We use two things in prayer: our mind to think of what we are saying to God, and our heart to mean really what we say. Prayer is a conversing with God, telling him all our miseries, and asking him for help and for mercy. We believe that he can and will help us; he has promised to do so, and we trust to this promise to obtain what we want through the merits of Christ. Prayer is a very great act of religion, because in it we acknowledge our weakness and misery and our complete dependence upon God. You should always pray when you are in trouble and want, when any temptation comes upon you, or when you have fallen into sin. You should also say your morning and night prayers. Never omit these. You will find a short form of morning and night prayers at the end of this book. If you have not been in the habit of praying, begin at once, and you will soon realize its good effect upon your daily life. I would recommend you to get Mgr. Segur's pamphlet, "Advice on Prayer."

[75] See q. 249ff, below.

142. **How do we raise up our mind and heart to God?**

We raise up our mind and heart to God by thinking of God; by adoring, praising, and thanking him; and by begging of him all blessings for soul and body.

This answer is clear, and requires no explanation.

143. **Do those pray well who, at their prayers, think neither of God nor of what they say?**

Those who, at their prayers, think neither of God nor of what they say do not pray well; but they offend God, if their distractions are willful.

It very often happens that, when we are saying our prayers, our mind begins to think of other things—of our work, for instance, or of any trouble that we have. This is what we call "being distracted." If it is not our fault, if we do not know at the time that we are distracted, it does not make the prayer bad. God knows how weak we are, and he does not refuse to listen to us; but if we notice the distractions in our mind, and do not take the trouble to get rid of them, then our prayer is bad, and, instead of listening to us, God is angry with us, because it is a kind of mockery of him.

144. **Which is the best of all prayers?**

The best of all prayers is the Our Father, or the Lord's Prayer.

145. **Who made the Lord's Prayer?**

Jesus Christ himself made the Lord's Prayer.

One day, after our Lord had been praying, his disciples asked him to teach them how to pray. He then taught them the Our Father. We should often say this prayer, for it contains all that we can possibly need from God.

146. **Say the Lord's Prayer.**

Our Father who art in heaven, hallowed be thy name; thy kingdom come; thy will be done on earth as it is in heaven; give us this day our daily bread; and forgive us our trespasses, as we forgive them that trespass against us; and lead us not into temptation; but deliver us from evil. Amen.

The catechism now gives a short explanation of all the petitions in the Our Father. As I think you will be able to understand them, it will not be necessary for me to add anything to them.

147. **In the Lord's Prayer, who is called "Our Father"?**
In the Lord's Prayer, God is called "Our Father."

148. **Why is God called "Our Father"?**
God is called "Our Father," because he is the Father of all Christians, whom he has made his children by holy baptism.

149. **Is God also the Father of all mankind?**
God is also the Father of all mankind, because he made them all, and loves and preserves them all.

150. **Why do we say "Our Father" and not "My Father"?**
We say "Our Father," and not "My Father," because, being all brethren, we are to pray not for ourselves only, but also for all others.

151. **When we say, "Hallowed be thy name," what do we pray for?**
When we say, "Hallowed be thy name," we pray that God may be known, loved, and served by all his creatures.

152. **When we say, "Thy kingdom come," what do we pray for?**
When we say, "Thy kingdom come," we pray that God may come and reign in the hearts of all by his grace in this world, and bring us all hereafter to his heavenly kingdom.

153. **When we say, "Thy will be done on earth as it is in heaven," what do we pray for?**
When we say, "Thy will be done on earth as it is in heaven," we pray that God may enable us, by his grace, to do his will in all things, as the blessed do in heaven.

154. **When we say, "Give us this day our daily bread," what do we pray for?**
When we say, "Give us this day our daily bread," we pray that God may give us daily all that is necessary for soul and body.

155. **When we say, "Forgive us our trespasses, as we forgive them that trespass against us," what do we pray for?**
When we say, "Forgive us our trespasses, as we forgive them that trespass against us," we pray that God may forgive us our sins, as we forgive others the injuries they do to us.

156. **When we say, "Lead us not into temptation," what do we pray for?**
When we say, "Lead us not into temptation," we pray that God may give us grace not to yield to temptation.

157. **When we say, "Deliver us from evil," what do we pray for?**
When we say, "Deliver us from evil," we pray that God may free us from all evil, both of soul and body.

Protestants add the words, "For thine is the kingdom, the power, and the glory, forever and ever. Amen." Catholics do not use these words, because our Lord did not teach them to his disciples; therefore, they are not part of the Lord's Prayer.

158. **Should we ask the angels and saints to pray for us?**
We should ask the angels and saints to pray for us, because they are our friends and brethren, and because their prayers have great power with God.

We have already seen[76] that the angels and saints have power to help us; it stands to reason, therefore, that we should avail ourselves of this power. They are God's chosen friends; they surround his throne in heaven, and are ever before him. You may say, "Well, I prefer to pray direct to God"; quite right, only do not blame those who prefer to ask the angels and saints to help them, believing that when these friends of God join their prayers to theirs, they have much more chance of being heard by God. After all,

[76] See q. 104, above.

this is only what we all do in this world's business. Suppose you wanted to get some government appointment, or some special post in a business house, you would not go directly and immediately to those in authority, with whom the appointment to the post rested. You would look about you and see if there were not someone amongst your friends and acquaintances who could speak for you, who knew the officials, and would have some influence with them. Well, I know that whatever I want must come from God; but if I ask him directly, God may say, "Well, you know you do not deserve this favor; you do not love and serve me as you ought to do," and God might refuse my petition. If I ask our Lady, or some saint, or my angel guardian to ask for me, God would be more inclined to grant my request, not for my sake, but for the sake of those who ask for me. Of course, you are not bound to ask the intercession of the saints; you can do as you like in the matter, but don't condemn those who do.

159. **How can we show that the angels and saints know what passes on earth?**
We can show that the angels and saints know what passes on earth from the words of Christ: "There shall be joy before the angels of God upon one sinner doing penance."[77]

Here our Lord himself speaks of the work the angels and saints do for us. He tells us, first, that they know when the sinner does penance, for they rejoice at his repentance; and, secondly, they take a deep interest in his repentance because, again, they rejoice to see it. If the devil rejoices at our downfall, why should not the angels rejoice at our repentance?

160. **What is the chief prayer to the Blessed Virgin which the Church uses?**
The chief prayer to the Blessed Virgin which the Church uses is the Hail Mary.

[77] Lk 15:10

161. **Say the Hail Mary.**

Hail Mary, full of grace, the Lord is with thee; blessed art thou amongst women, and blessed is the fruit of thy womb, Jesus. Holy Mary, Mother of God, pray for us sinners, now, and at the hour of our death. Amen.

162. **Who made the first part of the Hail Mary?**

The angel Gabriel and St. Elizabeth, inspired by the Holy Ghost, made the first part of the Hail Mary.

If you will open your Bible at St. Luke's gospel, you will there read these words: "And he [the angel] came in unto her [the Virgin Mary] and said, 'Hail, thou that art highly favored, the Lord is with thee'" (or, as the marginal note in the Bible says, "endued with grace").[78] The Catholic version of the Bible, translated by St. Jerome, and all the Latin fathers have, "Hail, full of grace"—(*gratia plena—plena*, "full of"; *gratia*, "grace"). So here we find the first words of the Hail Mary in the Bible; and they are words used by the angel Gabriel, who, as the Bible tells us, "was sent from God to a virgin…and the virgin's name was Mary." So, at any rate, we cannot do wrong if we address the same words to her as God's angel did. Then read on a little further and you will find these words, "And she [St. Elizabeth] lifted up her voice with a loud cry, and said, 'Blessed art thou amongst women, and blessed is the fruit of thy womb.'"[79]

St. Elizabeth, who was the mother of St. John the Baptist, was filled with the Holy Ghost when she said these words to the Blessed Virgin. The Holy Spirit inspired her to say them; therefore, I cannot see that we can be doing wrong in addressing the same words to our Lady.

Protestants generally speak of our Lady as "the Virgin Mary." Catholics always call her "the Blessed Virgin Mary." In the canticle of the Magnificat, our Lady says, "For behold, from henceforth all generations shall call me blessed."[80]

[78] Lk 1:28
[79] Lk 1:42
[80] Lk 1:48

163. **Who made the second part of the Hail Mary?**

The Church of God, guided by the Holy Ghost, made the second part of the Hail Mary.

The second part is a prayer composed by the Church in honor of our Lady. *Holy Mary.* Certainly she must have been holy to have been chosen by God to become the Mother of the Redeemer. *Mother of God.* She is called in the Bible "the mother of Jesus."[81] Now, Jesus was God, therefore Mary, being the Mother of Jesus, is truly the Mother of God: not, of course, of the divine nature, but of Jesus, God made man for us. *Pray for us sinners now.* We believe that in heaven Mary has great power with her divine Son. If we believe that the angels and saints can and do help us by their prayers, there is much more reason for believing that Mary, the greatest of all saints, helps us also. *And at the hour of our death.* It is then indeed that we shall need all the help and prayers we can get, for all depends on that last hour. We know the devil tries to disturb the dying by tempting them to despair of God's mercy, and if he is allowed to try and disturb the dying, surely the Blessed Virgin would have a greater power given to her by God to help and assist them.

164. **Why should we frequently say the Hail Mary?**

We should frequently say the Hail Mary to put us in mind of the incarnation of the Son of God; and to honor our Blessed Lady, the Mother of God.

165. **Have we another reason for often saying the Hail Mary?**

We have another reason for often saying the Hail Mary—to ask our Blessed Lady to pray for us sinners at all times, but especially at the hour of our death.

The first part of the Hail Mary is composed, as we have seen, of words which were used by the angel Gabriel and St. Elizabeth, and these words refer to the incarnation. So they remind us of that great mystery. We cannot think too frequently about it, for it was the beginning of our redemption.

[81] Jn 2:1

The latter part of the Hail Mary, being a prayer to Mary, shows how much we venerate her, and hope for her powerful intercession.

166. **Why does the Catholic Church show great devotion to the Blessed Virgin?** The Catholic Church shows great devotion to the Blessed Virgin, because she is the immaculate Mother of God.

And surely that is reason enough. No other creature has ever been raised to such an exalted dignity. God spoke about her, foretelling her greatness and dignity in the book of Genesis.[82] For thousands of years the earth was praying for the happy time to dawn when the Virgin should conceive and bring forth a Son. Every Jewish maiden hoped that she might be the one chosen by God to be the Mother of the Messias; and when Mary did appear on earth, chosen amongst all women to be the Mother of Christ, was it an ordinary position in creation that God gave to her? How could any such position ever again be conferred upon a creature? At the incarnation, she is saluted as "full of grace" by God's angel.[83] The Holy Spirit, through St. Elizabeth, proclaims her "blessed amongst women."[84] She herself, in the canticle of the Magnificat, says of herself, "For behold, from henceforth all generations shall call me blessed."[85] And yet protestants say that she was only an ordinary woman, and, in their incomprehensible aversion to her, try even to see in some of the words her divine Son spoke to her nothing but rebuke and indifference. We cannot forget that her divine Son had said, "Honor thy father and thy mother," and it seems a strange thing to be told that he acted and spoke as if he himself had but little love and respect for her.

I cannot understand how protestants do not see in her the same exalted creature that we do. I suppose it comes from misunderstanding, as, indeed, all bigotry does. They have some kind of idea that we worship her in the same way as we worship God. How could we possibly do such a thing? It would be real idolatry, for she is a creature like ourselves. We give divine

[82] Cf. Gn 3:15
[83] Lk 1:28
[84] Lk 1:42
[85] Lk 1:48

worship to no being but God, but we venerate and respect and love those whom God has exalted and loved. We love Mary, and have great confidence in her intercession, because Jesus loved her and obeyed her as a Son on earth, and because of her own special privilege and great merit.

Now that our Blessed Lady is in heaven, where all things are made perfect, where she sees her God face-to-face, and sees and realizes fully all that Jesus did to save us, we believe that she exercises her great power of intercession on our behalf, praying for us in all our necessities. On earth, at the marriage feast in Cana of Galilee,[86] she obtained by her prayers the changing of the water into wine; in heaven, would her divine Son turn a deaf ear to her, or not allow her to have the same power at least of praying for us that she had on earth? We must not forget she was his real Mother. It is a mother's place to command more than to ask. Heaven does not destroy the relationship between mother and son, between Mary and Jesus. This we know and believe, and hence we have the greatest confidence in Mary's prayers, for how could Jesus refuse her anything?

167. **How is the Blessed Virgin Mother of God?**

The Blessed Virgin is Mother of God, because Jesus Christ her Son, who was born of her as man, is not only man but is also truly God.

This has been explained already under Question 163.

168. **Is the Blessed Virgin our Mother also?**

The Blessed Virgin is our Mother also, because, being the brethren of Jesus, we are the children of Mary.

Jesus is our brother because he had a human nature like ours; he became man, and hence we look upon and call his Mother our Mother also. When Jesus was dying on the cross, he said to his Mother, "Behold thy son."[87] It is generally believed that by these words he intended to give all the human race, in the person of St. John, to his Mother to be her adopted children.

[86] Cf. Jn 2:1ff
[87] Jn 19:26

The Commandments of God

169. **What is charity?**

Charity is a supernatural gift of God, by which we love God above all things, and our neighbor as ourselves for God's sake.

There are two great laws given to us by God. "Thou shalt love the Lord thy God with all thy heart, and with all thy soul, and with all thy mind... And a second like unto it: Thou shalt love thy neighbor as thyself."[88] Everybody is bound to keep these two great commandments. We could not keep them unless God helped us by giving us the gift of charity—that is, the power and willingness to keep them through love of him, for his sake. Of our own power, we could not keep the ten commandments on account of the corruption of our fallen nature and the strength of temptation; nor could we love our neighbor as God wishes us to do unless, again, he helped us. I think we all feel this, for the love of our neighbor (at least that love that God requires from us) is very difficult; it is to love our enemies and to pray for those that persecute us.[89]

170. **Why must we love God?**

We must love God, because he is infinitely good in himself and infinitely good to us.

Two very good reasons indeed. First, God is so good in himself. We cannot realize this goodness in itself, for it is infinite; but we can realize it as far as it has been shown to us. God has shown this love by creating us, by redeeming us, by promising heaven to us, and by giving us all the help and grace we need to get there.

[88] Mt 22:37, 39

[89] Cf. Mt 5:44

171. **How do we show that we love God?**
We show that we love God by keeping his commandments, for Christ says, "If you love me, keep my commandments."[90]

God is not content by our merely saying, "Oh, my God, I love thee," but he requires this practical proof: that if we love him, we should keep his commandments. What would you think of a boy who was always telling his mother that he loved her, but at the same time disobeyed her in every way? Would you not say that that was a very poor sign of his love; that, if he really loved his mother, he would obey her? So it is with God: we cannot say that we love God if we break his divine laws. The reason why God has given us this test is because it is hard to keep the commandments; and if we really do it, it is a positive sign that we really do love him.

172. **How many commandments are there?**
There are ten commandments.

173. **Say the ten commandments.**
I am the Lord thy God, who brought thee out of the land of Egypt and out of the house of bondage.

1. Thou shalt not have strange gods before me. Thou shalt not make to thyself any graven thing, nor the likeness of anything that is in heaven above or in the earth beneath, nor of those things that are in the waters under the earth. Thou shalt not adore them nor serve them.
2. Thou shalt not take the name of the Lord thy God in vain.
3. Remember that thou keep holy the sabbath day.
4. Honor thy father and thy mother.
5. Thou shalt not kill.
6. Thou shalt not commit adultery.
7. Thou shalt not steal.
8. Thou shalt not bear false witness against thy neighbor.
9. Thou shalt not covet thy neighbor's wife.
10. Thou shalt not covet thy neighbor's goods.

[90] Jn 14:15

174. **Who gave the ten commandments?**

God gave the ten commandments to Moses in the old law, and Christ confirmed them in the new.

I do not intend to enter into much explanation of the commandments, partly because they are more or less clearly explained in the words of the catechism, but principally because my object in this little book is more to explain the doctrines of the Catholic Church, and to try to put them in their true light before those who unfortunately have had wrong impressions instilled into their minds about them. All Christians of all denominations believe the commandments to be binding upon their consciences, and all understand them more or less in the same way.

The First Commandment

175. **What is the first commandment?**

The first commandment is: "I am the Lord thy God, who brought thee out of the land of Egypt, and out of the house of bondage. Thou shalt not have strange gods before me. Thou shalt not make to thyself any graven thing, nor the likeness of anything that is in heaven above or in the earth beneath, nor of those things that are in the waters under the earth. Thou shalt not adore them nor serve them."

176. **What are we commanded to do by the first commandment?**

By the first commandment, we are commanded to worship the one, true, and living God, by faith, hope, charity, and religion.

By *religion* we mean believing all the truths which the Christian religion teaches us, and putting into practice all the duties and obligations it imposes upon us.

177. **What are the sins against faith?**

The sins against faith are all false religions, willful doubt, disbelief, or denial of any article of faith, and also culpable ignorance of the doctrines of the Church.

Once we are certain that God has revealed or made known certain truths, it would be a great sin to deny them or to disbelieve them, or even to doubt them, because we are made to know God. If we know or have a suspicion that the Catholic Church is the true one, we are bound in conscience to inquire into its teaching.

178. **How do we expose ourselves to the danger of losing our faith?**

We expose ourselves to the danger of losing our faith by neglecting our spiritual duties, reading bad books, going to non-Catholic schools, and taking part in the services or prayers of a false religion.

Spiritual duties. This means praying, hearing Mass, hearing instructions, and going to confession and Communion.

Bad books, especially books written against religion and immoral books. If a Catholic child is sent to a non-Catholic school, it cannot learn its religion, and it would be a grievous sin on the part of a parent to deprive a child of the knowledge of its faith. It is a sin for Catholics to attend other places of worship than their own for the purpose of worshipping God there, because they know that all other religions except their own are false.

179. **What are the sins against hope?**

The sins against hope are despair and presumption.

Despair means "having willfully given up all hope of God's mercy."

Presumption means "a rash expectation of getting to heaven, and of obtaining all the means necessary for us to get there, without doing what God requires of us," as, for instance, leading a bad life and persevering in it, and at the same time expecting to be able to make peace with God whenever we think proper. It really means contempt of God. For it is practically saying to him, "I will do just as I like and as long as I like, and, when I think proper to repent, I expect you to help me. When I am dying, you must give me the grace to die a good death and then take me to heaven." Surely this is a mockery of God's mercy and justice.

180. **What are the chief sins against religion?**
The chief sins against religion are the worship of false gods or idols, and the giving to any creature whatsoever the honor which belongs to God alone.

181. **Does the first commandment forbid the making of images?**
The first commandment does not forbid the making of images, but the making of idols—that is, it forbids us to make images to be adored or honored as gods.

This will need some explanation, for we Catholics are accused of worshipping images, and we are told God has forbidden us to make them. In the first place, God never forbade people to make images; nay, he commanded his own people, the Jews, to make them. "And the Lord spoke to Moses: '...Thou shalt make also two cherubims of gold, on the two sides of the oracle.'"[91] You remember the history of the brazen serpent. "And the Lord said to Moses: 'Make a brazen serpent, and set it up for a sign; whosoever being struck shall look on it, shall live.' Moses, therefore, made a brazen serpent."[92]

What God did forbid was to make images and adore them as gods, as they had done with the golden calf. "But," you say, "we see you Catholics kneeling in front of statues and praying to them." Yes, kneeling there and praying, but not to the statues; they are of wood or stone or metal; they cannot hear or see us, so what would be the use of speaking to them? But we are praying to the angels or saints whom these statues represent. Or it may be the crucifix. Well, at any rate, I find it easier to say my prayers with attention and devotion before a crucifix or a statue than before a bare wall. The crucifix reminds me of my Savior, and keeps my thoughts collected.

We have just seen that God commanded Moses to make a brazen serpent, and to put it upon a standard, and when the people were bitten by the poisonous snakes, their friends carried them to some place where they could see the brass figure of the serpent, and when they cast their eyes upon it, they were miraculously cured in an instant, and mind, this was all done

[91] Ex 25:1, 18
[92] Nm 21:8-9

by command of God. We do not expect anything like this, but remember this really took place, and what God did once he can do again if he sees fit. Sometimes people are astonished, or perhaps shocked to see candles burning in front of statues in Catholic churches, or to see flowers placed before them. Well, let these good people go and see Beaconsfield's statue on "Primrose Day." It is covered with garlands of flowers, and mind, it is only a statue of a man—a great statesman, it is true, and one who did much for his country. Surely you would not call this superstition or idolatry? These flowers are intended to honor the memory of a great statesman, and our flowers are intended to honor the great saints of God.

182. **Does the first commandment forbid dealing with the devil and superstitious practices?**

The first commandment forbids all dealing with the devil and superstitious practices, such as consulting spiritualists and fortune tellers, and trusting to charms, omens, dreams, and suchlike fooleries.

Catholics are often charged with superstitious practices, such as wearing a crucifix or a medal round the neck. Well, I cannot see what harm there is in it. I suppose there is no harm in wearing a locket containing a photo of anyone we love here on earth, and why it should be wrong to wear a representation of the crucifix or medal bearing the image of the Mother of God, or of our angel guardian, or of some great saint, I am at a loss to understand. Those who cry out against us would probably not scruple to hang up an old worn horseshoe behind their front door to bring good luck.

183. **Are all sins of sacrilege and simony also forbidden by the first commandment?**

All sins of sacrilege and simony are also forbidden by the first commandment.

Sacrilege is a violation or irreverent treatment of what is consecrated to God, whether of things, such as the sacred vessels used in the church, or of persons, such as priests or nuns, or of places, such as a church or cemetery. *Simony* means "buying or selling sacred things, and making profit out of them because they are sacred."

184. **Is it forbidden to give divine honor and worship to the angels and saints?**
It is forbidden to give divine honor or worship to the angels and saints, for this belongs to God alone.

185. **What kind of honor or worship should we pay to the angels and saints?**
We should pay to the angels and saints an inferior honor or worship, for this is due to them as the servants and special friends of God.

We have already spoken about this in the ninth article.[93] Let me repeat what the Catholic Church teaches us. "The saints who reign together with Christ offer up their prayers to God for men: it is good and profitable [it does not say necessary] suppliantly to invoke them, and to have recourse to their prayers, aid, and help for obtaining benefits from God through his Son, Jesus Christ, our Lord, who is our only Redeemer and Savior."[94]

We adore Christ, and we honor the saints. So do protestants, or they are supposed to do. Do they not dedicate their churches to them? We hear of St. Agnes's Church, St. Philip's, St. Jude's, St. Thomas's, All Saints' Church. There is a calendar of the saints at the beginning of the *Book of Common Prayer*; I suppose this means that the Church of England intends thereby to honor the saints. They ask, too, in the collect read on St. Michael's feast, that they may be succored and defended by the ministering spirits. Surely this means that they consider the angels worthy of honor and veneration, if they ask their help and assistance. This is all we do. To give them supreme or divine honor would be a great sin, but to give them the honor which is really due to them as the special friends of God is no sin, but only right and just. We not only honor the king, but also his ministers and judges, because from their position they are deserving of our honor and respect.

186. **What honor should we give to relics, crucifixes, and holy pictures?**
We should give to relics, crucifixes, and holy pictures a relative honor as they relate to Christ and his saints and are memorials of them.

[93] See q. 104, above.

[94] Council of Trent, Session 25, "On the Invocation, Veneration, and Relics, of Saints, and on Sacred Images"

The word *relics* means, in general, "something that is left to us"—something that belonged to an individual who is dead, or some articles that remind us of an action that has passed, like a battle, an expedition, etc. Madame Tussaud's exhibition is full of relics of persons and things. You will see Nelson's coat there, Wellington's snuffbox, Napoleon's carriage, etc., and they are very valuable, not in themselves, but because they were used by great men—it is this that makes their value. So, the relics that we have of saints have no value in themselves, but they are exceedingly precious on account of their having belonged to great saints. By *relics* we Catholics generally mean portions of the bones of the martyrs who laid down their lives for their faith, or anything that once belonged to one who is now a canonized saint in heaven, pieces of the true cross on which Jesus died, etc.

187. **Do we pray to relics or images?**
We do not pray to relics or images, for they can neither see nor hear nor help us.

This is plain enough.

The Second Commandment

188. **What is the second commandment?**
The second commandment is: "Thou shalt not take the name of the Lord thy God in vain."

189. **What are we commanded by the second commandment?**
By the second commandment, we are commanded to speak with reverence of God and all holy persons and things, and to keep our lawful oaths and vows.

In vain means "without necessity"—not to bring the name of God into ordinary conversation without need.

Holy persons are those who have consecrated themselves and their lives to the service of God, like priests and nuns.

Holy things means "all that belongs to the service and worship of God in religion"—the sacraments, the Mass and the ceremonies used in them, the sign of the cross, etc.

An oath is calling God to witness that what we say is true. *A vow* is a solemn promise made to God, to do something great and good in his honor—for instance, to build a church if we recover from an illness.

190. **What does the second commandment forbid?**

The second commandment forbids all false, rash, unjust, and unnecessary oaths; as also blaspheming, cursing, and profane words.

A false oath is calling God to witness that what we say is true when we know at the time it is false; it is also called "perjury." *A rash oath* is when we do not take the trouble to find out whether what we say is true or not. *An unjust oath* is swearing to do a thing which is forbidden by God. *An unnecessary oath* is an oath taken when there is no need for it. *Cursing* is very different to swearing, though many people think they are the same thing. Cursing means "calling down God's great anger upon ourselves or upon our neighbor, or wishing ourselves or our neighbor any great evil." We are never allowed to curse.

191. **Is it ever lawful to swear or to take an oath?**

It is lawful to swear or to take an oath, only when God's honor, or our own, or our neighbor's good requires it.

People are allowed, and sometimes are forced, to swear—as, for instance, in a court of justice—because the public good requires it; otherwise, people might not tell the truth, and justice would not be done.

The Third Commandment

192. **What is the third commandment?**

The third commandment is: "Remember that thou keep holy the sabbath day."

193. **What are we commanded by the third commandment?**

By the third commandment, we are commanded to keep Sunday holy.

The Jews' sabbath day was Saturday; we Christians keep Sunday holy. The Church, by the power our Lord gave her, changed the observance of Saturday to Sunday.

A word about Sunday. God said, "Remember that thou keep holy the sabbath day."[95] The sabbath was Saturday, not Sunday; why, then, do we keep Sunday holy instead of Saturday? The Church altered the observance of the sabbath to the observance of Sunday in commemoration of our Lord having risen from the dead on Easter Sunday, and of the Holy Ghost having descended upon the apostles on Whitsunday. Protestants who say that they go by the Bible and the Bible only, and that they do not believe anything that is not in the Bible, must be rather puzzled by the keeping of Sunday when God distinctly said, "Keep holy the sabbath day." The word *Sunday* does not come anywhere in the Bible, so, without knowing it, they are obeying the authority of the Catholic Church.

194. **How are we to keep the Sunday holy?**

We are to keep the Sunday holy by hearing Mass and resting from servile works.

The obligation of going to Mass on Sunday is explained in Question 232. Servile works are the works the slaves used to do, such as digging, ploughing, working in stone or iron, etc., and, for women, spinning, etc. It is not forbidden to play games on Sunday, such as croquet, tennis, golf, etc., but if we have reason to believe that we should scandalize our neighbor by so doing, it is better to avoid it.

195. **Why are we commanded to rest from servile works?**

We are commanded to rest from servile works that we may have time and opportunity for prayer, going to the sacraments, hearing instructions, and reading good books.

[95] Ex 20:8

The Fourth Commandment

196. **What is the fourth commandment?**

The fourth commandment is: "Honor thy father and thy mother."

197. **What are we commanded by the fourth commandment?**

By the fourth commandment, we are commanded to love, reverence, and obey our parents in all that is not sin.

A parent may not order a child to steal or to tell a lie. The child would not be bound to obey in that case.

198. **Are we commanded to obey our parents only?**

We are commanded to obey not only our parents, but also our bishops and pastors, the civil authorities, and our lawful superiors.

199. **Are we bound to assist our parents in their wants?**

We are bound to assist our parents in their wants, both spiritual and temporal.

200. **Are we bound in justice to contribute to the support of our pastors?**

We are bound in justice to contribute to the support of our pastors; for St. Paul says, "The Lord ordained that they who preach the gospel should live by the gospel."[96]

This is why there is a collection morning and evening in the churches on Sundays.

201. **What is the duty of parents toward their children?**

The duty of parents toward their children is to provide for them, to instruct and correct them, and to give them a good Catholic education.

[96] 1 Cor 9:14

202. **What is the duty of masters, mistresses, and other superiors?**
The duty of masters, mistresses, and other superiors is to take proper care of those under their charge, and to enable them to practice their religious duties.

203. **What does the fourth commandment forbid?**
The fourth commandment forbids all contempt, stubbornness, and disobedience to our parents and lawful superiors.

204. **Is it sinful to belong to any secret society?**
It is sinful to belong to any secret society that plots against the Church or state, or to any society that by reason of its secrecy is condemned by the Church; for St. Paul says: "Let every soul be subject to the higher powers; he that resisteth the power resisteth the ordinance of God; and they that resist purchase to themselves damnation."[97]

No Catholic may be a Freemason, because the society is a secret one, and is condemned by the Church, and, moreover, it is a kind of religion, for Freemasons have temples, chaplains, and a ritual; Catholics never take part in the services of another religion.

The Fifth Commandment

205. **What is the fifth commandment?**
The fifth commandment is: "Thou shalt not kill."

206. **What does the fifth commandment forbid?**
The fifth commandment forbids all willful murder, fighting, quarreling, and injurious words, and also scandal and bad example.

Many people have a very wrong impression about the meaning of the word *scandal* or *scandalizing*. They believe it has something to do with saying evil things about one's neighbor; but this is really calumny, or detraction. *Scandal* comes from a Latin word (*scandalum*) which means "a

[97] Rom 13:1-2

stumbling-block, something put in a person's way to trip him up and make him fall"; so, a spiritual scandal is something which is done to make, or which is likely to make, a person fall into sin. *Bad example* is very like scandal, but not quite so wicked. The amount of sin, both of scandal and bad example, depends upon the amount of injury we do to our neighbor's soul.

207. **Does the fifth commandment forbid anger?**
The fifth commandment forbids anger and, still more, hatred and revenge.

208. **Why are scandal and bad example forbidden by the fifth commandment?**
Scandal and bad example are forbidden by the fifth commandment, because they lead to the injury and spiritual death of our neighbor's soul.

The Sixth Commandment

209. **What is the sixth commandment?**
The sixth commandment is: "Thou shalt not commit adultery."

It is seldom that a sin against this commandment is only a venial sin. Nearly all sins against purity are mortal sins, and therefore you should keep this commandment very carefully. One of the best means of doing so is to put away at once any wicked thoughts which the devil brings before your mind. The sign of the cross and this little prayer, "Jesus, Mary, and Joseph, help me in my temptations," you will find very useful when you are tempted.

210. **What does the sixth commandment forbid?**
The sixth commandment forbids all sins of impurity with another's wife or husband.

211. **Does the sixth commandment forbid whatever is contrary to holy purity?**
The sixth commandment forbids whatever is contrary to holy purity in looks, words, or actions.

The eyes are called the "windows of the soul." Death enters into the soul through them. Keep them, therefore, away from what is impure or immodest. Evil conversation is a very fruitful source of sin. It is the weapon mostly employed by the devil to corrupt souls.

Avoid all those who use impure talk. They are called "bad companions." Actions of impurity are the result of temptations. Crush the temptation at once and the sin will be crushed too.

212. **Are immodest plays and dances forbidden by the sixth commandment?**
Immodest plays and dances are forbidden by the sixth commandment, and it is sinful to look at them.

213. **Does the sixth commandment forbid immodest songs, books, and pictures?**
The sixth commandment forbids immodest songs, books, and pictures, because they are most dangerous to the soul and lead to mortal sin.

The Seventh Commandment

214. **What is the seventh commandment?**
The seventh commandment is: "Thou shalt not steal."

215. **What does the seventh commandment forbid?**
The seventh commandment forbids all unjust taking away or keeping what belongs to another.

Mark the words *unjust taking away*. That means against the will of the owner, unless, of course, necessity compels it. It is not stealing to take away the bottle of poison or the revolver with which a person intends to take his life, though these things may really be his own property.

216. **Is all manner of cheating in buying and selling forbidden by the seventh commandment?**
All manner of cheating in buying and selling is forbidden by the seventh commandment, and also every other way of wronging our neighbor.

217. **Are we bound to restore ill-gotten goods?**

We are bound to restore ill-gotten goods if we are able, or else the sin will not be forgiven; we must also pay our debts.

God will never forgive a person who has stolen unless that person makes restitution for his theft if he is able to do so, or, if he is not able, has at least the will and resolution to do so when he is able. He has taken what did not belong to him, and that was a sin; and God does not forgive sin unless it is repented of. The true test of repentance is sorrow for what has been done. If the thief, therefore, is sorry, he will restore what he has taken. If he is no longer able to do this, he must at least have a sincere desire and intention to restore if ever he has the opportunity or the means of doing so.

Debt. It is not a sin to contract a debt, when we know that we shall have the means of paying it off, but otherwise it is a sin. Debts must be paid just as restitution must be made for theft.

218. **Is it dishonest in servants to waste their master's time or property?**

It is dishonest in servants to waste their master's time or property, because it is wasting what is not their own.

The Eighth Commandment

219. **What is the eighth commandment?**

The eighth commandment is: "Thou shalt not bear false witness against thy neighbor."

220. **What does the eighth commandment forbid?**

The eighth commandment forbids all false testimony, rash judgment, and lies.

False testimony means "giving false evidence against our neighbors."

Rash judgment means "judging that a certain person has been guilty of something wrong when we have no real ground to go upon for so judging."

Lies. There are several kinds of lies, but they may be divided into two classes—little lies and big lies. Little lies include lies of joke, lies of excuse, etc. Big lies are principally calumny and detraction.

221. **Are calumny and detraction forbidden by the eighth commandment?**
Calumny and detraction are forbidden by the eighth commandment, and also talebearing, and any words which injure our neighbor's character.

Calumny is saying something wicked against our neighbor which we know to be false. *Detraction* is saying something which is really true, but which is secret. Both calumny and detraction are mortal sins if we have done our neighbor a serious injury, and in that case we are bound, before God will forgive us, to undo the evil we have done, if we are able to do so.

222. **If you have injured your neighbor by speaking ill of him, what are you bound to do?**
If I have injured my neighbor by speaking ill of him, I am bound to make him satisfaction, by restoring his good name as far as I can.

We must restore a person's character just as much as, and indeed more than, his purse. When a person has robbed us of our purse and its contents we can replace them, but it is not so easy to regain our neighbor's good will when we have lost our character or good name.

The Ninth Commandment

223. **What is the ninth commandment?**
The ninth commandment is: "Thou shalt not covet thy neighbor's wife."

224. **What does the ninth commandment forbid?**
The ninth commandment forbids all willful consent to impure thoughts and desires, and all willful pleasure in the irregular motions of the flesh.

225. **What sins commonly lead to the breaking of the sixth and ninth commandments?**
The sins that commonly lead to the breaking of the sixth and ninth commandments are gluttony, drunkenness, and intemperance, and also idleness, bad company, and the neglect of prayer.

The Tenth Commandment

226. **What is the tenth commandment?**

The tenth commandment is: "Thou shalt not covet thy neighbor's goods."

227. **What does the tenth commandment forbid?**

The tenth commandment forbids all envious and covetous thoughts and unjust desires of our neighbor's goods and profits.

This tenth commandment does not forbid us to wish to have what our neighbor possesses, but to wish to get it by unjust or unfair means, or to deprive him of it.

The Commandments of the Church

We now come to another set of commandments—viz., those framed by the Church of Christ. Our Lord not only established a Church and entrusted his sacred doctrine to its keeping, but also gave that Church authority and power to make whatever laws it considered necessary for the better observing of his doctrine. "What things soever ye shall bind on earth shall be bound in heaven."[98] "He that heareth you heareth me."[99] These words were said by Christ to the apostles, and by these words he intended to give to them a power of making laws for the Church, which laws he would consider as his own.

228. **Are we bound to obey the Church?**

We are bound to obey the Church, because Christ has said to the pastors of the Church: "He that heareth you heareth me; and he that despiseth you despiseth me."[100]

[98] Mt 18:18
[99] Lk 10:16
[100] Ibid.

If anyone refuses to obey the Church, our Lord takes it as an act of disobedience to himself.

Now, what is the principle upon which the Church has made these six commandments?

There are many precepts which Christ gave during his public teaching which he never told us how to fulfill, nor when, nor how often we had to fulfill them. He left that to the Church to do. For example, God demands that we should adore and serve him. The Church says, "If you assist at Mass (the Christian sacrifice of adoration) on certain days, you will have fulfilled this precept." Again, Christ says, "If any man would come after me, let him deny himself, and take up his cross daily and follow me."[101] The Church steps in and says, "If you will abstain and fast on the days that I appoint, you will carry out this precept." Again, he said to his apostles, "Whosoever sins ye forgive they are forgiven unto them."[102] This power was given that people might get their sins forgiven. The Church says, "You must go to confession at least once a year." Again, he said, "Except ye eat the flesh of the Son of man and drink his blood ye have not life in yourselves."[103] How often must we receive his flesh and blood? He himself did not say. His Church says, "You must go to Holy Communion once a year at a certain time, and then you will fulfill this very important command of Christ." I think what I have said will explain my meaning. These precepts of the Church are not new commandments, but merely the Church telling us how and when we are to fulfill certain commands which Christ said we must fulfill. If, therefore, I refuse to carry out these precepts of the Church, I am committing a great sin against Jesus Christ, both because he gave the Church power to make them and because they are really his commands interpreted by the Church.

229. **What are the chief commandments of the Church?**

The chief commandments of the Church are:

[101] Lk 9:23
[102] Jn 20:23
[103] Jn 6:54

1. To keep the Sundays and holy days of obligation holy, by hearing Mass and resting from servile works.
2. To keep the days of fasting and abstinence appointed by the Church.
3. To go to confession at least once a year.
4. To receive the Blessed Sacrament at least once a year, and that at Easter or thereabouts.
5. To contribute to the support of our pastors.
6. Not to marry within certain degrees of kindred, nor to solemnize marriage at the forbidden times.

The First Commandment of the Church

230. **What is the first commandment of the Church?**

The first commandment of the Church is: "To keep the Sundays and holy days of obligation holy, by hearing Mass and resting from servile works."

231. **Which are the holy days of obligation observed in England?**

The holy days of obligation observed in England are: Christmas day, the Circumcision, the Epiphany, the Ascension, Corpus Christi, Sts. Peter and Paul, the Assumption of Our Lady, and All Saints.[104]

Days of obligation are certain great feasts of the Church which we keep like Sundays—that is, we are bound to go to Mass, and to keep from work; but this for many people is impossible, and therefore the obligation does not bind them.

232. **Is it a mortal sin to neglect to hear Mass on Sundays and holy days of obligation?**

It is a mortal sin to neglect to hear Mass on Sundays and holy days of obligation.

[104] In the United States, the holy days of obligation are: Christmas day, the Circumcision, the Ascension, the Assumption, All Saints, and the Immaculate Conception. In Scotland, they are the same as in England, with the addition of St. Joseph (March 19) and the Immaculate Conception. In Ireland, St. Patrick (March 17) and the Immaculate Conception are added to those for England.

The Mass is explained in Question 277. The reason why it is such a great sin to neglect to hear Mass on Sundays and days of obligation is simply this: we are bound by our very existence and dependence on God to adore and worship him. I suppose all Christians believe this. The Mass is the Christian's act of worship, and, therefore, we are bound to assist at it on the days appointed by the Church. If we miss it through our own fault, we are, as it were, depriving God of his worship; we are refusing to adore him; and this it is that makes the sin so great. There are, however, occasions when it is impossible to hear Mass, and then, of course, it is not a sin to be absent from it. For example, if you are confined to your room through illness, or you are bound to wait upon a sick person, or the church is too far distant, or if you stay at home to allow someone else to go, you cannot hear Mass: you are then dispensed from the obligation. It is difficult sometimes to get protestants to realize that they are bound to worship God, and that by religious worship. They have been accustomed, more or less, to do as they like about religion, and they cannot quite get rid of the idea that they are not bound to attend to it; but all this is very much opposed to what God requires. He did not leave it a matter of option or choice to us. His words are very strong and forcible: "He that believeth and is baptized shall be saved, but he that believeth not shall be condemned."[105] We are, therefore, bound, under pain of eternal loss, to believe all that God has taught us; and this means also doing all that he has told us to do, whether by his own divine lips or by the voice of his Church.

233. **Are parents, masters, and mistresses bound to provide that those under their charge shall hear Mass on Sundays and holy days of obligation?**
Parents, masters, and mistresses are bound to provide that those under their charge shall hear Mass on Sundays and holy days of obligation.

[105] Mk 16:16

The Second Commandment of the Church

234. **What is the second commandment of the Church?**

The second commandment of the Church is: "To keep the days of fasting and abstinence appointed by the Church."

The fasting that we are now going to explain must not be confounded with the fasting necessary before receiving Holy Communion.[106]

235. **What are fasting days?**

Fasting days are days on which we are allowed to take only one full meal.

This does not mean that no other food may be taken. The Church allows us to take a little food twice during the day apart from the full meal. The amount should be regulated by local custom.

Many Anglicans think that fasting and abstinence have nothing to do with them. They know that Catholics are bound by these observances, but they do not think that they concern them. If you have an Anglican *Book of Common Prayer* by you, just open it somewhere about the beginning, and you will find there, "Tables and Rules for the Feasts and Fasts through the Whole Year." Amongst these tables, there is one entitled, "A Table of the Vigils, Fasts, and Days of Abstinence to Be Observed in the Year." First, there come sixteen vigils: these are days before certain great feasts. A *vigil* means "a day of watching." In olden days, the Christians used to spend these days as days of preparation for the festival that came the next day; they were days of prayer, and generally spent in the church. According to their prayer book, therefore, Anglicans ought to prepare beforehand to celebrate the feasts of the saints mentioned in their book. There are two feasts of the Blessed Virgin mentioned. Surely this looks as if they were honoring the Blessed Virgin and the saints if they are supposed to prepare to celebrate their feasts. After the list of vigils, there comes a list of fasting and abstinence days to be observed. These days are about the same as the catechism gives, except that the *Book of Common Prayer* includes the three Rogation days before the Ascension. We do not observe these, so

[106] See q. 272, below.

that Anglicans really have three more fasting and abstinence days than we have.

236. **Which are the fasting days?**

The fasting days are the weekdays of Lent; certain vigils; and the Ember days.[107]

237. **What are days of abstinence?**

Days of abstinence are days on which we are forbidden to take flesh meat and soups made from meat.

Fasting and abstinence days differ in this: that on a fasting day, the quantity of food is limited. On an abstinence day, meat is forbidden, but we may take as much abstinence food as we like and as often as we like.

238. **Which are the days of abstinence?**

The days of abstinence are all Fridays, except any Friday on which a holy day of obligation falls; the Wednesdays of Lent (in England); the four vigils (unless one falls on a Sunday); and the Ember days.[108]

There is a little difference between the lists given here and in the Anglican prayer book, but very little.[109] Fridays are especially mentioned there as being days of abstinence, so that no Anglican who believes in his Church and prayer book is allowed to eat meat on Fridays. This may seem strange, but it is true—no Anglican may eat meat on a Friday unless it be Christmas day.

239. **Why does the Church command us to fast and abstain?**

The Church commands us to fast and abstain that so we may mortify the flesh and satisfy God for our sins.

[107] Lent ends at midday on Holy Saturday. The vigils are those of Pentecost, the Assumption, All Saints, and Christmas. When a vigil falls on a Sunday, but is transferred to a Saturday, it does not carry with it the obligation to fast or abstain.

[108] When December 26 falls on a Friday, the abstinence is at present dispensed in England. When one day of abstinence immediately follows another, leave is given to eat meat on the second, except in Lent. When a holiday of obligation occurs in Lent, e.g., St. Joseph or St. Patrick in Scotland or Ireland, neither fast nor abstinence is abrogated.

[109] See q. 235, above.

We must mortify and keep down our evil inclinations, or they will master us and lead us to hell. Besides getting our sins forgiven by God through repentance and the sacrament of penance, we must make satisfaction to God's justice for the injury we have done to it.

The Third Commandment of the Church

240. **What is the third commandment of the Church?**
The third commandment of the Church is: "To go to confession at least once a year.'"

Confession will be fully explained later on in Question 281, etc.

241. **How soon are children bound to go to confession?**
Children are bound to go to confession as soon as they have come to the use of reason, and are capable of mortal sin.

242. **When are children generally supposed to come to the use of reason?**
Children are generally supposed to come to the use of reason about the age of seven years.

Confession becomes an obligation when a person can really distinguish between right and wrong, and is thus capable of committing sin. It may seem strange that the Church should require confession at an early age from children, but you must understand that absolution, or the grace given in the sacrament of penance, not only forgives any sins that may have been committed, but also helps to preserve the soul from falling into future sin; it has a preserving power as well as a healing power.

The Fourth Commandment of the Church

243. **What is the fourth commandment of the Church?**
The fourth commandment of the Church is: "To receive the Blessed Sacrament at least once a year, and that at Easter or thereabouts."

The Church binds us not merely to go to Holy Communion once a year, but she also appoints the time during which that Communion must be received. Canon 859, par. 2, limits the time for paschal Communion as from Palm Sunday to Low Sunday, but the time may be anticipated in certain dioceses—viz., (as a rule) from the Fourth Sunday in Lent, and delayed till Trinity Sunday, both days included.

244. **How soon are Christians bound to receive the Blessed Sacrament?**
Christians are bound to receive the Blessed Sacrament as soon as they are capable of distinguishing the body of Christ from ordinary bread, and are judged to be sufficiently instructed.

On August 8, 1910, Pope Pius X issued a decree to the effect that children who have begun to use their reason should be carefully instructed and allowed to receive Holy Communion. It is now the custom for them to make their first Communion when they are about seven years old.

The Fifth Commandment of the Church

245. **What is the fifth commandment of the Church?**
The fifth commandment of the Church is: "To contribute to the support of our pastors."

246. **Is it a duty to contribute to the support of religion?**
It is a duty to contribute to the support of religion according to our means, so that God may be duly honored and worshipped, and the kingdom of his Church extended.

St. Paul says in the first epistle to the Corinthians, "Even so did the Lord ordain that they which [who] proclaim the gospel should live of the gospel."[110] To Catholic priests in England especially does this apply. They have no endowments and livings as the Anglican clergy have. The money which is now devoted to supporting the Established Church was for the most part once Catholic money. At the Reformation, it was taken from the Catholic Church. The Catholic Church in England is poor, and it naturally looks to its members to support it. The Catholic priest is forbidden

[110] 1 Cor 9:14

by the law of the Church to enter any profession or to engage in trade as a means of support. True it is: it does not need much to support him, for he has no wife nor children depending upon him; but as he has given up his life to God to work solely for him and to do his work among the people—in other words, as he lives for his flock, and is ready at any time of the day or night to do his duty as a priest for them, even at the risk of his life—so the Church requires that his flock should support him, and enable him to carry out the services of God in a fit and becoming manner. This is the reason why there are collections at the services on Sundays, seat rents, offerings for the Holy Mass, offerings for baptisms, churchings, etc.

The Sixth Commandment of the Church

247. **What is the sixth commandment of the Church?**

The sixth commandment of the Church is: "Not to marry within certain degrees of kindred, nor to solemnize marriage at the forbidden times."

All relationships up to second cousinship inclusively prohibit marriage; however, for very special reasons, the Church permits dispensations for marriage between even first cousins. If there is any difficulty about a marriage, a priest will readily tell you what can be done. It may be well to remark that those who have acted as godfathers and godmothers in baptism contract a spiritual relationship between themselves and the child baptized, and this spiritual relationship forbids marriage without a dispensation.

248. **Which are the times in which it is forbidden to marry with solemnity?**

The times in which it is forbidden to marry with solemnity without special leave are from the First Sunday of Advent till after Christmas day, and from Ash Wednesday till after Easter Sunday.

Not that people may not get married if they like during these times, but the marriages must be more or less private or quiet, and, in some dioceses, they must first get leave from the bishop. There must not be any marriage Mass or great ceremony about the service. However, the solemn nuptial blessing may be given for a special reason with the permission of the ordinary.

The Sacraments

We now come to the practical part of the life of a Catholic. Hitherto the catechism has been teaching us what we have to believe and what we have to do to save our souls; now it teaches us how we have to do it. All that we have learnt has now to be put into practice.

And first a word about the sacramental system, as it is called—that is to say, what the sacraments are, what they mean, and for what end they were instituted by Christ.

We Christians all believe in Jesus Christ; we believe in his existence as God made man. We believe that he redeemed us by his death on the cross, and thereby saved us from eternal ruin. But many are inclined to stop there, and to go no farther. Their idea of the sacrifice of the cross is that it has done all for us, and that we need not trouble ourselves anymore about our salvation. "Jesus died to save me," they say, "and why should I fear anymore? He has done all for me." "If this is true," I reply, "he has done all for everybody else also. Why, then, are any souls lost? Why are there any souls in hell? For our Lord died on the cross for them as well as for the souls who are in heaven. If his death has done all, why did it not save those that are lost? How comes it that some souls are lost and others saved?" There must be some mystery here, so let us go on and inquire.

What did Jesus Christ come to do for us when he came down from heaven? He came to reconcile us to our heavenly Father, he opened the gates of heaven to us by his death, he gave us a right to go there, and promised us help to get there—but he did not go beyond that. He would not, because he had given us free will, and he would not force us to be saved against our will.

There is, therefore, a part which we also have to take, something that we have to do, or else the death of Christ will be of no avail to us. We must get his death applied to our souls; his precious blood which was shed for us must really be applied to each soul individually, and wash and cleanse each soul, or the shedding of that blood on the cross is useless to it. If, like the poor Magdalen, we had knelt under the cross and seen our Lord's precious blood being shed for us, we should have felt as she did, that we were really redeemed; but we are living now many centuries after his death, and still the same precious blood must be as really applied to our souls as it was to the soul of that penitent sinner.

Now, how is this done? Our Lord thought of it and arranged it all in his own divine mind. In his love for us, he devised a means of applying to each one personally the full merits of his passion and death. He established and instituted the sacraments for this purpose, and gave to them the wonderful power of saving the soul from eternal loss, just as if he did it with his own divine hand.

Take that little baby that has just been born; it is in original sin, its soul is in danger of never seeing the face of God for all eternity; if it dies without baptism, it will never go to heaven. Christ has said so.[111] It can do nothing by itself, but cannot something be done for it? What is the one thing necessary to put its soul in such a state that it will go to heaven if it does die? It needs that the death of Jesus should be applied to it, for Jesus died for that child: the merits of the precious blood must touch it. It was shed for it. And how can this be done? By baptism. For our Lord instituted baptism especially as a means of applying his death to that child's soul. If any person pours water on that child's head, and at the same time says the words of baptism, intending to do what our Lord wishes by that act and those words, the merits of the redeeming blood of Jesus Christ are at once given to that soul; original sin is washed away and that soul is safe.

Again, take that poor man who is on his deathbed; his soul is deeply stained with mortal sin. In a short time, he will be in eternity. Can nothing save him? Only one thing can — the precious blood of our Lord. And how can it be applied to him, so as to drive that mortal sin out of his soul and save him before he dies? By the words of absolution given by the priest of God: "I absolve thee from thy sins in the name of the Father, and of the Son, and of the Holy Ghost." Our Lord himself appointed those words for that very purpose, and the moment they are pronounced over that penitent

[111] Cf. Jn 3:5

sinner by a real priest of God, the sin is taken away and the man will be saved, for God has forgiven him. "Whosesoever sins ye shall forgive, they are forgiven unto them."[112] These are his own words.

So, you see, we are not saved simply because our Lord shed his precious blood for us, but we need to have the merits of that blood applied to our souls, and that is done by the sacraments. The catechism now asks:

249. **What is a sacrament?**

A sacrament is an outward sign of inward grace ordained by Jesus Christ, by which grace is given to our souls.

Outward sign. Every sacrament has something about it that we see, some act that is done—for example, pouring water, as in baptism; anointing with oil, as in confirmation or extreme unction, etc. There must also be some words which are said while the act is being performed. When water is poured upon the child's head in baptism, the words *I baptize thee*, etc., are said. When the bishop anoints the forehead with the sacred oil in confirmation, he uses certain words;[113] so does the priest in giving extreme unction.[114]

Of inward grace. When the various acts are performed and the sacramental words are said at the same time, a particular grace is given to the soul by that act and those words. Each sacrament gives its own special grace or help. Baptism makes us Christians; confirmation strengthens us in the faith; the Holy Eucharist feeds the soul; penance forgives sin; and so on.

Ordained by Jesus Christ. Only God could give power to signs and words to give grace to souls.

By which grace is given to our souls, for it is through them, as I have already said, that grace, either to take our sins away or to help us to lead good lives, is given to us.

[112] Jn 20:23

[113] See q. 265, below.

[114] See q. 302, below.

250. **Do the sacraments always give grace?**

The sacraments always give grace to those who receive them worthily.

Naturally, our Lord would not give us his grace unless we came in a proper state to receive it; for instance, if a person came to confession and was not sorry for his sins, our Lord would not grant him forgiveness for his sins, because he promises pardon to those only who repent.

251. **Whence have the sacraments the power of giving grace?**

The sacraments have the power of giving grace from the merits of Christ's precious blood, which they apply to our souls.

This, I think, you can understand clearly from what has been already said above.

252. **Ought we to have a great desire to receive the sacraments?**

We ought to have a great desire to receive the sacraments, because they are the chief means of our salvation.

I suppose we all really want to be saved. Nobody in his right senses would say that he did not, no matter how wicked a life he was leading. Therefore, as the sacraments are the means instituted by Christ for saving our souls, it should be our most earnest desire to receive them: this is common sense.

253. **Is a character given to the soul by any of the sacraments?**

A character is given to the soul by the sacraments of baptism, confirmation, and holy order.

254. **What is a character?**

A character is a mark or seal on the soul which cannot be effaced, and therefore the sacrament conferring it may not be repeated.

There are two classes or divisions of the sacraments:

1. The sacraments of the living and the sacraments of the dead (not that the dead can receive any sacraments, for the sacraments are to give grace and help to the soul, not to the body; and once a person is dead, the soul has gone, for death is the separation of the soul from the body); but

by *the dead* are meant those who are dead in God's sight—that is, those who have lost his love and whose souls are in mortal sin. The sacraments of the dead are baptism and penance, because they are to bring us to life when we are dead in sin. By the word *living* is meant those who are living in the grace of God, who are leading good lives and who have no mortal sins on their souls. The sacraments of the living are confirmation, Holy Eucharist, extreme unction, holy order, and matrimony. When we receive these sacraments, the soul must be without mortal sin upon it, we must be living in a state of grace and pleasing to God. The sacraments of the dead are to get us out of sin; the sacraments of the living are to keep us out of sin and to strengthen us in God's grace.

2. The second division of the sacraments is: 1) Those which confer a character or mark upon the soul, and which can only be received once in a lifetime; these are baptism, confirmation, and holy order. Once a person is really baptized, confirmed by a real bishop, or validly ordained a priest, he cannot be baptized, confirmed, or ordained a second time. 2) Those which do not confer a character or mark on the soul, and therefore can be received more than once. Confession and Communion ought to be received frequently, extreme unction can be received as often as a person is in danger of death by sickness (for it is the sacrament of the dying), and marriage can be contracted more than once if one of the parties is dead.

255. **How many sacraments are there?**

There are seven sacraments: baptism, confirmation, Holy Eucharist, penance, extreme unction, holy order, and matrimony.

There have always been seven sacraments from the beginning of the Church. At the Reformation, five were discarded and only two retained—viz., baptism and the Lord's supper; but as the Anglican clergymen are not priests at all, there is really for them only one sacrament—viz., baptism. We know for certain from the Bible that our Lord established seven, and this will be seen when, treating of each sacrament in particular, we give the text upon which the institution of each sacrament rests.

There is a beautiful reason why our Lord made seven sacraments and not fewer nor more. You know the life of the body and the life of the soul are very similar to each other and have a very intimate relationship with each other. Now, in the life of the body (or natural life) there are, as it were, seven wants or necessities: 1) A man must be born in order to exist; so, in the life of the soul, a man must be born again of water and the Holy Ghost by baptism to exist as a Christian. 2) If he is to live, he must grow stronger; so, the spiritual life is strengthened by confirmation. 3) The body must be fed to preserve its life; so, the soul must be fed by the Holy Eucharist to keep God's life in it. 4) If the body falls sick, it must have medicine and other remedies to make it better again; so, the diseases of the soul, sins, are cured by penance. 5) When worn out, the strength of the body must be renewed and reinvigorated; so, extreme unction strengthens and comforts the soul at the approach of death. 6) There must always be an order of men, such as judges, magistrates, etc., to protect us and defend us from harm, robbery, etc.; so, there must be an order of men, selected and called by God and gifted with peculiar powers, to attend to the wants of our souls. And these men are fitted for their work by the sacrament of holy order; they are the bishops and priests. 7) The human race must be propagated by the natural means ordained by God; so, the sacrament of matrimony gives the husband and wife grace to bear the difficulties of their married life and to bring up their children in the love and fear of God.

Baptism

256. **What is baptism?**

Baptism is a sacrament which cleanses us from original sin, makes us Christians, children of God, and members of the Church.

Baptism is the first of the seven sacraments. It is the gate through which all must enter into the Church of God. Before a child is baptized, it is not a Christian. Baptism makes it one. It also takes away Adam's sin with which the soul is stained. It makes it a child of God, for it was a child of wrath and sin at first. Lastly, it makes it a member of the true Church and gives it a right to receive all the other sacraments. No sacrament can be given to an unbaptized person. From all this, you will understand what a terrible crime a parent commits by neglecting to have his child baptized.

257. **Does baptism also forgive actual sins?**

Baptism also forgives actual sins, with all punishment due to them, when it is received in proper dispositions by those who have been guilty of actual sin.

Sometimes, unfortunately, the baptism of children is neglected, and the child grows up without it. Through the providence of God, however, this may be discovered later on, and then the person is baptized as an adult. Of course, in infant baptism, instruction is impossible, for the child cannot understand, but before an adult can be baptized, he must be properly instructed in the Christian religion and make his act of faith in it.

Now, what takes place in his soul at baptism? First, the original sin which is still upon the soul is washed away, and with it every other sin, great and small, which he has committed since he came to the use of reason; for you cannot take away one particular sin and leave another—if one is forgiven, all are forgiven. Then, further, all the temporal punishment which is due to the justice of God[115] on account of his sins is taken away also, so that there is not the slightest vestige of the guilt of sin or punishment due to it upon that adult's soul, and, were he to die immediately after baptism, he would go straight to heaven. The proper dispositions of which the catechism speaks are 1) faith in what God has taught and 2) sorrow for sin.

258. **Who is the ordinary minister of baptism?**

The ordinary minister of baptism is a priest; but anyone may baptize in case of necessity, when a priest cannot be had.

Baptism is so absolutely necessary for salvation that our Lord allows anyone to baptize in case of necessity—that is, in case the proper person (the priest) cannot be obtained. Of course, this supposes that the child is dying, and there is no chance of getting a priest in time. Anybody's baptism is valid, provided it is done properly, and the person baptizing has the intention of doing what the Church requires. A Mahommedan or a heathen can baptize perfectly validly, even though they do not believe in baptism, so long as they intend in their minds to do what the Christians

[115] See q. 115, above.

do by that act, and that they pour the water properly, and at the same time say the right words, and in the right way.

Now, we sometimes hear people say, "so-and-so was baptized an Anglican, or a Wesleyan, or a Baptist," just as if there were various kinds of baptisms, or that a person became a member of a certain denomination because he was baptized by a minister of that sect or in a chapel belonging to that sect. There is only one real baptism—"One Lord, one faith, one baptism," says St. Paul in the letter to the Ephesians;[116] and that one baptism makes a child a member of God's one true Church—the one, holy, catholic, apostolic Church—that is, the Roman Catholic Church, for there is no other true Church and no other true religion. A child cannot be baptized a protestant, because protestantism is not a true religion, it is a protestation against the true religion: hence its name, *protest*-antism. Wesleyans, Baptists, etc., are sects which have broken off from the Church of England, and therefore, like their parent stock, are false forms of religion. Every child that is really baptized—no matter by whom—is thereby a Catholic and a member of Christ's Church. Baptism cannot make it a protestant or a Wesleyan or a Baptist because, once more, these are false religions.

259. **How is baptism given?**

Baptism is given by pouring water on the head of the child, saying at the same time these words: "I baptize thee in the name of the Father, and of the Son, and of the Holy Ghost."

There are three ways of baptizing, all, of course, with water—1) by immersion, or dipping; 2) by aspersion, or sprinkling; 3) by effusion, or pouring; and it is by this last method that the Church baptizes now.

The water must flow on the skin to signify the act of washing, for baptism washes original sin off the soul. Of course, baptism by immersion is all right if the proper words are used at the same time. Sprinkling is always dangerous, for very often the water does not flow off the child. Some protestant clergymen baptize by dipping their finger in water, and then tracing

[116] Eph 4:5

a cross on the child's forehead, whilst they pronounce the words. This is a very doubtful kind of baptism, as it means very often only damping the forehead instead of washing it, and the water does not really flow.

One cannot be too careful about baptism. It is absolutely necessary for salvation and there is only one right way of doing it; if it is not done that way, there is no baptism. Hence when a protestant or a member of any sect becomes a Catholic, it is usual to baptize such a one conditionally. The priest says, "John (or whatever the name may be), if thou art not baptized, I baptize thee in the name of the Father, and of the Son, and of the Holy Ghost." This makes all things safe in case he was not baptized properly before.

260. **What do we promise in baptism?**

We promise in baptism to renounce the devil and all his works and pomps.

That is, the godfather or godmother (for only one is necessary) makes this promise for us, and when we get old enough we must keep it. The office of godparent is to look after the child's faith and religious life in case the parents neglect it or in case they die whilst the child is young.

261. **Is baptism necessary for salvation?**

Baptism is necessary for salvation, because Christ has said: "Unless a man be born again of water and the Holy Ghost, he cannot enter into the kingdom of God."[117]

This has already been spoken about.[118] There is one thing about baptism which I should like to add. There are two other kinds of baptism besides that of water, and these, under certain circumstances, have the same effect as the baptism by water of which we have been speaking. They are called "the baptism of blood" and "the baptism of desire."

The baptism of blood took place in the martyrs, who proclaimed themselves to be Christians, and were put to death before they could really be

[117] Jn 3:5

[118] See q. 256, above.

baptized. They were baptized in the shedding of their blood for Christ, but at the same time God required from them an act of sorrow for their sins.

Even the infants who were put to death by Herod are honored by the Church as saints. They were not baptized with water, of course; but, because they were massacred for our Lord's sake, they suffered martyrdom, and were then baptized by the baptism of blood.

The baptism of desire is an ardent desire to be baptized on the part of one who is not baptized, when real baptism is not possible, as in the case of a person dying by drowning, or in a building which is on fire when escape is impossible; but again there must be joined to this desire a great sorrow for sins committed, and that sorrow must be perfect sorrow.[119]

Confirmation

262. **What is confirmation?**

Confirmation is a sacrament by which we receive the Holy Ghost, in order to make us strong and perfect Christians and soldiers of Jesus Christ.

The object of baptism is to make us Christians; the object of confirmation is to make us good and strong Christians. Baptism gives us the faith; confirmation strengthens it. The Holy Ghost is brought down upon us in this sacrament, as he came down upon the apostles and disciples on Pentecost day; and he brings with him all the graces we need, and which we shall need during our life, in order to profess our faith openly, and not to be ashamed of it, and to lead the lives of good, practical Catholics; so it is a very necessary sacrament. Of course, it is not absolutely necessary for salvation as baptism is, but still it would be a great sin to neglect to be confirmed if the opportunity presented itself, especially if the person were weak in his faith, or exposed to temptation against it.

Our Lord is generally supposed to have instituted this sacrament sometime between the resurrection and the ascension. We read of this sacrament being conferred by the apostles: "Now when the apostles, which were at Jerusalem, heard that Samaria had received the word of God, they sent

[119] See q. 287, below.

unto them Peter and John, who, when they were come down, prayed for them that they might receive the Holy Ghost, for as yet he was fallen upon none of them: only they had been baptized into the name of the Lord Jesus. Then laid they their hands on them, and they received the Holy Ghost."[120] Also, "And when Paul had laid his hands upon them, the Holy Ghost came on them and they spake with tongues and prophesied."[121]

263. **Who is the ordinary minister of confirmation?**

The ordinary minister of confirmation is a bishop.

He must be a real, validly consecrated bishop. Sometimes the pope gives permission to a simple priest to confirm, especially in missionary countries, in order that people may not be deprived of this sacrament.

264. **How does the bishop administer the sacrament of confirmation?**

The bishop administers the sacrament of confirmation by praying that the Holy Ghost may come down upon those who are to be confirmed; and by laying his hands on them, and making the sign of the cross with chrism on their foreheads, at the same time pronouncing certain words.

At the beginning of the ceremony, the bishop stretches out his hands over all who are to be confirmed, and prays that the Holy Ghost may come down upon them and bring his graces and gifts with him. Then each one kneels in front of the bishop, who makes the sign of the cross on his forehead with chrism, saying at the same time certain words.

265. **What are the words used in confirmation?**

The words used in confirmation are these: "I sign thee with the sign of the cross, and I confirm thee with the chrism of salvation in the name of the Father, and of the Son, and of the Holy Ghost. Amen."

The chrism is made of oil of olives and balsam, and is solemnly consecrated by the bishop every year on Holy Thursday, the day before Good Friday. Oil is used in confirmation as water is used in baptism. Water is

[120] Acts 8:14-17
[121] Acts 19:6

a sign of washing, oil is a sign of strengthening. We often hear of people strengthening weak joints by rubbing in oil, and as confirmation is a sacrament to strengthen us in our faith, the sacred oil is used as its sign, and, joined with the words and the imposition of hands, the anointing with the chrism really brings down the Holy Ghost upon us, in the same way as water, joined to the words of baptism, really makes us Christians. It is usual, though not necessary, to take another name when we are confirmed—the name of some angel or saint to whom we have a special devotion.

The Holy Eucharist

266. **What is the sacrament of the Holy Eucharist?**
The sacrament of the Holy Eucharist is the true body and blood of Jesus Christ, together with his soul and divinity, under the appearances of bread and wine.

We now come to a very important sacrament, one upon the reality of which Catholics and protestants hold very different views. We say that our Lord is really, truly, and substantially present, body and blood, soul and divinity in this sacrament—as really present there, as he is sitting on the right hand of God the Father in heaven. Most protestants deny this; they protest against this doctrine, and maintain that our Lord is only spiritually present, not really; only in figure, not in substance; and yet it is hard to reconcile this with the teaching of their *Book of Common Prayer*—in some parts of it, at any rate. Thus, in the catechism, the Anglican child is asked (speaking of the Lord's supper): "What is the inward part [of the sacrament] or thing signified?" The child's answer is: "The body and blood of Christ, which are verily and indeed taken and received by the faithful in the Lord's supper."

Again, in the Communion Service, just before the Communion is administered, the minister says in the name of the people, "Grant us, therefore, gracious Lord, so to eat the flesh of thy dear Son Jesus Christ, and drink his blood, that our sinful bodies may be made clean by his body, and our souls washed through his most precious blood." Delivering the Communion, the minister says, "The body of our Lord Jesus Christ, which was given for thee, preserve thy body and soul unto everlasting life"; and then he says, "The blood of our Lord Jesus Christ, which was shed for thee, preserve thy body and soul unto everlasting life." It seems as if the prayer book taught the real presence in some parts; and yet if we turn to the rubric at the end of the Communion Service, it distinctly states that the body of Christ is in heaven and not on earth. The rubric says, "Whereas it is ordained...that the communicants should receive the same kneeling,... yet, lest the same kneeling should by any person be misconstrued and depraved: it is hereby declared that thereby no adoration is intended or ought to be done either unto the sacramental bread or wine there bodily received, or unto any corporal presence of Christ's natural flesh and blood. For the sacramental bread and wine remain still in their very natural substances, and therefore may not be adored...and the natural body and blood of our Savior Christ are in heaven and not here; it being against the truth of Christ's natural body to be at one time in more places than one."

Martin Luther, who commenced the Reformation in Germany, says, "In vain I wished to have denied the real presence of Christ in the Eucharist, on purpose to have vexed the papists more effectually, but the words of the scripture are so plain and so strong in favor of the mystery, that I could never bring my mind to adopt the bold expedient."[122] Again, he says that among the ancient fathers of the Church there is not as much as one who ever entertained a doubt concerning the real presence of Christ in the Holy Eucharist.[123]

However, let us go on to the proofs of the real presence.

Just let us take the Bible and open it at St. John's gospel (chapter six). In this chapter, we have narrated to us the miracle of Christ feeding five thousand people with five barley loaves and two fishes; then the walking of Christ upon the sea; and, lastly, what we have to deal with—viz., the promise of the Holy Eucharist.

Let us commence at verse twenty-six. The Jews wanted more food, like that which they had had the previous day. Our Lord knew it and taxed

[122] Luther, *Ep. car. amico*

[123] Cf. Luther, *Defens. Verb. Caenae*

them with it, at the same time upbraiding them for their want of faith in him. "Ye seek me, not because ye saw signs [miracles], but because ye ate of the loaves and were filled. Work not for the meat which perisheth, but for the meat which abideth unto eternal life, which the Son of man shall give unto you." Here is our Lord's promise to give a food much superior to ordinary food—a food which will give them eternal life.

The Jews naturally were surprised and delighted, and replied: "What must we do that we may work the works of God?" Jesus answered and said unto them: "This is the work of God, that ye believe in him whom he hath sent." Here, you see, he asks for faith from them—faith in himself and in his words. This the Jews understood, for they immediately ask, "What, then, doest thou for a sign, that we may see and believe thee?" forgetting already the miracle of the day before. Then they remind our Lord of the manna which their forefathers ate in the desert, as though they thought that this new food would be the same. But our Lord tells them that the manna did not really come from heaven, but that his Father will give them the true bread from heaven. Then the Jews at once replied: "Lord, evermore give us this bread." Jesus then speaks plainly, and says, "I am the bread of life." This rather astonishes them, and they began to murmur at him, and said to each other: "Is not this Jesus, the son of Joseph, whose father and mother we know? How doth he now say, 'I am come down out of heaven'? What does he mean by saying that he came down from heaven?" But our Lord takes no notice of their murmuring. Again, he asks them to believe in him, and then repeats what he has already said: "I am the bread of life...I am the living bread which came down out of heaven. If any man eat of this bread he shall live forever." And now our Lord tells them plainly what that bread is. "And the bread which I will give is my flesh for the life of the world."

The Jews understood perfectly what our Lord meant—that is, that he would give them his flesh to eat—for they ask at once: "How can this man give us his flesh to eat?" Our Lord does not answer that question, for he knew that they understood him perfectly well, but they would not believe him. Now he apparently gets angry with them and threatens them: "Verily, verily, I say unto you, except ye eat the flesh of the Son of man and drink his blood, ye have not life in yourselves. He that eateth my flesh and drinketh my blood hath eternal life, and I will raise him up at the last day. For my flesh is meat indeed, and my blood is drink indeed..."

Now many of the Jews when they heard this said: "This is a hard saying. Who can hear it?" They would not believe our Lord, and many of them left him, and walked away; and Jesus let them go, knowing that they distinctly understood him to mean that someday he would give his real body and his real blood to be the food of their souls.

Now I ask you one question. If Jesus had only meant that they were to receive a figure of his body and blood (not the real body and blood), do you not think he would have called them back and said so? Would he have let them go away with a wrong impression, especially on so important a matter? Our knowledge of our Lord's goodness certainly forbids our thinking so. No. The Jews understood him well enough, but they would not believe.

Then our Lord turned to his twelve apostles, and asked them if they too were going away. "Lord," replied St. Peter, "to whom shall we go? Thou hast the words of eternal life." We know thy words are true, though we cannot understand everything, "and we have believed and know that thou art the holy one of God." (The real words are: "That thou art the Christ, the Son of God.") So you see that this is a sacrament of faith, and *faith* means "believing what God has said, even though we do not understand it, or see how it is, or can be, done."

Now we come to the fulfillment of Christ's promise that he would give his body and blood as the food of our souls.

Just turn to the description of the last supper as recorded in St. Luke's gospel:[124] "And he took bread, and when he had given thanks, he brake it and gave to them, saying, 'This is my body which is given for you: this do in remembrance of me.' And the cup in like manner after supper, saying, 'This cup is the new covenant in my blood, even that which is poured out for you.'" Now turn to St. Paul's first epistle to the Corinthians:[125] "For I received of the Lord that which also I delivered unto you, how that the

[124] Lk 22:19-20

[125] 1 Cor 11:23-25

Lord Jesus in the night in which he was betrayed, took bread, and when he had given thanks, he brake it, and said, 'This is my body which is [broken] for you. This do in remembrance of me.' In like manner, also the cup after supper, saying, 'This cup is the new covenant in my blood. This do as often as ye drink it in remembrance of me.'" Again, in the same epistle, St. Paul says, "The cup of blessing which we bless, is it not a communion of the blood of Christ? The bread which we break, is it not a communion of the body of Christ?"[126]

Now one or two remarks on these passages of the Bible. First, the words of our Lord at the last supper. He takes the bread in his sacred hands, and says, "This is my body." He does not say, "This is a figure of my body," nor, "This bread is my body," but, "This [which I hold in my hand] is my body." In the same way does he speak and act with the wine, saying that it is his blood. Remember, Jesus Christ was the God who made the world out of nothing; surely, then, his omnipotent power could change one substance into another. Again, he was alone with his apostles, and for the last time. He had looked forward to that last supper with eagerness. "With desire I desired to eat this passover with you before I suffer."[127] Surely our Lord would speak plainly to them then, and not leave them, or their successors, any room to doubt the meaning of his words. If he really meant to change the bread and wine into his body and blood, could he have chosen plainer words or plainer language? Well, many non-Catholics do admit that our Lord did really change the bread and wine into his body and blood, but they say that he meant them and others only to take bread and wine in remembrance of him. "He uses the very word *remembrance*," they say, "and when we take the sacrament, we remember what our Lord did for us." Precisely; but what did our Lord really say before the word *remembrance*? "Do this," he said, "in remembrance of me."

"Do what?" we may ask. "Do what I have done," our Lord would reply. What had he just done? He had changed the bread and wine into his real body and blood, and he tells his apostles to do it—to do the same—viz.,

[126] 1 Cor 10:16
[127] Lk 22:15

to take bread and wine, and by the power which he then gave them in those words, "Do this," to change the bread and wine into his real body and blood. This is the meaning of our Lord's words, and this is what the apostles did. This is what St. Paul alludes to when he says, "The cup which we bless, is it not a communion of the blood of Christ; and the bread which we break, is it not a communion of the body of Christ?"[128]

Of course, whenever they did it, it made them remember what our Lord had done at the last supper. So you see the force of our Lord's words does not lie in the words, *in remembrance*, but in the words, *Do this*.

Protestants, then, are wrong, and pervert Christ's meaning, when they say it is only a remembrance. No; it is a reality. When the apostles consecrated the bread and wine, Christ's living body and blood were there truly, really, and substantially on the altar. When the bishops and priests of the Church, who are the successors of the apostles, say Mass, they are doing what the first priests (the apostles) did; and when they consecrate, Christ's body and blood are as equally, truly, really, and substantially present upon the altar; and when they give Holy Communion to the people, they give them the real, living body and blood of Christ. This is how the people can fulfill the command which Christ gave in St. John's gospel: "Except ye eat the flesh of the Son of man, and drink his blood, ye have not life in yourselves. He that eateth my flesh and drinketh my blood hath eternal life, and I will raise him up in the last day."[129]

This explanation of the Holy Eucharist has been rather long, but it was necessary to enable you to understand the words of the catechism.

In Holy Communion, the appearances of the bread and wine still remain. By the *appearances*, I mean that it looks like bread and wine, it tastes like them, it feels like them. It is not the outward form or appearances that are changed, but only the substance concealed under these appearances. If you had seen the infant Jesus in the stable at Bethlehem, you would have seen only the outward appearance of a child, yet that child was God. In the same way, if you had been present at the crucifixion, you would have seen

[128] 1 Cor 10:16
[129] Jn 6:54-55

only the outward form of a dying man, yet that dying man was your Savior the Son of God, who was redeeming you and saving you from eternal loss. So, in the Blessed Eucharist you do not see the real presence, but only the outward appearance of it, the outward form of the bread and wine—but it is really Jesus Christ's body and blood because he has said so.

267. **How are the bread and wine changed into the body and blood of Christ?**
The bread and wine are changed into the body and blood of Christ by the power of God, to whom nothing is impossible or difficult.

268. **When are the bread and wine changed into the body and blood of Christ?**
The bread and wine are changed into the body and blood of Christ when the words of consecration, ordained by Jesus Christ, are pronounced by the priest in the Holy Mass.

The words of consecration used by the priest are: "This is my body. This is the chalice of my blood of the new and eternal testament, the mystery of faith, which shall be shed for you and for many to the remission of sins." The instant these words are pronounced by a real, validly ordained priest, the substance of the bread and wine is changed into the substance of the living body and blood of Christ. This doctrine of the Church is called "the doctrine of transubstantiation," which means "the changing of one substance into another."

269. **Why has Christ given himself to us in the Holy Eucharist?**
Christ has given himself to us in the Holy Eucharist to be the life and the food of our souls. "He that eateth me, the same also shall live by me...He that eateth this bread shall live for ever."[130]

Our Lord well knew the terrible evil original sin had caused in the soul of man. He knew how darkened his intellect had become, how weak his will was, how powerless it was to fight against temptation and sin by itself. He knew that it would need a supernatural and a divine power to assist it

[130] Jn 6:58-59

in its struggle, and that is why he gave it his own body and blood to be its food and strength.

270. **Is Christ received whole and entire under either kind alone?**
Christ is received whole and entire under either kind alone.

One great objection that protestants have against us is that the cup is not given to the laity, and they cannot understand why it should be denied to them.

In the first place, I reply, it is not necessary from a Catholic point of view, because Christ did not give that as a precept to the laity. "Drink ye all of this," was addressed to the apostles, who had been ordained priests at the last supper. Secondly, Catholics believe that the Holy Eucharist is the living body of Jesus Christ. In receiving Communion, therefore, under the form of bread only, they receive the living body of our Lord. Now, if the body is living, it must have the precious blood joined with it, otherwise it would be a dead, lifeless body, but Christ "dieth no more";[131] therefore, in their Communion under the form of bread, they receive both the living body and blood of Christ, and there is no necessity to receive the cup. This is merely a matter of discipline. The history of the Church about it has been the following:

Up to the fifth century, Christians were free to receive under both kinds, or under one kind only. During the existence of the Manichean heresy, which taught that wine was a creature of the devil, those infected with this heresy received Holy Communion under the form of bread only, and no one could detect their heresy. In order to correct this, Pope Leo I, in the year 443, and Pope Gelasius, in 496, issued a decree that all should communicate under both kinds. When the heresy ceased, the people were free to receive under either kind as before.

By degrees, the custom of receiving under the form of bread only prevailed and became general. In the fifteenth century, it became a strict law of the Church that the laity should receive Holy Communion under the form of bread only. Some protestants will say, "Did not Christ say, 'Drink

[131] Rom 6:9

ye all of this' at the last supper, and does not this constitute a command to receive the cup?" Well, we have already said these words were not addressed to the laity, but to the apostles, who were priests. Besides, the same Jesus Christ said: "If any man eat of this bread" (he says nothing here about the cup) "he shall live for ever";[132] also, "The bread which I shall give is my flesh for the life of the world."[133] St. Paul speaks very plainly in his first epistle to the Corinthians: "Wherefore, whosoever shall eat the bread or drink the cup of the Lord unworthily shall be guilty of the body and the blood of the Lord."[134] Before the protestant Bible was revised, this passage used to be "and drink," etc. The reformers changed the word of God, and substituted the word *and* for the real word *or* in order to suit their own views. Now it is changed back in the Revised Version to its original text.

Further, although Christ instituted the Holy Eucharist at the last supper under both kinds, yet, when he appeared to the two disciples going to Emmaus, he administered Communion to them under the form of bread only.[135] In the Acts of the Apostles, the Communion under one kind is again alluded to.[136] Lastly, if it were a strict command to receive Holy Communion under both kinds, how difficult it would be for the sick or the paralyzed to receive it; for if the consecrated wine were spilt, remember it would be the blood of Jesus Christ, and the profanation would be terrible. Of course, in the protestant Communion, as it is only ordinary wine, an accident would not be of much consequence; but, with the real precious blood of Christ, it is a very serious difference.

271. **In order to receive the Blessed Sacrament worthily, what is required?**

In order to receive the Blessed Sacrament worthily, it is required that we be in a state of grace and fasting from midnight.

[132] Jn 6:52
[133] Ibid.
[134] 1 Cor 11:27
[135] Cf. Lk 24:30
[136] Cf. Acts 2:42; 20:7

272. **What is it to be in a state of grace?**

To be in a state of grace is to be free from mortal sin and pleasing to God.

There are two things requisite to make a good Communion. One regards the body—viz., that we should be fasting from food or drink; that is, that we should not have taken anything by way of food or drink from midnight until we receive Communion next morning. Even supposing a person is taken ill during the night and is obliged to take medicine, that breaks the fast. If anything be taken accidentally, without thought, during the night, the fast is broken, and the person may not go to Communion that day. In case of dangerous illness, Communion may be received when the fast has been broken. It is then called the "viaticum," which means "food for a journey." The object of the fast is to show reverence to the Blessed Sacrament, which should be the first thing we receive into our bodies. The fast before Communion was not enforced immediately after our Lord's time, but on account of the abuses which crept in even in the time of the apostles,[137] it soon became obligatory and has continued so ever since. An alteration was recently made (December 7, 1906) regarding the Communion of the sick. Up to that time, the sick who desired to receive Communion were bound to receive it fasting. Now, however, all persons confined to their homes by reason of indisposition may, on the advice of their confessor, receive Communion even if they are not fasting, provided 1) they have been sick for a month; 2) that there is no certain hope of a speedy recovery; 3) that only liquid food or medicine be taken. When these conditions exist, Communion may be given once or twice a week.

The second condition concerns the soul. There must not be any mortal sin of which we are conscious on the soul. If a person is in a state of mortal sin and still wishes to go to Communion, he must go to confession first and receive absolution; then he may go.

How often ought we to receive Holy Communion? The Church has recently changed her discipline very considerably in the matter. Now anybody may go to Communion, even daily, provided they are in a state of grace and they have a right intention in going—viz., to get more grace for

[137] Cf. 1 Cor 11:21

their souls, to lead a more perfect life. It would, of course, be wrong to go out of vanity or to be thought well of by others, or merely through custom or because others are going.

273. **Is it a great sin to receive Holy Communion in mortal sin?**

It is a great sin to receive Holy Communion in mortal sin; "for he that eateth and drinketh unworthily eateth and drinketh judgment to himself."[138]

I suppose this would be the greatest sin a person could commit, for it would be forcing the God of holiness to descend into a soul which was at that moment his enemy.

274. **Is the Blessed Eucharist a sacrament only?**

The Blessed Eucharist is not a sacrament only; it is also a sacrifice.

275. **What is a sacrifice?**

A sacrifice is the offering of a victim by a priest to God alone, in testimony of his being the sovereign Lord of all things.

276. **What is the sacrifice of the new law?**

The sacrifice of the new law is the Holy Mass.

We now come to the second end for which our Lord instituted the Holy Eucharist—viz., to be the Christian's act of worship. This is what we mean by the Mass. God has always wished to be worshipped by sacrifice. In the fourth chapter of Genesis, we read of Cain and Abel offering sacrifices to God—the one of the fruits of the earth, the other of the firstlings of his flock. When Noah went out of the ark after the flood, he built an altar and sacrificed to God, according to God's own appointment, birds and beasts which had been preserved in the ark for that very purpose.[139] Melchisedech offered bread and wine in sacrifice, "for he was priest of the most high God."[140]

[138] 1 Cor 11:29
[139] Cf. Gn 8:20
[140] Gn 14:18

In the law of Moses, there were four kinds of sacrifice, all ordered by God—viz., the holocaust, the eucharistic sacrifice, and the propitiatory and impetratory sacrifices. These sacrifices were instituted to enable man to fulfill his four great duties toward God. The holocaust (a whole burnt offering) was to acknowledge that God was his supreme Lord and master; the eucharistic sacrifice was offered to thank God for his benefits; the propitiatory (appeasing) to obtain the pardon of sin; and the impetratory (begging) to ask for all the blessings he stood in need of.

Man, therefore, has four duties to God: 1) to worship him, 2) to thank him, 3) to beg his forgiveness for his sins, 4) to ask for what he wants for body and soul. And the Jews were commanded to offer and assist at these sacrifices to fulfill these four duties. This is how God intended they should worship him—viz., by sacrifice.

Now, we Christians have, of course, these same duties toward God, and we have to worship him in the same way as the Jews did—viz., by sacrifice. The true Christian religion, therefore, must have a true Christian sacrifice, at which the people can and must assist in order to worship God. All the sacrifices of the Jews were only types and figures of the true sacrifice of the new law. The prophet Malachias foretold that the Jewish sacrifices would be done away with, and that another sacrifice (a pure oblation) would be substituted in their place. "I have no pleasure in you, saith the Lord of hosts, neither will I accept an offering at your hand, for, from the rising of the sun even unto the going down of the same, my name is [or shall be] great amongst the Gentiles; and in every place incense and a pure oblation are [shall be] offered unto my name, for my name is great amongst the Gentiles, saith the Lord God of hosts."[141] The Catholic version says, "And in every place there is sacrifice and there is offered to my name a clean oblation for my name is great among the Gentiles, saith the Lord of hosts."

Here the prophet of God foretells (for he is speaking of the future) that among the Gentiles (that is, amongst us) there shall be offered to God a clean or pure oblation in every part of the world. These words of the prophet must be fulfilled. So the pure, clean sacrifice is in existence now,

141 Mal 1:10-11

and in existence in every place; it must be offered everywhere. The prophet cannot have meant only the death of Jesus Christ on the cross, for this took place only once and in one place. Now, what is this sacrifice which the prophet speaks of? It is the Mass, the act of worship of the Catholic Church. The Mass is the continuation of the sacrifice of the cross; for although Christ does not really die and shed his blood in the Sacrifice of the Mass, yet he does so in appearance, for after the words of consecration pronounced by the priest ("This is my body; this is the chalice of my blood") the living body and blood of Christ are really present on the altar, and appear to be separated from each other as if Christ were really sacrificed and dead. This is what St. Paul alludes to when he says in his first epistle to the Corinthians, "As often as ye eat this bread and drink this cup, ye proclaim [or show forth] the death of the Lord until he come."[142]

277. **What is the Holy Mass?**

The Holy Mass is the sacrifice of the body and blood of Jesus Christ, really present on the altar under the appearance of bread and wine, and offered to God for the living and the dead.

This is, then, the pure, clean offering or sacrifice which the prophet Malachias foretold should be offered to God in every place, for the Mass is said all over the world. By assisting at this sacrifice, Christians can properly fulfill their four duties to God.

1) In the Mass, they can really worship God; the offering of the body and blood of Jesus Christ gives God supreme worship, for Jesus takes our worship and joins it to his own and makes it worthy of God; 2) we cannot properly thank God of ourselves, so Jesus Christ does it for us in the Mass, and our thanksgiving, too, becomes worthy of God; 3) we cannot of ourselves be properly sorry for our sins, so Jesus Christ offers his sorrow for ours and obtains the gift of real sorrow for us; and, lastly, 4) it is only through him that all good can come to us, and this is why we always end our prayers "through Jesus Christ our Lord."

[142] 1 Cor 11:26

Now, I think you can understand why we are commanded under pain of sin to assist at the Mass on certain days—because we are bound to adore and worship God, and the Mass is the means appointed by God for that purpose; therefore, we must assist at it. If we refuse to do so we are refusing to adore God, to thank him for his benefits, to ask his forgiveness and to acknowledge our dependence upon him, and this is a great sin.

278. **Is the Holy Mass one and the same sacrifice with that of the cross?**
The Holy Mass is one and the same sacrifice with that of the cross, inasmuch as Christ, who offered himself, a bleeding victim, on the cross to his heavenly Father, continues to offer himself in an unbloody manner on the altar, through the ministry of his priests.

On the cross and in the Mass there is the same victim, Jesus Christ. He was really on the cross. He is really present on the altar. The sacrifice of the cross redeemed us, the Sacrifice of the Mass applies that redemption to our souls and gives us the means of fulfilling our four essential duties to God.[143] There is but one difference, and it is this: on the cross, Jesus really shed his precious blood and he died; in the Mass, he sheds his blood mystically, in appearance, and does not really die, but only mystically and in appearance. If you could see on the altar after the consecration, you would see the consecrated bread and wine separate from each other; it seems as if the body and blood of our Lord were separated from each other as if he were really dead. St. Paul says, in the first epistle to the Corinthians, "As often as ye eat this bread and drink this cup, ye proclaim [or show forth] the Lord's death till he come."[144] Therefore, when the apostles did what our Lord told them to do at the last supper, they proclaimed, they showed forth, they represented his death, and this has to go on "till he come"—that is, till the end of the world—so the proclaiming or showing forth or representing of the death of our Lord must always go on, and this it does in the Mass. The Mass, therefore, cannot be "a blasphemous fable," as protestants make it out to be.

[143] See q. 276, paragraph 3, above.
[144] 1 Cor 11:26

One word more. In vain do we look for anything like a sacrifice in the protestant religion. They have a Communion Service—the relics, the remains of the Mass which at one time was the Christian act of worship in Catholic England. The reformers abolished the Mass and called it "a blasphemous fable," but they substituted no act of worship in its place. Where there is no sacrifice, there are no priests, and a religion which has no sacrifice nor priests cannot be the religion of Christ. Ritualists are beginning to celebrate what they call "Mass," but the Church of England, whose ministers they are, calls it "a fable"; if three hundred years ago they had done what they are now doing, they would have been hanged, drawn, and quartered as priests, and their heads put up on London Bridge by the very authors of their own religion.

279. **For what ends is the Sacrifice of the Mass offered?**
The Sacrifice of the Mass is offered for four ends—first, to give supreme honor and glory to God; secondly, to thank him for all his benefits; thirdly, to satisfy God for our sins and to obtain the grace of repentance; and fourthly, to obtain all other graces and blessings through Jesus Christ.

This we have already spoken of. No further explanation seems necessary.

280. **Is the Mass also a memorial of the passion and death of our Lord?**
The Mass is also a memorial of the passion and death of our Lord, for Christ at his last supper said, "Do this for a commemoration of me."[145]

It was at the last supper, as we have already explained, that Christ gave his apostles power to change bread and wine into his body and blood, and to offer him up to his heavenly Father in sacrifice, by saying, "Do this." Whenever the apostles performed this great act, they remembered what our Lord had done—they commemorated his great sacrifice.

One thing that often puzzles protestants is our having our services, like the Mass or benediction or baptism or the burial service, etc., in Latin. Well, there are some serious reasons for it; let me give you one or two. You

[145] Lk 22:19

know that the Latin language and the meanings of its words never change, and the Church has kept it as her language so as to prevent any change in her doctrine. The meanings of words in our modern languages change very much; for instance, the word *worship* in its present meaning refers to the worship of God, divine worship; but, formerly, it simply meant "respect" or "reverence." In the marriage service, the bridegroom says to the bride, "With my body I thee worship"; it simply means "reverence" there, for no one would think of giving divine honor to a creature.

Again, we speak of "His Worship the Mayor"—that does not mean that the mayor ought to be worshipped; so this one word *worship* has completely changed its meaning.

Moreover, when a Catholic goes abroad, he finds the Mass just the same as he has it in England. He is quite at home at once, and can attend to his Mass just as easily as he could in his own church here, even though he does not know a word of the language of the country he is visiting.

Moreover, in all our prayer books, you always find the English translation side by side with the Latin words, so that you can follow all that the priest is saying.

Penance

281. **What is the sacrament of penance?**

Penance is a sacrament whereby the sins, whether mortal or venial, which we have committed after baptism are forgiven.

I have already explained a good deal about the forgiveness of sin, and it would be well for you just to turn back for a few moments and read what I have said about it under the tenth article of the Creed.[146] We have now to deal with the forgiveness of actual sins, mortal or venial[147]—viz., those which are committed by a person who has already been baptized. A person cannot be baptized a second time for the remission of these sins;

[146] See q. 110ff, above.

[147] See q. 121-127, above.

some other sacrament is necessary for that. This sacrament is called the sacrament of penance.

282. **Does the sacrament of penance increase the grace of God in the soul?**
The sacrament of penance increases the grace of God in the soul, besides forgiving sin; we should, therefore, often go to confession.

The sacrament of penance has a twofold effect upon the soul of the sinner—1) it remits, or takes away, the sins which have been committed, provided, of course, the sinner is properly prepared for receiving pardon; and 2) it gives a special grace and help not to commit the same sins again. It increases the grace of God—that is, it strengthens the soul so as to enable it more easily and more readily to fight against temptations. So you see why, as the catechism says, it is a good thing to go to confession often, because the oftener we receive absolution, the more strength we get, and the more we are able to resist sin. The Church only binds us to go once a year, but that is hardly sufficient to help a person to lead a good life. A dinner now and then will scarcely keep your body in a good state of health; you must feed it regularly, otherwise it grows weak and is liable to fall into illness.

283. **When did our Lord institute the sacrament of penance?**
Our Lord instituted the sacrament of penance when he breathed on his apostles, and gave them power to forgive sins, saying: "Whose sins you shall forgive, they are forgiven."[148]

Let us for a moment turn to the old testament and see what was the custom amongst the Jews about the forgiveness of sins. In the book of Numbers, we read: "And the Lord spake unto Moses: 'When a man or woman shall commit any sin that men commit, to do a trespass against the Lord, and that soul be guilty; then they shall confess their sin which they have done: and he shall make restitution for his guilt in full.'"[149] Also in the book of Joshua: "Joshua said unto Achan, 'My son, give, I pray thee, glory to the Lord, the God of Israel, and make confession unto him, and

[148] Jn 20:23
[149] Nm 5:5-7

tell me now what thou hast done, hide it not from me.'"[150] You see from these two passages that confession of sin was used in the old testament. But it is, of course, with the words of our Lord in the new testament that we have to deal principally.

Our Lord instituted this sacrament of penance on the occasion of his first apparition to his disciples after the resurrection. "Jesus, therefore, said to them again: 'Peace be unto you: as the Father hath sent me, even so send I you.' And when he had said this, he breathed on them, and saith unto them: 'Receive ye the Holy Ghost: whosesoever sins ye forgive, they are forgiven unto them; whosesoever sins ye retain, they are retained."[151] In these words we have a distinct power given by our Lord to his apostles to forgive sin, and a distinct engagement that the sins forgiven by his apostles should be forgiven by him; he would ratify in heaven the sentence of forgiveness pronounced by them over the sinner on earth.

Moreover, a second power he gives them, and a second engagement too: that if the apostles refused to forgive (retain) the sins, he, too, would refuse to forgive (or would retain). From this it follows that forgiveness of sin could only be obtained by applying for it to the apostles of our Lord, and to them alone; for to no other people did our Lord give this power of forgiving sins. This power did not expire or die with the apostles; it was given as much for us as for the people of those days; therefore, this power must have been handed down to all those who have succeeded the apostles in their work as God's ministers, and these successors are the bishops and priests of the Catholic Church.

Some people, especially protestants, while agreeing that the power of forgiving sins exists on earth, seem to think that our Lord left it optional, or as a matter of choice, to us to go to confession or not, just as we like. Well, I suppose we all agree that we must get our mortal sins forgiven somehow before we die, or we shall be lost. If confession is a matter of choice, our Lord must have left some other means of getting rid of sin. But what means? What are these means? He said to his apostles (and this he meant,

[150] Jo 7:19
[151] Jn 20:21-23

of course, for their successors as long as the Church should last) that if they (and their successors) retained the people's sins, he should retain them too; therefore, there was no forgiveness except through them, nor is there any forgiveness now except through their successors. Hence we are bound to confess our sins to a priest of God's true Church if we want them forgiven.

Now, let me give you a few more instances of the power of forgiving sins mentioned in the new testament. Look for a moment at St. Matthew's gospel.[152] There we read the history of the "man sick of the palsy, lying on a bed: and Jesus seeing their faith said unto the sick of the palsy, 'Son, be of good cheer, thy sins are forgiven.' And, behold, certain of the scribes said within themselves, 'This man blasphemeth.' And Jesus knowing their thoughts said, 'Wherefore think ye evil in your hearts? For whether is it easier to say, Thy sins are forgiven; or to say, Arise and walk? But that ye may know that the Son of man hath power on earth to forgive sins' (then saith he to the sick of the palsy), 'Arise, and take up thy bed and go unto thy house.' And he arose, and departed to his house. But when the multitudes saw it, they were afraid, and glorified God which had given such power unto men." Our Lord here performs a wonderful miracle to prove that, as the Son of Man, he had power to forgive sin. The scribes took him to be a man, and said so: "This man blasphemeth." Our Lord does not correct them, but leaves them under that impression—viz., that as man he had received power from God to forgive sin—and the people glorify God for having given power to man to forgive sin. Surely if this impression had been wrong, if God never intended to give this power to man, our Lord would have corrected their impression at once, as he always did if the people mistook him or his meaning.

In St. Paul's second epistle to the Corinthians, the apostle says that he forgives the wicked Corinthian "in the person of Christ."[153] In the first epistle of St. John, the apostle says: "If we say that we have no sin, we deceive ourselves, and the truth is not in us. If we confess our sins, he is faithful and righteous to forgive us our sins, and to cleanse us from all

[152] Cf. Mt 9:2-8
[153] 2 Cor 2:10

unrighteousness."[154] Lastly, turn to the epistle of St. James and you will read these words: "Confess, therefore, your sins one to another, and pray for one another, that ye may be healed" (that is, saved).[155]

284. **How does the priest forgive sins?**
The priest forgives sins by the power of God when he pronounces the words of absolution.

285. **What are the words of absolution?**
The words of absolution are: "I absolve thee from thy sins in the name of the Father, and of the Son, and of the Holy Ghost."

Of course, as a man, the priest has indeed no more power to forgive sin than any other individual, but at his ordination to the priesthood, this special power of forgiving sins was given to him to use as part of his priestly office, just in the same way as one of His Majesty's judges condemns a man to death or acquits him, not of his own power as Mr. So-and-so, but by the power which the King conferred upon him when he appointed him one of his judges. The King alone in this kingdom has the power to condemn a man to death (God alone has the power to forgive sin); but the King can delegate his power of life and death to others (God can give his own power of forgiving sin to others). When a judge condemns a murderer to death or acquits him, he (the judge) really does it. He does not say, "The King sentences you to death" or "acquits you," but, "I do it." So the priest in absolution does not say, "God absolves thee from all thy sins," but, "I absolve thee"; but, of course, it is done in God's name and by God's power.

In the same way, in baptism we do not say, "God baptizes thee in the name of the Father," etc., but, "I baptize thee," etc.

286. **Are any conditions for forgiveness required on the part of the penitent?**
Three conditions for forgiveness are required on the part of the penitent: contrition, confession, and satisfaction.

[154] 1 Jn 1:8-9
[155] Jas 5:16

The penitent is the person who goes to confession. The first of the three conditions for the forgiveness of sin is contrition: it is the first and the most important; so important, indeed, that without it God cannot and will not forgive any sin, no matter how trifling it may be.

287. **What is contrition?**

Contrition is a hearty sorrow for our sins because by them we have offended so good a God, together with a firm purpose of amendment.

The doctrine of the Catholic Church about contrition, or sorrow for sin, is that "it is a grief of mind and a detestation (hatred) of sin committed, with a resolution of not sinning for the future...This contrition contains not a cessation from sin only, but likewise a detestation of the old (sins)."[156]

How different all this sounds from the popular idea of protestants about confession—viz., that all a man has to do is to confess his sins and then go and commence committing them again! No wonder they cry out against it and say it is wicked and an abomination; so, indeed, it would be if their idea were true, for confession then would simply amount to a mockery of God. But, in the mind of a Catholic, confession means something very different; it means that a man must be sincerely and truly sorry for his past sins, and must have made up his mind not to commit them again, and, further, to avoid all occasions, such as persons and places, which have led him into those sins before.

It means a complete alteration of his life and habits. He knows that, and is prepared for it when he goes to confession. Those Catholics who cannot make up their minds to leave off sin, stop away from confession; they know full well that it would only be tempting and mocking God to presume to approach this sacrament in that state. Now, the catechism says that contrition is a hearty sorrow. This word does not mean that a man has to shed tears or feel the sorrow that he would feel if his wife or child died; that is only human sorrow, and is of no use for confession. He must have a sincere, thorough "grief of mind"—that means that he must realize in his mind how grievous a thing sin is before God; and then, when his

[156] Council of Trent, Session 14, "Doctrine on the Sacrament of Penance," Ch. 4

mind does realize this, it influences his will, and he says to himself, "Well, as sin is such a terrible thing, I will not commit it again, and because such-and-such a person or such-and-such a place has been the cause of my past sin, I will leave that company and that place, and this will be a practical proof to God that I am really sorry for my sins." This is the sorrow we must bring with us when we go to confession, and it is the one condition on which God will forgive us.

There is one thing that people sometimes make a mistake about, and that is about feeling sorry; they think they are not sorry for their sins because they do not feel sorry. Sorrow has nothing whatever to do with the human feelings, which often deceive us. What we must try to make sure of is that we detest sin in our minds, as I have already said, that if we had our time to come over again we would not do the same sins again, and that we are determined with God's help to avoid them for the future.

288. **What is a firm purpose of amendment?**

A firm purpose of amendment is a resolution to avoid, by the grace of God, not only sin but also the dangerous occasions of sin.

A firm purpose does not mean merely a wish or desire to be better, but a real, sincere determination to be better for the future; and, as I have already said, it must include a determination to break with whatever has led us into sin in the past, no matter how dear that occasion of sin has been to us.

It may happen, sometimes, that we cannot possibly get away from whatever has been the cause of sin to us; then, at least, we must be prepared to do all that the priest advises us to do to make that occasion of sin less dangerous to us. A priest can always tell you how to keep out of sin, and how to avoid it, for it is not merely a priest's work in confession to absolve us from our sins, but also to guide and direct us as to the proper means of leading a good life for the future.

289. **How may we obtain a hearty sorrow for our sins?**

We may obtain a hearty sorrow for our sins by earnestly praying for it, and by making use of such considerations as may lead us to it.

It is not, of course, always an easy thing for a man to be really sorry for his sins, and to do all that real sorrow requires of him. A man, for instance, who is fond of drunkenness, or fond of any crime, will find it desperately hard to begin all of a sudden to hate and detest what he has loved for so long, and yet he must detest the sins he has committed before God will forgive him. The Council of Trent distinctly says that sorrow is a "detestation of sins committed."[157] What, then, must he do if he wants to make himself right with God? He must begin to pray, and to pray hard to God for the sorrow which is so necessary for him. Many people assist at Mass several times before going to confession, because in the Sacrifice of the Mass our Lord himself intercedes for them, and then God gives a most abundant sorrow. To his prayers the man must add some thoughts or reflections in his mind as to the terrible evil sin has done in his soul, and how it has grievously offended his God, who made him to love and serve him. The catechism now puts before our minds three thoughts that will help us to understand the wickedness of sin.

290. **What consideration concerning God will lead us to sorrow for our sins?** This consideration concerning God will lead us to sorrow for our sins: that by our sins we have offended God, who is infinitely good in himself and infinitely good to us.

This is the highest and best reason for our sorrow, and pleases God most. The power of love is very great. We feel ready to do almost anything for those whom we love on account of their goodness, and nothing pains us more than to feel that we have forfeited their love. To do anything that would make us forfeit God's love ought to be a source of intense sorrow to us. And, besides, God has been, and is, so good to us. He made us, and redeemed us, and has promised heaven to us for all eternity. Could he have done more? Deliberate, grievous sin despises and rejects God's love for us.

[157] Ibid.

291. **What consideration concerning our Savior will lead us to sorrow for our sins?**

This consideration concerning our Savior will lead us to sorrow for our sins: that our Savior died for our sins, and that those who sin grievously "crucify again to themselves the Son of God, making him a mockery."[158]

Our Lord Jesus Christ died in bitter agony on the cross to expiate sin, to reconcile us to God, and to save us from being lost in hell. He was not bound to suffer as he did. One tear shed by him, one act of sorrow made by him for our sins would have expiated them and the sins of ten thousand worlds. Why, then, did he suffer so much pain? Simply to show the excess of his love for us. When we commit mortal sin, we make a mockery of his sufferings; we render them powerless and useless to us. One of the tortures of the souls in hell for all eternity will be the knowledge of what Jesus Christ had done to save them, and how easy it would have been for them to have been saved: they had every help, but they would not use it. Their damnation is their own doing, for they have spurned and despised their Savior's love.

292. **Is sorrow for our sins, because by them we have lost heaven and deserved hell, sufficient when we go to confession?**

Sorrow for our sins, because by them we have lost heaven and deserved hell, is sufficient when we go to confession.

There is a third reason to be sorry for our sins—viz., the fear of God and his punishments, the fear of losing heaven and being condemned to hell. This sorrow is not so perfect as those we have already spoken of, because it includes a less perfect love of God, and we are looking more to our own interests than to those of God, hence it is called "imperfect contrition," or "attrition."

293. **What is perfect contrition?**

Perfect contrition is sorrow for sin, arising purely from the love of God.

[158] Heb 6:6

294. **What special value has perfect contrition?**

Perfect contrition has this special value: that by it our sins are forgiven immediately, even before we confess them; but nevertheless, if they are mortal, we are strictly bound to confess them afterward.

You can readily understand that the first kind of sorrow I spoke of is the best,[159] because it has the highest motive. It is called "perfect contrition," and it has a very marvelous power with God, for it induces God to forgive us our mortal sins even before we confess them, provided we have a desire at the time to go to confession. It might happen to a person who is in mortal sin to be face-to-face with death, say by shipwreck, or from fire or some sudden accident. If that person could make an act of perfect contrition, and had at the same time a sincere desire to go to confession if he could, his soul would not be lost. So you see how useful it is always to try to make the best act of contrition for our sins; to be sorry for sin, not from the fear of hell, but from the love of God. If a person in mortal sin made an act of contrition for his sins simply from fear of being lost, God would not forgive him without absolution, because that act of sorrow is not earnest enough to merit forgiveness. Let me give you a short act of perfect contrition and then one of imperfect contrition, or attrition as it is called, and then you will see the difference.

An act of perfect contrition: "O my God, I am sorry that I have sinned against thee, because thou art so good, and I will never sin again and will carefully avoid all that has led me into sin."

An act of imperfect contrition: "O my God, I am sorry that I have sinned against thee, because by my sins I have lost heaven and deserved hell, and I will not sin again and will carefully avoid all that has led me into sin."

One word more about perfect contrition. If the person escapes from the danger of death, even though his sins had been forgiven by the act of contrition joined with the desire of confession, he would be bound to confess his mortal sins at the first opportunity he had, because all mortal sins must be confessed.

[159] See q. 290, above.

295. **What is confession?**

Confession is to accuse ourselves of our sins to a priest approved by the bishop.

The fact of our Lord having given power on earth to his priests to forgive sins means that the priests must know what sins have been committed, and this they cannot do unless the sins are confessed to them. A priest cannot give absolution to everybody that comes; he must be morally sure in his mind that the penitent is sorry for what he has done, and has made up his mind to change his life and do better; and how can a priest be certain of this unless he knows what that penitent has done?

Supposing a person went to confession and said, "Father, I am a great sinner, I am sorry, and I want absolution," that man might be leading a very dishonest life, making money by evil means, pilfering from his master, etc. And this might have been going on for years. Perhaps he had thought of the obligation of restitution; perhaps he had not or, if he had, did not intend to fulfill it. If he does not restore, God will not forgive him. If the priest gives him absolution, the man goes on leading the same bad life, and thieving continues; and instead of helping him to overcome his sin and to lead an honest life, confession only tends to encourage him in sin, for he thinks that, because the words of absolution have been said over him, all is right, and he can go on as he did before. What a mockery confession would be in that case! But if he makes known that sin of dishonesty in confession, then the priest sees the evil that is going on in that soul, and can stop it. He will speak to the penitent of the grievousness of his sin, and of the judgment of God which must inevitably fall upon him; he will urge him to restore what he has stolen as far as may lie in his power. If the penitent refuses to do this, the priest will refuse him absolution, and, go where he may, no priest in this wide world would absolve him. He is not sorry for his sin, and on that account he cannot be forgiven. The man knows this, and if he really wishes to be reconciled to God by forgiveness he knows he can only effect this reconciliation by repentance and the intention to restore.

Supposing a man goes to a doctor, and says, "Doctor, I am ill, please cure me," the first question the doctor would ask him would be, "What is the matter with you? Have you any pain anywhere? What makes you think you are ill?" And supposing the man replies, "That has nothing to do with it. You are a doctor, and I come to you because I am ill; don't expect me to tell you anything about my illness or pains; your business is to give me medicine that will do me good." The doctor naturally would decline to have anything to do with such a man, how could he possibly treat him with any degree of certainty unless he knew what his ailment was? So also a priest cannot help a man's soul and reconcile it to God unless he knows what is the matter with that soul.

Some people imagine, because they come across certain negligent Catholics who do not go to confession, that therefore they do not believe in it. Just the very opposite; assuredly they believe in it, but they stop away from it simply because they know that if they do go to confession they will have to amend their lives and leave off sin, and this they are hardly prepared to do. Their stopping away from confession is rather a proof of their faith in the sacrament than otherwise. They know they cannot trifle with it.

Again, you find people who say, "Oh, it is all very well for the priests to hear the confessions, but if they had to go to confession themselves they would not like it." Well, bishops and priests and the pope himself have all to go to confession, just like any other Catholic. They are human and may fall into sin, and they need the grace of the sacrament as much as, nay more than, anyone else. They have to lead very holy lives, and they must make even more use of the means of God's grace (prayer and the sacraments) than others.

Now what sins are we bound to confess? 1) Only those deliberate mortal sins of which we find ourselves guilty after carefully examining our conscience. 2) Those circumstances which change the nature of a sin, and make it different and more grievous. For instance, to steal a large sum of money is, of course, a grievous sin; but to steal this money out of a church to which it had been given for the service of God would make that theft a sacrilege, therefore a much greater sin. 3) The number of times, as far as we can tell, that we have committed each mortal sin.

296. **What if a person willfully conceal a mortal sin in confession?**

If a person willfully conceal a mortal sin in confession, he is guilty of a great sacrilege, by telling a lie to the Holy Ghost in making a bad confession.

Better for a person not to go at all than to make a mockery of so holy an institution. A man may deceive the priest and make him believe that he is sorry for his sins, but he cannot deceive God, who knows and sees the secrets of all hearts. Besides, what would be the use of going to confession and concealing a sin? The priest's absolution would be no use, God would not ratify it, and that man would go away a worse sinner than he was before.

Some people may say that shame would prevent them from telling all their worst sins. Why should it? They have not been ashamed to commit them and thereby run the risk of losing their souls to all eternity; why, then, should they be ashamed to acknowledge them, when by that humble confession of them they can get rid of them and become God's friends again?

"What will the priest think of me," others say, "when he knows all my secret life?" He will think none the worse of you, I assure you, but rather bless God that you have had the courage to make a good confession. The worse you have been, the more interest he will take in your soul. The greatest joy and happiness of a priest's life is to reconcile a poor sinner to his God. He feels he has done something really great for his divine master.

Is a priest ever allowed to say anything about the sins of his penitent? Most emphatically, "No." He is bound by most stringent laws to maintain an absolute silence about what has been told him in confession, and there is not a priest in the Church of God that would not suffer death sooner than reveal what he knows from confession. Tell me, have you, or has anybody else, ever heard of a priest breaking "the seal of confession," as it is called? There is scarcely a crime on this earth of which priests have not been accused at one time or another, but never of that. It is to me a standing miracle, and a proof of the truth of the Catholic Church, that out of all the priests who have existed, no one has been convicted of that crime.

297. **How many things have we to do in order to prepare for confession?**

We have four things to do in order to prepare for confession: first, we must heartily pray for grace to make a good confession; secondly, we must carefully examine our conscience; thirdly, we must take time and care to make a good act of contrition; and fourthly, we must resolve by the help of God to renounce our sins, and to begin a new life for the future.

You will see from this answer that going to confession is a serious matter; it is not a thing that we can treat lightly.

In every Catholic prayer book, you will find a prayer specially to help you to make a good confession. You will also find an examination of conscience on the ten commandments, the commandments of the Church, and the seven deadly sins. This examination will bring to your mind all the sins you may have committed.

The third and fourth parts of the preparation are the most important — viz., the act of contrition and the resolution to begin a new life. Without these two, the confession is useless.

One word more: a person should never be afraid of not being able to make a good confession, or of forgetting certain sins; the priest, who has been specially trained for his work as a confessor, will help him and make things very easy for him. If a mortal sin has been forgotten, the penitent must mention it in the next confession: he need not go to confession sooner in order to confess that forgotten sin, but when he does go he must mention it, if he remember it.

298. **What is satisfaction?**

Satisfaction is doing the penance given us by the priest.

When a person has finished his confession, the priest speaks to him about the state of his life, telling him what sins he has particularly to avoid, and how to avoid them. Then, before he gives him absolution, he tells him to say certain prayers or to do certain things as a penance for his sins; the penitent then makes his act of contrition, and, whilst he is making it, the words of absolution are pronounced by the priest and the sins are forgiven.

Now, a word about this penance. You will remember that when speaking about purgatory[160] I explained how after every sin, even though the guilt of it be forgiven by God, there remains a debt of temporal punishment

[160] See q. 107, above.

due to the justice of God, and that, if we do not pay this debt in this world, we shall have to pay it in purgatory in the next. One means of getting rid of this temporal punishment in this life is by saying the penance given us by the priest in confession; and perhaps it is the most effectual means we have, because it is sacramental; it is part of the sacrament of penance, and, therefore, it has the merits of the precious blood of Jesus Christ joined to it. If the penance we receive is imposed for mortal sin, we are guilty of mortal sin if we do not perform it.

299. **Does the penance given by the priest always make full satisfaction for our sins?**

The penance given by the priest does not always make full satisfaction for our sins. We should, therefore, add to it other good works and penances and try to gain indulgences.

The three good works specially recommended are prayer, fasting, and giving alms to the poor.

300. **What is an indulgence?**

An indulgence is a remission, granted by the Church, of the temporal punishment which often remains due to sin after its guilt has been forgiven.

Indulgences. This word has a very unpleasant sound in protestant ears. From want of knowing better, they believe that it means a license or a permission to commit sin given by the priest on condition he is paid so much money, and that the amount of money to be paid is regulated by the amount of sin to be committed! It is hard to see how people with any sense in their heads can be induced to believe such rubbish. However, one must not blame them too much; they have been taught from their childhood that everything Catholic is wicked, and perhaps nothing more wicked than indulgences.

Now, an indulgence is not a permission to commit sin; it has nothing whatever to do with sin; in fact, an indulgence for the remission of any punishment due to sin cannot be obtained until the sin itself is forgiven by repentance. Remember there are two things in sin — viz., its guilt and its punishment. The guilt of sin is removed by absolution, and the eternal punishment due to mortal sin is changed into a temporal punishment which the sinner must undergo either in this life or in purgatory. Now turn back to the answer to Question 107, and see what has been said about temporal punishment.

An indulgence is the remission or letting off of part or of the whole of this temporal punishment, on condition that some prayers are said or good works are done by the sinner. In the early ages of the Church, penitents had to do very severe public penances for their sins—for instance, a murderer had to do penance for twenty years for his crime; theft was punished with two years' penance, perjury with eleven years; and an apostate, or one who fell away from the faith during the time of the persecutions, had to do penance for that sin for the remainder of his life. And, mind, people did those penances, for they had real faith in those days, and understood much better than we do the great debt which is due to God's justice on account of sin. Sometimes the Christians who were awaiting death in prison used to petition the bishops to let these poor sinners off part of their penance. In return for their constancy in being ready to give their lives for Christ, the bishops used to accede to their request and grant this remission, or, as we say, grant the penitents an indulgence or a letting off from their penance. In these days, we could not do these long penances; and so the Church, like a good mother, has become more indulgent or more easy with us, and, on condition of our doing certain acts of charity or saying certain prayers, she remits the penances which we deserve for our sins, but the sins themselves must have been forgiven first.

There are two kinds of indulgences granted by the Church: 1) the plenary and 2) the partial indulgence. A plenary indulgence means the taking away of all the punishment due to our sins, and this indulgence is very hard to gain, as it means that we must be absolutely free from all sin and any affection for sin; for, so long as there is any guilt on the soul, the punishment due to it sticks to it, as it were, and cannot be separated from it. To gain a plenary indulgence, we must make a good confession and Communion as a means of getting our souls free from all sin, and also faithfully fulfill any other condition the Church may have imposed. A partial indulgence does not require us to be in such a perfect state; still, it requires that there should be no mortal sin on our souls. I think now you can understand how an indulgence is not only not a permission to commit sin, but that no indulgence can be obtained unless we are free from sin. And really, without thinking of it, people are constantly asking for and gaining indulgences in ordinary life. Supposing you have a married sister who has a boy, say, of ten years of age, and one day you go to pay her a visit. You miss the boy, and you ask where he is. "Oh," replies the mother, "he has been very naughty, and I have been obliged to punish him. He told me a deliberate lie; of course, I have forgiven him because he said he was sorry, but I felt bound to punish him in some way to show him how wrong it is to deceive his mother." Naturally you would feel very sorry, and you would ask if, for your sake, he might not be released from all further punishment. I suppose the answer would be: "Very well, as you ask for him, I will let him off all." The mother would in that case grant the boy an indulgence. The "letting off" would not be from the lie, for that was pardoned, but from the consequences of it. So long as the boy persisted in his lie and refused to ask forgiveness, no good mother would let him off his punishment because the lie or sin remained, but as soon as this was removed, she would be more inclined to remove the punishment.

Sometimes you will find in a Catholic prayer book words like these: "To this prayer is attached an indulgence of 300 days, or 7 years," etc., or simply in brackets "300 days' indulgence," etc. Surely this does not mean that the person who says this prayer is allowed to commit some sin for three hundred days! Well, perhaps you say that he gets off three hundred days of purgatory? No, it does not mean that, but simply this: that if you had been one of the early Christians and had been condemned to do three hundred days' penance as a punishment for sin, you gain the same amount of remission of your temporal punishment by saying this prayer now, devoutly and with sorrow for sin in your heart, as you would have done if you had actually done these three hundred days of penance. Of course, this is a great act of mercy and clemency and indulgence on the part of the Church, for she knows we could not do these long penances now.

From whom did the Church get this wonderful power? From her founder, Jesus Christ, in those words which he said to St. Peter: "Whatsoever thou shalt loose on earth shall be loosed in heaven."[161] Here our Lord gives to St. Peter, as chief pastor of his Church, and to St. Peter's successors, a power of conducting the faithful to heaven by loosing them from whatever may prevent their going there. Two things keep souls out of heaven—the guilt of sin and the punishment due to it; and Christ has given to his Church power and authority to remove both—sin by absolution, temporal punishment by indulgences.

Extreme Unction

301. **What is the sacrament of extreme unction?**

The sacrament of extreme unction is the anointing of the sick with holy oil, accompanied with prayer.

In his infinite goodness and mercy, our Lord has provided for the needs of our soul at the hour of death, and has instituted a sacrament to give us at that time the strength we need to resist the attacks of the devil and to die well. The devil knows when death is approaching, and if he never loses an opportunity during life of ruining our souls, we may well suppose that he redoubles his efforts to get us to fall into sin at the hour of death; if he can do nothing else, he will try to make us despair of God's mercy by bringing before our minds the memory of our past sins.

302. **When is extreme unction given?**

Extreme unction is given when we are in danger of death by sickness.

When a Catholic is taken seriously ill, the priest is sent for if he does not already know of the illness. He takes with him the Blessed Sacrament (which is always kept in the church) in order to give the sick person Holy Communion, and a little vessel containing the oil of the sick. He first hears the confession of the dying person, gives him absolution and then Holy Communion. After this, he anoints him with the sacred oil, or gives him, as we say, extreme unction, or the last anointing with the sacred oil. He makes the sign of the cross upon the eyes, the ears, the nostrils, the lips,

[161] Mt 16:19

the hands, and the feet of the dying person, saying during each anointing: "By this holy anointing and by his most loving mercy, may the Lord forgive thee whatever thou hast committed by the sight, by the hearing," etc. This sacrament is given only to those who are in danger of death from sickness or accident. A soldier who is going into action, even though there is every probability of his being killed, cannot be anointed; if he is mortally wounded and is dying, he can then receive this sacrament.

303. **What are the effects of the sacrament of extreme unction?**
The effects of the sacrament of extreme unction are to comfort and strengthen the soul, to remit sin, and even to restore health when God sees it to be expedient.

Each of the seven sacraments has its own effect upon the soul or its own particular work to do in the soul. Extreme unction gives to the dying a feeling of comfort and peace, and the special strength needed to fight against temptation. If there be any sin upon the soul, it forgives it, if the person be sorry for it. It also takes away the relics of sin—I mean: indisposition to pray or to make acts of virtue, the evil attraction we feel for sin, weakness of soul, and the fear of death and of eternal salvation. Not unfrequently, too, the anointing even affects the bodily health and helps nature to revive. Every priest who has had much to do with the dying can testify to this extraordinary effect of the sacrament.

304. **What authority is there in scripture for the sacrament of extreme unction?**
The authority in scripture for the sacrament of extreme unction is in the fifth chapter of St. James, where it is said: "Is anyone sick among you, let him bring in the priests of the church; and let them pray over him, anointing him with oil in the name of the Lord. And the prayer of faith shall save the sick man: and the Lord shall raise him up; and if he be in sins they shall be forgiven him."[162]

Here is a matter which has always puzzled me—perhaps you may be able to explain it: it is that though extreme unction is distinctly mentioned

[162] Jas 5:14-15

in the Bible, it is never practiced by protestant clergymen. The words of the Revised Version of the Bible are slightly different from those of the Catholic version, but they are substantially the same. The protestant Bible says: "Is any among you sick? Let him call for the elders of the Church, and let them pray over him, anointing him with oil in the name of the Lord; and the prayer of faith shall save him that is sick, and the Lord shall raise him up, and if he have committed sin it shall be forgiven him." Why, let me ask you, is not this done? People are never tired of telling us Catholics that we do not read the Bible, that we do not believe in it, and that we do not do what it teaches. I think it is our turn to retort and ask why those who profess to believe in the Bible as the word of God, and who say that it is their only rule of faith—why these people, I say, do not carry out what the Bible says distinctly must be done in case a person falls sick. If a protestant is taken ill, he ought to send for the clergyman. The clergyman ought, according to the *Book of Common Prayer*,[163] to move the sick man to make "a special confession of his sins" and then to give him absolution; then he ought to give him Communion or the sacrament,[164] and then, according to the Bible, anoint him with oil. The Catholic priest, at any rate, always does this, and more, for he gives the dying person the "apostolic blessing for the hour of death"—that is, he has received power to give him a plenary indulgence. Of the two, then, who does all that God has instituted for the dying—the Catholic priest or the protestant clergyman?

Holy Order

305. **What is the sacrament of holy order?**

Holy order is the sacrament by which bishops, priests, and other ministers of the Church are ordained and receive power and grace to perform their sacred duties.

Our Lord came down from heaven 1) to redeem us and 2) to help us to get to heaven by instituting the means of having his redemption applied to

[163] See "The Visitation of the Sick."

[164] See "Communion of the Sick," following "The Visitation of the Sick."

our souls. He could not always remain visibly on earth himself to save our souls, so, before ascending into heaven, he chose twelve apostles, to whom he communicated his own divine powers, and he also gave them a power to hand down these same divine powers to others by ordaining them bishops and priests. He gave his apostles power to preach the gospel, to teach all nations, and to baptize;[165] also to change bread and wine into his sacred body and blood and to offer the Sacrifice of the Mass, when he commanded them at the last supper to do what he had just done;[166] and, lastly, to forgive sins.[167] These powers the apostles were to hand down to their successors till the end of time. No one can exercise these priestly powers unless he has been validly ordained for that purpose. If anyone presumed to assume the office of a priest without real ordination, he would be an intruder into the sacred office and would be guilty of terrible sin.

I suppose you have heard something about what is called "the question of Anglican orders"—that is, as to whether Anglican clergymen are really priests, as we are, or not. You know there are a certain number of clergymen in the Anglican Church who for many years have been rather tired of the cold, uninteresting services of their Church, and have been making things much brighter. They have more services now, better singing, candles on the altar, etc.; and some have gone so far as to imitate the services and ritual of the Catholic Church. They have what they call "Mass," prayers for the dead, devotions in honor of the Blessed Virgin and the saints, images, banners, processions, etc. And now these clergymen call themselves "Catholic priests" and try to make their congregations believe that they are real priests. Is this all true? Are they really priests? Can they say real Mass and give real absolution, or is all this only a make-believe? I think the best proof that they are not priests is the conduct of the authors of the Reformation regarding the Mass and other Catholic services which the present Anglican ministers have adopted of late years.

1. *The doctrine of the reformers.*—The thirty-first "Article of Religion," as contained in the *Book of Common Prayer*, says: "The sacrifices of Masses, in

165 Cf. Mt 28:19; Mk 16:15

166 Cf. Lk 22:19

167 Cf. Jn 20:23

which it was commonly said that the priest did offer Christ for the quick [the living] and the dead, to have remission of pain or guilt, were blasphemous fables and dangerous deceits"; and now these Anglican ministers, who have subscribed to this article at their ordination, do attempt to say Mass.

2. *The actions of the reformers.*—They did everything they could to get rid of the idea of *priest* and *sacrifice*. The Catholic priests were put to death if they were caught saying Mass. The altars were pulled down, and the altar stones, on which the Mass had been said, were turned to profane uses—some were made into hearthstones, and many were let into the pavement of the churches so that the people should walk on them. There is one to this day in the protestant church at Irnham, in Lincolnshire. "Tables" were erected in the place of the Catholic altars, and the minister was forced to stand at the side instead of with his back to the people, so that all could see what he was doing. Therefore, from the teaching of the authors of the protestant religion and from their actions, too, we have a certain proof that the first protestant bishops had not the slightest intention or idea of ordaining men to be priests—that is, of giving them power to say Mass and to forgive sins—for the real Catholic priests, who did say Mass and did forgive sins, were put to death for this very reason. A hundred years ago, no Anglican minister would have dared to have attempted to say Mass or hear confessions. If it is right to do so now, why should it not have been right for them to have done it during the last three hundred years? It was either the right thing to do or it was not. If it were, why did they not do it? If it were not, how can it be right now? Men who at their ordination called the sacrifices of Masses "blasphemous fables" should either stick to their word now or leave the church, and not deceive their congregations by trying to make them believe that they are real priests. It is an awful thing to play at being priests of the most high God and at being representatives of Jesus Christ on earth.

Matrimony

306. **What is the sacrament of matrimony?**

Matrimony is a sacrament which sanctifies the contract of a Christian marriage, and gives special grace to those who receive it worthily.

Marriage is the means God has instituted for the propagation of the human race. God has sent all mankind into the world for one end—viz., to know, to love, and to serve him here, and afterward to be happy with him forever in heaven; and as marriage is the means of bringing us into the world, it was just and right that God should surround it with all the aids necessary to make it carry out its great end of helping parents to save their own souls and the souls of their children. Married life has its own difficulties and trials, and it needs a particular grace and assistance from God. This is why our Lord raised it to the dignity of a sacrament, that those who entered upon that state should have a right to claim from God the graces they needed.

307. **What special grace does the sacrament of matrimony give to those who receive it worthily?**

The sacrament of matrimony gives to those who receive it worthily a special grace to enable them to bear the difficulties of their state, to love and be faithful to one another, and to bring up their children in the fear of God.

The difficulties of married life generally result from the difference of character and disposition of the husband and wife, from jealousy, poverty, sickness, etc., and the great tact and patience required in the training of children.

308. **Is it a sacrilege to contract marriage in mortal sin, or in disobedience to the laws of the Church?**

It is a sacrilege to contract marriage in mortal sin, or in disobedience to the laws of the Church, and, instead of a blessing, the guilty parties draw down upon themselves the anger of God.[168]

[168] For the marriage of a Catholic to be valid there must be present 1) either the bishop or the parish priest, or another priest duly delegated, and 2) two witnesses.

A sacrilege means "the profanation of a sacred thing." Marriage is a sacrament, and therefore to contract it when one or the other of the parties, or perhaps both, are in a state of mortal sin makes the reception of that sacrament a great sin, but at the same time the parties are really married. Since Easter Sunday, 1908, very serious alterations have been made by the Church regarding Catholic marriages in protestant churches and in the offices of civil registrars. Up to the above date, these marriages were in England and some other countries admitted to be valid, but the contracting of them in this manner was always condemned as sinful. Since the new decree of Pope Pius X, these marriages are not only sinful but they are invalid—that is to say, they are not real marriages in the sight of God. For a marriage to be valid and lawful now (whether it be a mixed marriage or one in which both parties are Catholics) it must be contracted before the parish priest of the district, or the bishop of the diocese, or some priest delegated by either of them to perform the ceremony. There must also be two witnesses to the marriage. Unless there be some reasonable excuse, the marriage should always be celebrated before the parish priest of the district in which the bride resides. Both parties must be prepared to produce evidence of "freedom to marry"—that is to say, that they are not already married to someone else. Your parish priest or the priest who instructs you will always be able to answer any difficulties you may have in the matter.

309. **What is a mixed marriage?**

A mixed marriage is a marriage between a Catholic and one who, though baptized, does not profess the Catholic faith.

In general, it means a marriage between a Catholic and a protestant. The difference of religion forms an impediment or barrier to marriage and makes it unlawful.

310. **Has the Church always forbidden mixed marriages?**

The Church has always forbidden mixed marriages, and considered them unlawful and pernicious.

Few people, I suppose, would feel inclined to question the wisdom of the Church in forbidding mixed marriages. One must remember that marriage is for life; it cannot be ended just when people like, or because they do not or cannot agree. The parties are bound to each other until one or the other dies. Everyone knows what a little it takes sometimes to make marriage a terrible misery, and there are few things about which people are so tenacious or quarrelsome as religion. For two people to start in life with different religious opinions is, indeed, to make a bad start. Quarrels must inevitably arise concerning the children's baptism or in what religion they are to be brought up. Then, again, there is the danger of the Catholic party not being able to follow his or her religion; Mass, Friday's abstinence, confession, and Communion are gradually neglected, and not unfrequently the end is loss of faith and religion.

311. **Does the Church sometimes permit mixed marriages?**
The Church sometimes permits mixed marriages by granting a dispensation for very grave reasons and under special conditions.

The difficulty of finding a suitable Catholic partner, especially in a small town, and the probable conversion of the protestant party are sometimes considered by the bishop reasons sufficient for granting a dispensation.

The conditions on which the bishop grants a dispensation in the case of a mixed marriage are that 1) both parties promise in writing that all the children of both sexes that may be born of their marriage shall be baptized in the Catholic Church, and shall be carefully brought up in the knowledge and practice of the Catholic religion. 2) The non-Catholic party promises (also in writing) that he or she will not interfere with the religious belief of the Catholic party, nor with his or her full and perfect liberty to fulfill all his or her duties as a Catholic. 3) The Catholic party promises *viva voce*—that is, "by word of mouth"—that he or she will in future leave no stone unturned to bring about the conversion of the non-Catholic party by good example and gentle persuasion.[169]

[169] See also q. 308, above.

312. **Can any human power dissolve the bond of marriage?**

No human power can dissolve the bond of marriage, because Christ has said: "What God hath joined together let no man put asunder."[170]

This means that no human power can divorce a lawfully married man and wife in such a way as to allow them to marry again during each other's lifetime. The law of the land unfortunately allows it, but it is simply adultery. No Catholic priest would ever tolerate such a thing.

I have now come to the end of the explanation of the catechism, as far as I intended to carry it. The rest of the catechism follows; you can read it and probably understand it fairly well. My object has been to give you a simple and plain explanation of the doctrine and practice of the Catholic religion, and to try to remove some of the many prejudices which still exist against it.

You must have been struck by the idea this little book has given you of our holy religion, an idea very different indeed from the one you had formed about it yourself or that someone had given you, possibly himself in ignorance of its real teaching. If you have seen and acknowledged the truth, do not stop there. Get some Catholic friend to introduce you to a priest, and ask him to explain anything you may not have quite understood. If you have no friend to help you, go alone to the priest and tell him your difficulties. Do not be afraid; there is nothing to fear. Remember you have a soul to save. You must not leave it to take its chance. God has given you a religion by means of which you can most certainly save it. That religion is the one taught by the Church of Christ, the one, holy, catholic, and apostolic Church. Embrace that religion and practice it faithfully, and all will be safe with you at the day of judgment.

[170] Mt 19:6

Of Virtues and Vices

313. **Which are the theological virtues?**
The theological virtues are faith, hope, and charity.

314. **Why are they called "theological virtues"?**
They are called "theological virtues," because they relate immediately to God.

315. **What are the chief mysteries of faith which every Christian is bound to know?**
The chief mysteries of faith which every Christian is bound to know are the unity and trinity of God, who will render to every man according to his works, and the incarnation, death, and resurrection of our Savior.

316. **Which are the cardinal virtues?**
The cardinal virtues are prudence, justice, fortitude, and temperance.

317. **Why are they called "cardinal virtues"?**
They are called "cardinal virtues," because they are, as it were, the hinges on which all other moral virtues turn.

318. **Which are the seven gifts of the Holy Ghost?**
The seven gifts of the Holy Ghost are:
1. Wisdom.
2. Understanding.
3. Counsel.
4. Fortitude.
5. Knowledge.
6. Piety.
7. The fear of the Lord.

319. **Which are the twelve fruits of the Holy Ghost?**

The twelve fruits of the Holy Ghost are:

1. Charity.
2. Joy.
3. Peace.
4. Patience.
5. Benignity.
6. Goodness.
7. Longanimity.
8. Mildness.
9. Faith.
10. Modesty.
11. Continency.
12. Chastity.

320. **Which are the two great precepts of charity?**

The two great precepts of charity are:

1. Thou shalt love the Lord thy God with thy whole heart, and with thy whole soul, and with thy whole mind, and with thy whole strength.
2. Thou shalt love thy neighbor as thyself.

321. **Which are the seven corporal works of mercy?**

The seven corporal works of mercy are:

1. To feed the hungry.
2. To give drink to the thirsty.
3. To clothe the naked.
4. To harbor the harborless.
5. To visit the sick.
6. To visit the imprisoned.
7. To bury the dead.

322. **Which are the seven spiritual works of mercy?**

The seven spiritual works of mercy are:

1. To convert the sinner.

2. To instruct the ignorant.
3. To counsel the doubtful.
4. To comfort the sorrowful.
5. To bear wrongs patiently.
6. To forgive injuries.
7. To pray for the living and the dead.

323. **Which are the eight beatitudes?**

1. Blessed are the poor in spirit: for theirs is the kingdom of heaven.
2. Blessed are the meek: for they shall possess the land.
3. Blessed are they that mourn: for they shall be comforted.
4. Blessed are they that hunger and thirst after justice: for they shall have their fill.
5. Blessed are the merciful: for they shall obtain mercy.
6. Blessed are the clean of heart: for they shall see God.
7. Blessed are the peacemakers: for they shall be called the children of God.
8. Blessed are they that suffer persecution for justice' sake: for theirs is the kingdom of heaven.

324. **What are the seven capital sins or vices and their contrary virtues?**

The seven capital sins or vices and their contrary virtues are:

	Contrary virtues
1. Pride.	1. Humility.
2. Covetousness.	2. Liberality.
3. Lust.	3. Chastity.
4. Anger.	4. Meekness.
5. Gluttony.	5. Temperance.
6. Envy.	6. Brotherly love.
7. Sloth.	7. Diligence.

325. **Why are they called "capital sins"?**

They are called "capital sins," because they are the sources from which all other sins take their rise.

326. **Which are the six sins against the Holy Ghost?**

The six sins against the Holy Ghost are:

1. Presumption.
2. Despair.
3. Resisting the known truth.
4. Envy of another's spiritual good.
5. Obstinacy in sin.
6. Final impenitence.

327. **Which are the four sins crying to heaven for vengeance?**

The four sins crying to heaven for vengeance are:

1. Willful murder.
2. The sin of Sodom.
3. Oppression of the poor.
4. Defrauding laborers of their wages.

328. **When are we answerable for the sins of others?**

We are answerable for the sins of others whenever we either cause them or share in them through our own fault.

329. **In how many ways may we either cause or share the guilt of another's sin?**

We may either cause or share the guilt of another's sin in nine ways:

1. By counsel.
2. By command.
3. By consent.
4. By provocation.
5. By praise or flattery.
6. By concealment.
7. By being a partner in the sin.
8. By silence.
9. By defending the ill done.

330. **Which are the three eminent good works?**

The three eminent good works are prayer, fasting, and almsdeeds.

331. **Which are the evangelical counsels?**

The evangelical counsels are voluntary poverty, perpetual chastity, and entire obedience.

332. **What are the four last things to be ever remembered?**

The four last things to be ever remembered are death, judgment, hell, and heaven.

The Christian's Rule of Life

333. **What rule of life must we follow if we hope to be saved?**

If we hope to be saved, we must follow the rule of life taught by Jesus Christ.

334. **What are we bound to do by the rule of life taught by Jesus Christ?**

By the rule of life taught by Jesus Christ, we are bound always to hate sin and to love God.

335. **How must we hate sin?**

We must hate sin above all other evils, so as to be resolved never to commit a willful sin for the love or fear of anything whatsoever.

336. **How must we love God?**

We must love God above all things and with our whole heart.

337. **How must we learn to love God?**

We must learn to love God by begging of God to teach us to love him: "O my God, teach me to love thee."

338. **What will the love of God lead us to do?**
The love of God will lead us often to think how good God is; often to speak to him in our hearts; and always to seek to please him.

339. **Does Jesus Christ also command us to love one another?**
Jesus Christ also commands us to love one another—that is, all persons without exception—for his sake.

340. **How are we to love one another?**
We are to love one another by wishing well to one another, and praying for one another, and by never allowing ourselves any thought, word, or deed to the injury of anyone.

341. **Are we also bound to love our enemies?**
We are also bound to love our enemies; not only by forgiving them from our hearts, but also by wishing them well and praying for them.

342. **Has Jesus Christ given us another great rule?**
Jesus Christ has given us another great rule in these words: "If any man will come after me, let him deny himself, and take up his cross daily, and follow me."[171]

343. **How are we to deny ourselves?**
We are to deny ourselves by giving up our own will, and by going against our own humors, inclinations, and passions.

344. **Why are we bound to deny ourselves?**
We are bound to deny ourselves because our natural inclinations are prone to evil from our very childhood; and, if not corrected by self-denial, they will certainly carry us to hell.

[171] Lk 9:23

345. **How are we to take up our cross daily?**
We are to take up our cross daily by submitting daily with patience to the labors and sufferings of this short life, and by bearing them willingly for the love of God.

346. **How are we to follow our blessed Lord?**
We are to follow our blessed Lord by walking in his footsteps and imitating his virtues.

347. **What are the principal virtues we are to learn of our blessed Lord?**
The principal virtues we are to learn of our blessed Lord are meekness, humility, and obedience.

348. **Which are the enemies we must fight against all the days of our life?**
The enemies which we must fight against all the days of our life are the devil, the world, and the flesh.

349. **What do you mean by *the devil*?**
By *the devil*, I mean Satan and all his wicked angels, who are ever seeking to draw us into sin that we may be damned with them.

350. **What do you mean by *the world*?**
By *the world*, I mean the false maxims of the world and the society of those who love the vanities, riches, and pleasures of this world better than God.

351. **Why do you number the devil and the world amongst the enemies of the soul?**
I number the devil and the world amongst the enemies of the soul, because they are always seeking, by temptation and by word or example, to carry us along with them in the broad road that leads to damnation.

352. **What do you mean by *the flesh*?**
By *the flesh*, I mean our own corrupt inclinations and passions, which are the most dangerous of all our enemies.

353. **What must we do to hinder the enemies of our soul from drawing us into sin?**
To hinder the enemies of our soul from drawing us into sin, we must watch, pray, and fight against all their suggestions and temptations.

354. **In the warfare against the devil, the world, and the flesh, on whom must we depend?**
In the warfare against the devil, the world, and the flesh, we must depend, not on ourselves, but on God only: "I can do all things in him who strengtheneth me."[172]

The Christian's Daily Exercise

355. **How should you begin the day?**
I should begin the day by making the sign of the cross as soon as I awake in the morning and by saying some short prayer, such as, "O my God, I offer my heart and soul to thee."

356. **How should you rise in the morning?**
I should rise in the morning diligently, dress myself modestly, and then kneel down and say my morning prayers.

Short Morning Prayers

+ In the name of the Father, and of the Son, and of the Holy Ghost. Amen.

Our Father. Hail Mary. The Apostles' Creed.

Blessed be the Holy and undivided Trinity now and forever. Amen.

O my God, I believe in thee; do thou strengthen my faith. All my hopes are in thee; do thou secure them. I love thee with my whole heart; teach

[172] Phil 4:13

me to love thee daily more and more. I am sorry that I have offended thee; do thou increase my sorrow.

O my God, how good thou hast been to me, and how little have I done for thee! Thou hast created me out of nothing, redeemed me by the death of thy Son, and sanctified me by the grace of thy Holy Spirit. Thou hast called me into thy Church, and thou givest me all the graces necessary for my salvation. Thou hast preserved me during the night past, and given me the present day, wherein I may serve thee. What return can I make thee, O God, for all that thou hast done for me? I will bless thy holy name, and serve thee all the days of my life.

I offer to thee, O my God, all my thoughts, words, actions, and sufferings; and I beseech thee to give me thy grace, that I may not offend thee this day, but that I may faithfully serve thee and do thy holy will in all things.

357. **Should you also hear Mass if you have time and opportunity?**
I should also hear Mass if I have time and opportunity, for to hear Mass is by far the best and most profitable of all devotions.

358. **Is it useful to make daily meditation?**
It is useful to make daily meditation, for such was the practice of all the saints.

359. **On what ought we to meditate?**
We ought to meditate especially on the four last things and on the life and passion of our blessed Lord.

360. **Ought we frequently to read good books?**
We ought frequently to read good books, such as the holy gospels, the lives of the saints, and other spiritual works, which nourish our faith and piety and arm us against the false maxims of the world.

361. **And what should you do as to your eating, drinking, sleeping, and amusements?**
As to my eating, drinking, sleeping, and amusements, I should use all these things with moderation and with a desire to please God.

362. **Say the grace before meals.**
"Bless us, O Lord, and these thy gifts which we are going to receive from thy bounty, through Christ our Lord. Amen."

363. **Say the grace after meals.**
"We give thee thanks, Almighty God, for all thy benefits, who livest and reignest, world without end. Amen."

+ May the souls of the faithful departed, through the mercy of God, rest in peace. Amen.

364. **How should you sanctify your ordinary actions and employments of the day?**
I should sanctify my ordinary actions and employments of the day by often raising up my heart to God whilst I am about them, and saying some short prayer to him.

365. **What should you do when you find yourself tempted to sin?**
When I find myself tempted to sin, I should make the sign of the cross on my heart, and call on God as earnestly as I can, saying: "Lord, save me, or I perish."

366. **If you have fallen into sin, what should you do?**
If I have fallen into sin, I should cast myself in spirit at the feet of Christ and humbly beg his pardon by a sincere act of contrition.

367. **When God sends you any cross or sickness or pain, what should you say?**
When God sends me any cross or sickness or pain, I should say, "Lord, thy will be done; I take this for my sins."

368. **What little indulgenced prayers would you do well to say often to yourself during the day?**
I should do well to say often to myself during the day such little indulgenced prayers as:

Glory be to the Father, and to the Son, and to the Holy Ghost; as it was in the beginning, is now, and ever shall be, world without end. Amen.

In all things may the most holy, the most just, and the most lovable will of God be done, praised, and exalted above all forever.

O Sacrament most holy, O Sacrament divine, all praise and all thanksgiving be every moment thine.

Praised be Jesus Christ, praised forevermore.

My Jesus, mercy; Mary, help.

369. **How should you finish the day?**
I should finish the day by kneeling down and saying my night prayers.

Short Evening Prayers

+ In the name of the Father, and of the Son, and of the Holy Ghost. Amen.

O my God, I believe that thou art here present; and that thou observest all my actions, all my thoughts, and the most secret motions of my heart. I adore thee, and I love thee with my whole heart.

I return thee thanks for all the benefits which I have ever received from thee, and particularly this day. Give me light, O my God, to see what sins I have committed this day, and grant me grace to be truly sorry for them.

(Here examine whether you have offended God during the day, by any thought, word, or deed, or by neglect of any duty.)

O my God, who art infinitely good in thyself, and infinitely good to me, I am sorry, and beg pardon for all my sins, and detest them above all things, because they deserve thy dreadful punishments, because they have crucified my loving Savior Jesus Christ, and, most of all, because they offend thine infinite goodness; and I firmly resolve, by the help of thy grace, never to offend thee again and carefully to avoid the occasions of sin.

(Here put yourself in the disposition you desire to be found in at the hour of death.)

O my God, I accept death as an act of homage and adoration which I owe to Thy Divine Majesty, as a punishment justly due to my sins, in union with the death of my dear Redeemer, and as the only means of coming to thee, my beginning and last end.

Into thy hands, O Lord, I commend my spirit; Lord Jesus, receive my soul.

O Holy Mary, be a Mother to me.

May the Blessed Virgin Mary, St. Joseph, and all the saints, pray for us to our Lord, that we may be preserved this night from sin and all evils. Amen.

O my good angel, whom God has appointed to be my guardian, watch over me during this night.

All ye angels and saints of God, pray for me.

May our Lord bless us, and preserve us from all evil, and bring us to life everlasting. Amen.

And may the souls of the faithful departed, through the mercy of God, rest in peace. Amen.

370. **After your night prayers, what should you do?**

After my night prayers, I should observe due modesty in going to bed; occupy myself with the thoughts of death; and endeavor to compose myself to rest at the foot of the cross, and give my last thoughts to my crucified Savior.

The Rosary

Every Catholic knows that the rosary is a form of supplication which unites in itself mental and vocal prayer. It consists of fifteen meditations on the principal events of our Lord's life and the life of his holy Mother.

The fifteen meditations are divided into three equal parts. The first part brings before the mind the chief mysteries which gave joy to the world—viz., the annunciation, the visitation, the birth of our Lord, his being offered in the Temple as a child, and his being found there as a boy of twelve: these are called "the joyful mysteries." The second part of the rosary is called "the sorrowful mysteries," because it introduces to our pious notice the sorrows of our Lord's life, which culminated in his sacred and saving death: the agony and prayer in the garden, his being scourged at the pillar, his thorn-crowning, his carrying the cross from the place of judgment to Calvary, and finally his death upon the cross for the redemption of men. In the third division of the rosary, we are led to the contemplation of his triumph, and hence it is called by the name of "the glorious mysteries": these mysteries comprise his glorious resurrection from the dead, his triumphant ascension from earth to heaven, the coming down of the Holy Spirit upon the infant Church on Pentecost day, the assumption of our Lady into the kingdom of her Son, and then her solemn coronation as Queen of earth and Queen of heaven.

The rosary has been called "an epitome of the gospel," recalling to us as it does the incarnation of Jesus Christ, the consoling doctrine of the redemption by the sacred blood-shedding, and the hopeful and helpful teaching of the future rewards. "This is life eternal: to know thee, the one true and living God, and him whom thou hast sent, Jesus Christ."[173] St. Paul gives us a commentary upon these words of the divine master: "For he that cometh to God must believe that he is, and is a rewarder of them that seek him."[174] The mysteries of the rosary remind us that he is—that

[173] Jn 17:3
[174] Heb 11:6

he is our Savior and our Redeemer, and that he is our rewarder; that he came into the world "for us men and for our salvation"; that he left the world, because it was expedient for us that he should go;[175] and that he has gone "to prepare a place" for us,[176] so that his word may be realized: "Where I am, there shall my minister be."[177] This is the doctrinal part of the rosary; these are the subjects proposed for our meditation, thus supplying spiritual food for the mind, lifting up the intellect to God, keeping alive and strengthening the theological virtues of faith, hope, and love.

The rosary mysteries, like fifteen faithful mirrors, reflect back to us the ways and life, the words and actions, the joys, the sorrows, and the triumphs of our Lord. As fifteen lifelike pictures, they reveal to us, as in a cinematograph, the scenes and incidents of which the gospel is the faithful record, and the historic personages who took part in them. We see Mary and Joseph and Elizabeth, and the two Johns, and Anna, and Simeon, and the doctors of the law, Pilate and Herod, the Jews and the Roman soldiers and the centurion, the apostles, and the angels on earth and in heaven; but above them all—like Saul "head and shoulders above the prophets"[178]—we see Jesus, the central figure around which all revolve, the sun which illumines all, the sheaf before which all fall down in lowly adoring love. As an eloquent preacher, of eloquence beyond the power of words, the rosary preaches to us "the way, the truth, and the life."[179] As a most convincing teacher, it impresses upon us, in a manner which we cannot gainsay, "the wonderful ways of God."[180]

Such is the devotion as a mental prayer or meditation, consecrating the mind at once and the heart. But the lips have to be dedicated to God as well as the intellect and the will, and hence, as Leo XIII expresses it, St. Dominic "combined, and, as it were, interlaced the subjects to be meditated with the Angelical Salutation and with the prayer to God and the

[175] Cf. Jn 16:7
[176] Jn 14:2
[177] Jn 12:26
[178] 1 Kgs 9:2
[179] Jn 14:6
[180] Acts 2:11

Father of our Lord Jesus Christ."[181] Whilst we meditate upon the sublime truths, and while our hearts are made to "leap up to God," to use St. Augustine's expressive word, "and in our meditation a fire—the fire of divine love—breaks out,"[182] we unite the voice to the mind and heart, vocal prayer to mental prayer, saying, as we think of each mystery, one Our Father, ten Hail Marys, and one Glory be to the Father, thus fulfilling our Lord's injunction: "When you pray, pray thus: 'Our Father,'" etc.[183]—thus again reechoing the angel's word to Mary: "Hail, full of grace," etc.[184]—thus once more vying with the angels in holy rivalry, and singing with them honor and praise and glory to the blessed three: Father, Son, and Holy Ghost. Each of these divisions is called a decade.

And lest our mind should wander from our subject, lest we should be distracted by the counting of the prescribed prayers, we hold the bead-string in our hands and pass a bead through our fingers for each *Pater*, *Ave*, and *Gloria* that we say, so that we may know when our holy task is done. We sanctify the mind by sacred thoughts, the heart by acts of sorrow and love, the lips by the inspired words of sacred prayer, and the fingers by contact with the blessed beads. With reason then does the sovereign pontiff exclaim in the encyclical already quoted: "Let the Christian people cling more and more to the practice of the rosary, to which our ancestors had recourse as to an ever-ready refuge in their distress, and as a glorious pledge of Christian faith and devotion."

181 Leo XIII, *Supremi apostolatus officio*, September, 1883

182 Ps 38:4

183 Mt 6:9ff

184 Lk 1:28

The Scapular

(By a Carmelite Father)

The scapular, a garment worn by religious of various orders, is a broad strip of cloth hanging from the shoulders (*scapulae*) both in front and behind and reaching to the ankles. Originally, it merely served the purpose of an apron, but in the year 1250, it received a more mystical meaning. The general of the Carmelites, St. Simon Stock, an Englishman, living at that time at Cambridge, besought the Blessed Virgin, patron of his order, to protect it against the violent attacks of its adversaries and bestow upon it some mark of her favor. On the night of July 16, she appeared to him, holding in her hand the scapular, and saying: "This shall be your privilege; whosoever dies in this shall not suffer eternal fire." She also appeared to Pope John XXII (1322), promising to free from the flames of purgatory on the first Saturday after death all those who should wear the scapular, observe chastity according to their state of life, and abstain from the use of flesh meat on all Wednesdays and Saturdays in addition to Fridays, or else recite daily the little office (in Latin). This is called "the Sabbatine privilege," the apparitions and promises having been repeatedly confirmed by the Holy See. In order to bring these favors within the reach of all, a Confraternity of the Scapular was founded as far back as the thirteenth century, the members of which wear a small scapular consisting of two pieces of brown cloth held together by strings and hanging from the shoulders to the breast and the back. It is necessary to be enrolled by a Carmelite Father or a priest having power to that effect (as have at present nearly all priests), and to have one's name inscribed in a register kept at a Carmelite monastery or convent. The scapular should never be taken off, but, when unfit for use, may be replaced by another without a new blessing. No special prayers are prescribed, but the wearers of the scapular are exhorted to practice some devotion toward our Lady. Those desirous of enjoying the Sabbatine privilege, but unable to observe the abstinence or recite the office, should ask a priest who has faculties for a dispensation or commutation with regard to these obligations. Wearing the scapular does not, of course, imply that one may lead a wicked life and yet be certain of salvation, which would be sinful presumption, but, that, being clothed in the livery of our Lady and leading a good Christian life, one has a right to her protection during life and at the hour of death, when she will certainly obtain for her children the grace of receiving the last sacraments or of making an act of perfect contrition.

ABOUT THIS SERIES

Tradivox was first conceived as an international research endeavor to recover lost and otherwise little-known Catholic catechetical texts. As the research progressed over several years, the vision began to grow, along with the number of project contributors and a general desire to share these works with a broader audience.

Legally incorporated in 2019, Tradivox has begun the work of carefully remastering and republishing dozens of these catechisms which were once in common and official use in the Church around the world. That effort is embodied in this *Tradivox Catholic Catechism Index*, a multi-volume series restoring artifacts of traditional faith and praxis for a contemporary readership. More about this series and the work of Tradivox can be learned at www.Tradivox.com.

SOPHIA INSTITUTE

Sophia Institute is a nonprofit institution that seeks to nurture the spiritual, moral, and cultural life of souls and to spread the Gospel of Christ in conformity with the authentic teachings of the Roman Catholic Church.

Sophia Institute Press fulfills this mission by offering translations, reprints, and new publications that afford readers a rich source of the enduring wisdom of mankind.

Sophia Institute also operates the popular online resource CatholicExchange.com. *Catholic Exchange* provides world news from a Catholic perspective as well as daily devotionals and articles that will help readers to grow in holiness and live a life consistent with the teachings of the Church.

In 2013, Sophia Institute launched Sophia Institute for Teachers to renew and rebuild Catholic culture through service to Catholic education. With the goal of nurturing the spiritual, moral, and cultural life of souls, and an abiding respect for the role and work of teachers, we strive to provide materials and programs that are at once enlightening to the mind and ennobling to the heart; faithful and complete, as well as useful and practical.

Sophia Institute gratefully recognizes the Solidarity Association for preserving and encouraging the growth of our apostolate over the course of many years. Without their generous and timely support, this book would not be in your hands.

www.SophiaInstitute.com
www.CatholicExchange.com
www.SophiaInstituteforTeachers.org